W9-BZA-362

CRA, B MACHINE

3 4694 00102160 9

Contributed by your local
Edward Jones representative.

INNER VISION

THE STORY OF THE WORLD'S GREATEST BLIND ATHLETE

Published by Addax Publishing Group
Copyright © 1997 by Craig MacFarlane
Designed by Randy Breeden
Cover Design by Jerry Hirt
Edited by John Lofflin

All rights reserved. No part of this book may be reproduced or transmitted in
any form or by any means, electronic or mechanical, including photocopying,
recording, or by any information storage and retrieval system, without the
written permission of the Publisher.

For Information address:
Addax Publishing Group
8643 Hauser Drive, Suite 235, Lenexa, KS 66215

ISBN: 1-886110-30-1

Distributed to the trade by Andrews McMeel Publishing
4520 Main Street
Kansas City, MO 64111

1 3 5 7 9 10 8 6 4 2
Printed in the United States of America

Library of Congress Cataloging-in-Publication Data

MacFarlane, Craig, 1962-
        Inner vision : the story of the world's greatest blind athelete /
by Craig Mac Farlane with Gib Twyman.
        p. cm.
        ISBN 1-866110-30-1
        1. MacFarlane, Craig, 1962-   . 2. Blind athletes—Canada-
-Biography. 3. Blind athletes—United States—Biography.
I. Twyman, Gib. II. Title.
HV1807.M33A3   1998
362.4'1'092—dc21
        [B]   97-52666
                                                   CIP

INNER VISION

THE STORY OF THE WORLD'S GREATEST BLIND ATHLETE

By Craig MacFarlane
with Gib Twyman

Foreword by George Bush

ADDAX
PUBLISHING
G R O U P

Lenexa, Kansas

"Craig has proven you can accomplish anything through hard work, dedication and a lot of spirit."
Wayne Gretzky

"As I've come to know Craig MacFarlane, I'm deeply impressed with his intensity. I know he, too, is a true champion."
Evander Holyfield

"I can't tell you what a privilege it is to know this fella. He stands as an inspiration to everybody, to all the kids out there."
Paul Newman

"Just watching his desire to excel and do anything anyone else does - and better - is totally uplifting to me."
Mario Andretti

"Craig captures his audience with an uplifting message of courage and determination (through) his positive attitude and zest for life."
David Glass
Chairman & CEO,
Wal-Mart Stores, Inc.

"Over the years I have had many enjoyable experiences with Craig, from whitewater rafting in West Virginia to letting him drive my Formula speed boat in the Gulf of Mexico. Craig's not a bad captain of a boat as long as you don't mind driving in circles!"
David B. Skinner
Regional Leader
Edward Jones

"A lot of things that people do in their lives can make a difference for others. Craig's story is an example of this."

Tim Allen
Actor

"Craig is a hoot, a laugh a minute. I think I know him inside and out. Behind all of the laughter is a driven guy, the 'ultimate survivor.' I will never forget a one liner he told me after he lost a job, his marriage, and a home within a thirty day period, 'Wow, am I ever glad that's behind me.'"

Dick Schultz,
Friend and Confidant
St. Petersburg, FL

"For twelve years I've witnessed the energy and inspiration of Craig MacFarlane. Some may look at Craig and feel sorry for him. I look at Craig and feel a sense of jealous admiration. We all dream of leaving this world having made it a better place. The irony is that Craig has not only done that, but actually does it on a daily basis."

Rick Sherman
President/CEO
Fortune Hotels

"Craig is more than a motivational speaker, he is an inspiration to all who hear his words. Many individuals have the ability to motivate. Few are blessed with the gift to inspire."

Shawn Daily
General Partner
Edward Jones

DEDICATION

To my parents, Joyce and Earl, for always being there for me and to my son, Dalton, for enriching my life.

Table of Contents

Acknowledgments

When you've lived a life like mine, it's hard to know where to start saying thanks. Here's a "short" list. No doubt I will accidentally leave out someone who's been important to me in my life, or important in preparing this book.

Top of the list has to be my employer, Edward Jones Investments. Today Edward Jones has become a major player in the investment industry. In my heart and mind there's no company in the financial industry that better serves the needs of the individual investor from a customer service standpoint, than Edward Jones. Their genuine warmth and compassion for people of all ages is what impresses me most.

Many people at Edward Jones are important to me. I have to start with Jim Schmidt, who started me down this path. Dave Lane, Dave Skinner, Shawn Daily, Price Woodward, Terry Eskind, Barb Dothage and John Philpott are good buddies. Thank you to Becky Maddox and Greg Spady for all of the times we spent together. Jim Weddle invited me to become a limited partner and I was deeply honored. I must wholeheartedly thank John Bachmann for having the vision to create a spot for me on his team. I've enjoyed working with John Beuerlein, Amy Cox and the rest of the Edward Jones team.

Thanks to all those who helped me achieve one of my greatest accomplishments, passing the Series 7 exam. This allowed me to become a licensed stockbroker which entailed eighty-eight hours of audio-cassettes. Let me tell you, whoever wrote the Series 7 book had no sense of humor. I took the six-hour exam orally. What a test of concentration! Thankfully, I passed. Edward Jones gave me the opportunity to engage this challenge.

When you accumulate the air miles I do, you have thanks galore for those who help you rest at night. Start with Rich Sherman, president of Fortune Hotels TradeWinds Resort, St. Petersburg Beach, one of my favorite places. Steve Shalit, general manager of the Westin La Paloma in Tucson and Rich Masucci, general manager of the Bethesda, Maryland Hyatt have always treated me first class. Thanks to the staff of the Skydome Hotel, Toronto and for the comfort added to my busy schedule by the 100 nights a year or so that I stay in Marriott Hotels.

Thanks, as well, to David Glass, the outstanding CEO and chairman of Wal-Mart. Thanks also to Bob Costas who narrated the video of my life.

Thanks to Jon Saraceno of *USA Today* who introduced me to my

ACKNOWLEDGEMENTS

---

childhood hero Mario Andretti and his family, and to friends Paul Newman, Tim Allen and Gordie Howe who have always encouraged me. I appreciate the support given by Robert L. Crandall, chairman of the board and president of American Airlines.

To the employees of Air Canada and Canadian Airlines, many thanks for your hospitality.

I am honored to be able to extend thanks to former President George Bush and his lovely wife Barbara.

I'd like to express special appreciation for the expertise of my photographer, Ed Tyreman. Ed tells me his photographs are great and I'll just have to trust him on that. To Susan Brennen, my hairstylist and someone else that I have to trust, thanks for such a great job over the years.

Thanks as well to Patti Everson for countless hours devoted to this book.

Thanks, and a sigh of relief, to Bob Snodgrass, Darcie Kidson, John Lofflin and the crew at Addax Publishing Group.

A special thank you to Anna and Tony Mauris, Mike and Roberta Theisen, my lawyer Don Cohn and my accountant Duane Janssen.

My deepest appreciation to all my loyal fans in Sault St. Marie, Ontario and the surrounding area who have followed and believed in me since I was a child; also to Ray Gingras and family who helped me so much while I attended Korah Collegiate.

I must give special thanks to my main man, Dick Schultz, his kids, Lindsey and Aaron and his wife, Beverly. Dick has been there when I needed him.

Heartfelt thanks to my mom and dad, Earl and Joyce, for their patience and commitment in helping me write this book. To my brother Ian, my nephew John and my niece Crystal - thanks for being there.

To my son, Dalton, my closest friend and companion in life. Thinking of the great times we have spent together helps me through the days we're apart.

Aunt Shirley and Fred, thank you for your support.

To Paul Hendrick and his family, many thanks for the continued belief in me over the years.

Thanks to Nikkie Federico, a terrific friend.

I should also thank the wonderful students who have written me touching letters across the years. You know who you are.

And how do you ever thank all of the unsung heroes that have touched my life along the way.

Craig MacFarlane

FOREWORD
BY GEORGE BUSH

It is my pleasure and privilege to tell you about a truly
remarkable person, Craig MacFarlane. I first met Craig in 1984
when President Reagan invited him to carry the Olympic Torch
through Washington, D.C., on its way to the Los Angeles Games.
Craig is a young man whose own inner flame of determination,
boundless energy, and courage served as a point of light in
countless lives. That is why we asked Craig to join our Reagan–
Bush All Star Team during the 1984 Republican National
Conventions. Each time, Craig carried, with dignity and clarity
his inspirational message that through hard work, dedication,
strength of character, and purpose, we all can achieve our goals.
Despite being blinded in a tragic accident at age 2, Craig's
accomplishments in a wide variety of sports are incredible. He
exemplifies the kind of indomitable spirit that makes America
great; and over the past 12 years, Craig MacFarlane has taken his
message of PRIDE – Perseverance, Respect, Individuality, Desire,
Enthusiasm – to youth in over 1600 high schools. Barbara and I
are proud to call Craig a friend. I invite you to meet him
yourself in these pages of "Inner Vision" and discover the fire
within that can touch and inspire us all.

George Bush
41st President of the United States of America

WINNER
BY JAMES BRUCE JOSEPH SIEVERS

I met him only briefly
but still I felt I knew
This young man was very special
and so I listened to
All the kidding and laughing and joking
that hid the person inside.
He was more than what he displayed
and so again I tried
To see if I could see
what pushed him so very hard.

He had fulfilled so many dreams
and come so very far
But there was still a hunger,
a constant, burning drive,
Like a lion on the hunt
...it made him come alive.

There was an energy all around him
that came from deep inside
This was the key to Craig MacFarlane
...the word he used was pride.

Perseverance and respect,
individualism and desire.
These were the fuel that gave him the chance
...enthusiasm lit the fire.

WINNER

Nature isn't always fair
She made this young boy blind
Yet in so doing, she made him better
...She forced him to use his mind.

It's not our faults that make us fail
or our talents that mean success.
It's what we do with what we've got
that separates one from the rest.

Somewhere along life's highway
some winds will have to blow.
Some will dwell in the mud and the slush
...A winner sees fresh fallen snow.

One man is angry if he doesn't have
what other men have got.
A winner develops just what he has
...A loser complains he has not.

And Craig MacFarlane has always been a winner
in the biggest event of them all...
This young man sees life as it is
and simply refuses to fall.

Craig sees all of his problems as raindrops
instead of storms.
He just smiles and smells the roses
...ignoring all the thorns
And so to himself he has proven
success is all in the mind.
Craig sees life as a marvelous challenge
I wonder...which of us is blind?

13

Riding the chairlift with my guide, I "sensed" the vastness of the mountain in the sounds of skiers below, in the cold thin air, and in the way I could hear forever. It was a real "eye opener."

CHAPTER ONE
CONQUERING MOUNTAINS

The hush that speaks to you only on top of a mountain was talking loudly to me now.

I heard it as I pointed my skis down the slope.

"I can do this. I can do this," the voice kept repeating in my ear.

Whispers of encouragement blew out of the pine trees breathing heavy gusts of wind in my face and sending skiffs of snow swirling around my head.

The mountain seemed to drop off into a vast nothingness, a void eager to swallow up my courage and resolve, especially because I cannot see.

I had already taken one run down the mountain in the 1983 U.S. Blind National Snow-Ski Championships downhill competition in Alta, Utah. And the left knee, the one that had been so badly injured in a training run the day before, the one they said I couldn't stand or walk on, much less ski on — the one I'd had to sneak out of a Salt Lake hospital, just to make it to the top of the hill today — now felt like it would betray me. The throbbing sliced up into my shoulder blades.

The mountain seemed to shrug its own brawny shoulders. I felt a shadow of intimidation fall over me. Alta opened its craggy jaws and yelled into my ears:

"No, Craig. You can't."

I searched for some way to stop the churning in my belly. I remembered something someone once told me when I was becoming a national champion wrestler and sprinter back in high school in my native Canada: "The trick is to get a thousand butterflies to fly in unison inside you."

I gritted my teeth, trying to will those butterflies into formation. And then an old ally joined me, marshalling my forces.

The unknown.

Many people have a great fear of the unknown. I welcome it. I'd forgotten how welcome the unknown had been in my life as I stood there with my skis aimed down the mountainside. Suddenly I remembered how I'd always loved the challenge, the experience, the visualization process that goes with taming the unknown. I'd forgotten about what it was like to be out there on the edge, feeling it, wrapping my arms around it, harnessing it and then conquering it.

I had absolutely thrived on that all my life.

And now the unknown spoke louder than the hush and the wind. It made my blood run quicker. It flicked the shadow from my shoulders, stilled the spasms in my stomach and transformed the void from a threat into an open invitation. Yes, I remembered.

It is walking on the edge, taking it to the limit, pushing through the envelope — it is not knowing what will happen next — that has always fueled my fire.

This was just the very best time of all the times in my life that I'd discovered it.

Suddenly, I didn't care that my knee was swollen like a balloon pulling my leg almost too tight to bend and I didn't care if the pain knifing up my back cut me in two. I didn't care if I left my leg on the side of the mountain that day.

Energized, electrified, pulsing with the moment, I pushed with all my strength out of the starting gate and launched myself straight down the mountain, down the snow that had turned into an icy sheet — maximum speed, maximum risk, just the way I like it — down toward fifteen zigzagging gates, down toward the gold medal at the bottom which no one in the skiing world ever thought I had a chance to win.

Ok, Alta, it's you and me, baby. Two minutes, toe-to-toe. You've given me your best shot. Now let me show you what I've got.

DAY ONE: A NOVICE IN A SNOW DRIFT

I took up snow-skiing for the first time in my life only four scant months before the blind national championships in Alta, Utah. In itself, that is amazing.

I had moved to the United States on September 19, 1982. I was working for the Hartford Whalers Hockey Club and, quite frankly, I was a little bored. I'm such a high-strung, driven person and you have to realize that I was twenty and this was the first fall that I had been away from athletic competition since I was seven.

I was still in great physical condition, closing in on 100 gold medals of various kinds in different sports. The majority came in wrestling, but I had also won gold in track and field, where my main events were the sprints.

My job with the Whalers was community relations, but I also skated with them toward the end of their practices. Occasionally I would take a few shots on their goalie.

I was skating with hockey legend Gordie Howe at the end of those practices; at the time I was living with Gordie and his wife in a Hartford suburb. But practice skating wasn't enough to fill the chasm inside that athletes sometimes feel when they stop competing. I was still extremely hungry for a new challenge to bring back that old feeling of competition.

For a blind person, athletic opportunities beyond high school are rare. Professional opportunities are even more rare. Most blind athletes participate in individual sports, most professional opportunities are on teams. I was trying to resign myself to that reality but not having much success.

I am not a person who will sit there when he's forty and say,

"Gosh, was there anything else I could have done?" I've always been hell-bent for action, occasionally to my detriment, but more often than not in a beneficial way.

My trademark has always been, "I'll try anything and I'll give it everything." If I'm going to do something, I'm going to give it my best effort. That comes from my own wanting to achieve, my internal drive, and my fear of failure.

But why skiing?

It was new. It was exciting. It was different. I didn't know anything about blind people doing it. I also thought that it would be an incredible rush.

Just the noise I'd hear of the skis coming down the slope when I'd listen to *Wide World of Sports* on television seemed exciting. The chatter on the snow, the vibration of it and the way they explained it and the swish of them going by, had always intrigued me. I thought, "Wow, that would be an incredible thing to try."

I was grateful for the job with the Whalers. It was fulfilling. But I decided to give skiing a try because of the same thing that had always motivated me. I wanted more. I wanted something that matched my personality. And although wrestling fulfilled part of that, it didn't completely fill the void — not even being good enough to win over ninety percent of more than 500 career matches, often against sighted opponents.

Danger? Is that a good word for what I was seeking? I suppose. Living in the danger zone.

If you don't take risks, you don't fully maximize your potential, I'd always felt. I guess that was as good a reason as any to try snow-skiing.

I knew snow-skiing was pretty rare for a blind athlete. But I didn't realize how rare until I started calling different ski resorts to find out what was available.

I chased around various leads for two or three days. I learned they were heavily into blind skiing in Kirkwood, California, around Lake Tahoe, and in Winter Park, Colorado. But I didn't have the resources to go to either place. So I had to pull my horns in and settle for something closer. Smuggler's Notch, up in Vermont.

Smuggler's Notch was the closest place in the East where they taught blind people to snow-ski. And one of the guys there told me about one particularly good instructor named George Spangler.

It was a fantastic stroke of fortune to hook up with both Smugglers and George, even if just for four days of training. I told him who I was, some of the things I'd done and how I didn't want to ski for leisurely purposes. I told him I wanted to learn to race.

In exploring the possibilities for blind skiers I'd discovered a United States Blind National Snow-Skiing Championship that would be held in April in Alta, Utah.

Now I'm sitting in Hartford, it's the first part of December, and I'm not able to go up to Smuggler's until the first of January, 1983. I guess I should have had more patience about getting involved in those championships. They were only a little more than three months away and I was still a beginner. But I'd never even begun to calculate it like that. In my mind, if I was going to ski, I was going to do my best to win. That is the only way I have known how to do things.

But, to be sure, I was very naive about what was involved in the sport of snow-skiing. The Howes thought I was totally and completely crazy. Even Gordie, who may be the most competitive human being who ever lived, thought I was nuts.

"Number one, Bat," he said, he always affectionately called me "Bat," as in blind-as-a, "Number one, you're probably going to kill yourself up there on the mountains. That's all we need is a dingbat on skis."

Colleen, Gordie's wife, was like a mother to me. She thought I should take a scholarship at Yale and study undergrad law or political science.

"You're new in America. You have a job," she said. "That's why you're here, to make a career for yourself. Snow-skiing is not going to enhance it. What's another championship going to do? You have so many of those."

She was right, of course. Gordie probably was, too.

I could well kill myself up on a mountain, trying to race down it without the slightest idea where the hell I was going. I couldn't even imagine it myself — and I can imagine myself doing almost anything.

So playing it safe and just trying to nurture the secure job I had made sense, as Colleen said. But I just couldn't. It was the newness of skiing, the excitement of it, the semi-impossibility of it, that beckoned me.

It was like putting a ten-year-old kid in a go-kart and saying, "You can sit here, but you can't start it and you can't drive it."

I had my mind made up. I wanted to ski and I wanted to ski fast. Truthfully, I don't think the Howes were fully aware of my athletic capabilities. They knew I'd done some things in the past, but they'd never seen me in action.

Also, I think no one understood the importance of what athletics had meant to me. Gordie, who is synonymous with the word "athlete," of course knew as well as anyone what I was feeling. But not even he felt it as deeply as I.

Athletics had been the springboard that had continuously catapulted me forward, whether it was acceptance into a mainstream school in Canada, going to Carleton University in Ottawa, or coming to America.

Athletics was the foundation and core of who I was. Add to that the thought of blasting down a mountain at fifty miles-per-hour when you come from wrestling and running track, flatland sports. A mountain painted a new image in my mind. It provided a new aura of excitement. The great vastness of it, not knowing exactly what lay before me, was compelling.

On the telephone, George Spangler said that he would donate his time, which was incredibly kind and generous of him. With the financial aspect settled, nothing could deter me from going to Smugglers Notch.

CONQUERING MOUNTAINS

I remember riding the Greyhound bus up there. I got a pair of skis and boots and ski pants, donated from a local shop in Hartford. I'd been pricing clothing and just kind of explained what I was going to try to do. And boy, this ski shop was so supportive. I wish I could tell you the name of the place, but they've gone out of business — maybe they gave away too many ski boots, bless their hearts.

I've been blessed with people who gave me huge helping hands like this all my life. Handouts, I hate. Hands up, I love. I never could have gotten anywhere without them…like most people.

While I was riding to Smugglers, I was remembering how the skis felt back in the store when I tried them on. I couldn't believe how long they were. The ski boots, I remember trying them on in the shop and they were cumbersome. So big, so bulky. So darned uncomfortable.

I still had that kid-with-a-new-toy excitement riding up there. I got off the bus and immediately was struck by what a great human being George was. He was such a man of patience. Boy, was I blessed with George.

He gave me a hug of greeting and said something like, "Holy smoke, you're built to take a tumble. This is going to be a piece of cake." That was a nice thought.

I came from the world of wrestling so I'm not afraid to take a spill. And, you know, that helped a lot, because he knew he could push me a little faster, a little harder. He didn't have to be afraid that if I fell hard I would give up. He wasn't exactly getting my mother's fine china.

He was dealing with a guy who's spent a considerable amount of time on his face, backside, ear, elbows, knees, nose — I'd had just about every conceivable piece of anatomy smashed or flattened or snapped at one time.

It was evening before I got into Smuggler's Notch, so we stayed there in a lodge at the foot of the mountain that night. By the way, you might wonder if blind people can tell day from night. The answer is yes, and by obvious ways, when you think of it.

It's not light or dark. I am completely blind. I can see no shadow or color or image, or any kind of subtle way of explaining vision. But, I notice night in the density of the air. The air gets thicker at night, and heavier. It's damper. The noises of the night, be it cicadas or the eerie droning of transports on a highway, all are different than in the day. The smell of the air is different. I can smell the night. I can almost taste the dampness or the dew.

And, of course, I know the night by its stillness, not everywhere, but especially in the country.

Being evening, anyway, George and I grab a bite at the chalet where we're staying. I hear the fireplace crackling, smell the oak and hickory coming from the fire and the warm aroma of steaks and other food off the grill, the soups and coffees in the air, the heat coming from the fireplace — I hear the lively chit-chat of men and women sitting around who have obviously spent a day on the slopes. It was all so cozy and warm. I thought, "What camaraderie."

It felt like the authentic log cabin my dad built back in Northern Ontario, but amplified 200 or 300 times. It was a big place and I thought, "What a mecca, what a beautiful, majestic setting." It brought such a feeling of exhilaration to me.

I thought it was really cool. So this is what you do in the evenings when you ski. After we had some Vermont sugar pie for dessert George introduced me to all kinds of people and kind of bragged to them on my accomplishments, which was nice of him to do. I have to admit it made me feel pretty good.

I've always been a social, outgoing person. In that moment, I was feeling the opposite. I had a quiet resolve that I was looking forward to the next morning and this wonderful experience.

The morning couldn't come quickly enough for me. I was up at about 4:30 a.m., humbled by the challenge, quietly preparing for the day. When morning finally arrived, George looked at me and said, "Well, this is it. Let's go out and have fun." I thought to myself, "What a great attitude." That became our motto: "Let's have fun."

"I'm ready. Let's do it," I said.

We chowed a nice breakfast, pancakes and some Vermont maple syrup — but just out of loyalty I prefer my homemade syrup, which we tap on the trees at my folks' property in Northern Ontario.

Then we got out there and we started putting the stuff on. Literally, I had to be shown: This is how a boot straps on, here's where it goes in the ski. Here's what you snap to keep it on. We spent probably two hours at the bottom, just with the skis on, George showing me what snowplowing is, how you ski.

For much of this, George did not have his skis on. He was physically moving me. At times he would want me to feel him. This is how you bend over. When we're going on a right-hand turn, this is how I want you to do it. Weight on the downhill ski and so forth.

It was a great way of teaching a blind person. It was creating the mental picture in my mind before I ever attempted it.

Then came something I didn't like. George said, "Hey, we gotta put on these orange bibs."

I said, "What for?"

"Yours says, 'Blind Skier,'" he said. "Mine says, 'Sighted Guide.'" So I said to him, "OK. Let's trade."

We both laughed.

But it still bummed me out. I understood the need for safety. People needed to know I was coming up on them. Instead of turning properly, I might screw up and ski into them. But the bib was the same thing as the white cane and the dog. I never used them. I had spent a lifetime avoiding them. I had spent a lifetime trying to ignore or suppress the label of "Blind Anything."

I had accepted my blindness and I was willing to live with it, but I didn't want always to be categorized as the "blind whatever" and here I was wearing it on my chest and on my back.

The other thing I didn't like: I think all of us when we're twenty years old are aware of our looks and our image. I was thinking, "Gosh, I wonder what the girls are going to think when they see this 'Blind Skier.' Are they going to think he's not cool or different or something?"

Still another thing — I had always programmed myself to attack anything I did, and here I had to accept the mindset: You've got to crawl before you walk before you run.

So it was painful in the beginning. I'd had my successes in sports but here — at twenty — I was learning what skiers learn at six. I was humbled by the magnitude of the mountains and the job I had ahead. Eventually, I came to grips with this fact: "Hey, my friend, this bib is for your own good." As I'd gotten to appreciate the sport and the mountain, I did an about face and I understood what a wonderful idea the bib is. Because some people come flying down the mountain like missiles and they kind of need a heads-up.

Also, it helped that Smugglers was a place where people may not look at you twice if you're blind. A lot of other blind people learn to ski there, so the orange bibs are no surprise. That gave me comfort.

As I'm interacting with George for a couple of hours at the bottom of the mountain, people are going up the chairlift and swishing around me, going here, going there. I'm thinking, "Man, it would be awesome to do what they're doing, the creme de la creme."

Once I got through being quite so overwhelmed at the size of the mountain, I began to love the size of it. I also loved the sound of the skis. In Vermont, in January, the snow is hardpack and crunchy underfoot. Just to hear skiers stopping sort of reminded me of a stop you would make on ice skates. It was a little different sound, not as smooth as the sound you make on skates. George used my experience as an ice skater growing up in Canada to teach me snow-skiing techniques. He said, "You're going to draw from some of that."

Conquering Mountains

No matter what I drew from, I felt hopeless in the beginning.

The first time we went up the tow rope on the bunny slope, the tips of my skis crossed and I crumpled and wiped out. I thought, "Oh God, I'm holding up some other people. What a fool I am." I haven't gone five feet and I'm on my face. Great. I hated that.

Blind people are often hypersensitive about looking inept or foolish — myself included. Of course, everyone in the world feels the same about looking stupid, but sometimes I think it's just more acute with me because I detest people pitying me or seeing me as some dysfunctional freak.

But George kept telling me, "Hey, you can't see it, but I'm tellin' ya, there's people falling, there's people crashing and slipping and sliding all over the place out here. Not just you."

That made me feel better.

These were the days when George was skiing behind to guide me. He'd kind of call out, "Ok, Ok...you're Ok, keep goin'." It was rough around the edges because I was new and he was new to doing this with me. So we just kind of ad-libbed it.

The very first time down the bunny slope I did not fall. The second time down I did. Both times, I was skiing with the element of fear, like I was going to hit something, and if I did, it would be head-first. I wasn't skiing with any confidence at all.

Things hardly got smoother when we took the chair-lift up for the first time.

George said, "I'm gonna give you a countdown, three...two...one, and that'll mean the chair is right under you, and you can sit down."

Only trouble was, I heard the three...two...one thing and I sat down, but George didn't. He was so concerned about seeing that I got on, he missed getting on the chair with me.

I reach my hand over.

Geez. No George.

I'm thinking, God, this is strange. This must be some kind of joke. Does it come back and get George or what?

But, of course, he had jumped on the chair behind me and

he yelled out, "Hey, I got a little tangled up. But don't worry about it. When we get to the top, I'll give you three...two...one. Slide off at the end of the ride. Give me a few seconds and I'll come along side you."

But I was thinking, "Man, I just heard this three-two-one business. It didn't work."

Meanwhile, my skis were hanging in the air and the chair was rocking back and forth and I was thinking all the way up, "What happens if this darn thing breaks? I'm toast. I'm gonna fall X number of feet. And X is gonna mark the spot where I hit."

I could get a general feel for how high it was because people are skiing underneath me as well as off in the distance, and I can hear the swishing sound going down.

Despite my uncertainty and the confusion, I managed to say to myself, "Wow. This is awesome.

"If I could see, now, what would I see?"

It was just one of the most beautiful feelings of my life. Although I couldn't see it, I imagined these snow-capped mountains, riding up a chair-lift and skiers coming down of all sizes and shapes and colors and clothing.

Before I knew it, time had arrived for the three-two-one drill again. We got to the end of the lift and George called out, "Three...two...one.."

I got off the chair and stepped into...

Nothing.

I don't know if I jumped too early or he counted too fast or he couldn't see me properly. There was a little snow falling at the top of the mountain. But I fell about ten feet and landed in a huge snowdrift.

I was lying there in a sense of agony and frustration, thinking, "Golly, do people really enjoy this sport?"

It was the age old story of hurting my pride more than hurting myself. I'd stung my shoulder because I landed in a heap. Of course, my skis came off and one of them kind of went skidding partway down the hill. I thought, "Oh my God. This is humiliating."

Two girls and a guy came over to me and saw the "blind skier" vest and they said, "Whoa. Are you Ok?"

"Yeah. Yeah. I'm Ok," I said.

I remember the guy saying, "Well, what happened?"

I said, "I don't know. It's my first time on a chair lift. Tell me something. Is that how everyone gets off?"

"No. You came off early," he said with a laugh.

I found that to be a considerable relief, believe me.

"You're supposed to glide on the snow and then get off," he said.

I said, "Geez, I was beginning to think you needed a parachute for this sport."

I was thinking, man, I heard getting down the mountain was kind of an adventure. I never knew getting up was such a challenge.

By now George and these new acquaintances had taken their skis off and everyone was helping me get my skis on and put Humpty Dumpty together again.

George thanked the folks and so did I.

And then the one guy said, "Boy, you've got a lotta guts because if you could see down this thing, you might not be comin' down it."

Which was true but I said, "Gee, thanks for the vote of confidence, pal."

I thought at that moment, you often struggle in life through the valleys so you can have the opportunity to climb the mountains. Then when you start to climb, you meet all kinds of setbacks, the mountains are full of moguls and boulders and pitfalls. It's how you deal with those that determines your success. Such an awful beginning would have stopped some people. But, in my life, I could never let myself be stopped by something that got in the way. I could be embarrassed, maybe, but not stopped.

I got back on my feet. I realized for the first time, "I'm finally at the top of a mountain."

"Man, is it this steep all the way down?" I asked George.

"There's parts where its steeper and parts where it's less steep," he said.

I felt like I was just going to fall away somewhere off the side of the mountain. It was a huge eye-opener to me. It was like, oh my God, I didn't really envision that mountains were this big.

I sensed the enormity of it, because I'd ridden the chairlift for so long to get up there. The coldness up there bit deeply into my bones, even for a Canadian. The air was thin. I could hear forever. This was such an amazing mountain. I had never stood so high.

We started down on our first trip from the top. I was less graceful than I wanted to be and my skis sometimes flared up or parted wider than they should. It almost had me singing soprano a couple times. But what George preached to me was, "We're going to keep tight corners." In other words, we're not going to let you build up speed. We're not going to let you run. It's basically going to be turn-to-turn. Turning left, ski, ski, ski, turning right — we're going to keep you very controlled. We're going to do one or two corners and then we're going to stop.

Then we're going to talk about it.

And of course on those first turns, my uphill ski would be dancing around a little bit because I had all my weight on the downhill ski. My sense of balance helped a lot. It was a balance I seemed to have naturally and was enhanced by my years of wrestling and just navigating through life without sight. I was nowhere near smooth, but I didn't fall on the first two or three corners. George was really pumped.

As we're coming down on the first run, we link several turns together and as we linked maybe five or six turns, building more speed because of the natural terrain of the mountain, suddenly I went scooting off the trail.

George hollered, "Sit, sit, sit."

So I sat down. I was kind of in between two trees off the groomed part of the course. I could reach out one hand and reach out the other and touch them.

Conquering Mountains

"Say `Hi' to that big pine on your left," George called out.

The trees were no more than five to six feet apart. I was zinging along between 'em like a human football splitting the uprights. Fortunately, I didn't hit one. But, it was frustrating. You had to concentrate on so many things. I remember getting done with the first run and being so mentally and physically drained. My quadriceps burned like fire. My muscles ached. My whole body ached. I had a brain-cramp. It was because of the incredible amount of concentration it took to get to that point.

"Wow, that was-one run," I told myself. "Imagine how hard it's going to be to do more."

I had fought to utter exhaustion in wrestling. But because of my stiffness skiing, and the fact that I couldn't make myself relax mentally that first day, I found skiing far more draining than wrestling.

In skiing, you're not only concentrating on everything you're supposed to do, you're concentrating on the voice that provides your sense of direction. So if you start daydreaming, a split second later, boom, you're going between two trees. Or you smack headlong into one. Fortunately, I didn't nail a tree on the first run.

The second trip down the mountain, we did get on the chairlift together and that was a majestic ride, because now George was with me, explaining how the mountain goes up, explaining how the groomed trail is narrow. The trail wound around down through the trees, with snow that had gently fallen that day clinging to the branches like someone had emptied a shaker of powdered-sugar on them. George described the different outfits the skiers were wearing, the brilliant reds, oranges, yellows, pinks and purples.

Just to create that dreamy, wonderful snowy scene was really breathtaking, even to a blind person. I thought, "Wow, this snow-skiing stuff is part of my Canadian roots and heritage, and I'm out here and I'm doing it." And that helped me a lot mentally.

I could hear such an enormous distance up there, like to the next peak and the next. It gave me this sense of the majesty of the mountains.

We turned in a solid first day of skiing. I was fairly happy, considering that I hadn't fallen every single time down the mountain and hadn't smashed into anything face-first.

But there was still something not right. At first, I couldn't grasp what that was. I knew I was skiing afraid and hesitant, thinking, "It's only a matter of time until I hit something."

Then, an instructor came up to George and me and asked how it went. I said, "Great, I didn't fall much."

And he said, "Sounds like a lousy day. If you're not falling, you're not pushing yourself enough."

I realized that this was part of the learning process, your spills. I had been more concerned with not looking foolish than truly extending. That kind of thinking had held me back.

The second day, I turned up the volume on everything. I went down the mountain with a lot more speed and ran into objects with a lot more regularity.

The worst was the first run of the second morning. We had come down, eight turns and stopped. We certainly weren't to the stage where we actually zoomed all the way down a run. But we were getting to where we're starting to float along pretty well actually.

I was beginning to take skiing for granted, to enjoy it more. I was relaxing. Again, that's always a bad idea doing any sport, much less skiing.

George told me to turn left. I did. But I didn't totally loop it and start coming back up out of the turn. I went straight down. And suddenly, the mountain was falling away from me, like 100 degrees. I was burning this thing.

For a split instant I thought, "This is cool. This is like flying."

And I vaguely heard George saying, "You gotta turn. You gotta turn."

And then he screamed, "Sit! Sit!"

But I was frozen in time. I was in that place where you know what you're supposed to do, but your mind won't let you do it. Next thing I know — whoom — I pop up over this frozen little bank and then a three-foot drop and my skis land — bam — I didn't know where at first...but it was in the parking lot.

And now I'm smashing into something metal. And I'm thinking "What the heck is a car doing on the ski slope? This isn't right."

I had, indeed, smashed into a car, but it was not full-force. I was lucky.

And actually, I was relieved. What had been going through my mind and freaking me out a second earlier was: Maybe I'm going over a twenty-foot drop. Maybe I'm gonna go over a cliff.

That was always one of my fears, that I was going to go over a huge cliff into utter nothingness. I couldn't know it was coming. No one could shout at me quickly enough to stop me. When you're blind, you don't know if that air you just jumped into is three feet or thirty-five feet.

But of course, my fantasies and fears aside, I had just gone into a three-foot orbit, and after deflecting off the end of the one car in the parking lot I was still alive and well.

So was the car. We didn't need to talk about damage...again, fortunately. I could just see the owners turning that one into the insurance man.

"What do you mean a blind skier hit your car in the parking lot?"

The second trip down that second day, I was sailing along and I just walloped this girl and sent her flying. I ended up staying on my skis. My two skis went across her two skis and it was almost like a body check in hockey, hip-to-hip, and I just launched her out of her skis. My left hand went to the snow as I fought to maintain my balance and I pushed myself back up. I finished my loop and stopped. I was still standing. She wasn't.

By the time I got stopped, George was already over where the girl was saying, "Gosh, are you OK?"

It made me feel worse that it was a girl instead of a guy,

although hitting her, I guess, was a step up from a Buick. When I got over there and heard her glasses were broken, I guess I was surprised they were all I had fractured.

I was so sorry and embarrassed that I'd clocked her. She said her name was Beth and I said, "Oh, gosh, Beth, I really apologize. You know, I'll pay for the glasses."

She said, "No, you don't have to." She would not let me pay for them. She was totally sweet about it.

Obviously she saw our bibs designating us a blind skier and his guide and she knew we were stumbling around. George explained it was my second day on skis. George told me that I had turned a little tighter than normal and he also told Beth, "You gotta be a little more heads-up, not just for blind skiers, but for any skiers. When you're coming through like that, you need to be aware of other people on the mountain."

He spread the responsibility around, which made me feel a little better though not much. But I had to take full responsibility for the next thing I hit, because it couldn't get out of the way.

A snow hydrant.

I rocketed right into it, chest-first, and it was like being kicked by a workhorse. I mean, holy buckets. It nearly broke me in two. But I pulled myself together and went on. I was well schooled in pushing past pain through my wrestling trials. After we finished runs four and five that second day, I went to a hospital where they took X-rays. The pictures showed a cracked rib. I also was sporting some nice bruises for effect.

A cracked rib makes you feel like you can't take a deep breath. But not only were my ribs hurting, my spirits were cracked, too. Back in the lodge after the trip to the hospital, in the warmth of the fireplace, I turned to George in desperation and said, "I need you to ski in front of me." I felt that's what was holding me back. The uneasy feeling I had about our progress after the first day came down to this: I'm racing down the mountain sightless with nothing between me and the trees, cars and other skiers, but my nose. I simply couldn't let go, the way I was used to letting go in sports.

He was resistant, because if we skied that way he wouldn't be able to see what I was doing. He felt he couldn't see to coach me. He'd have to constantly ski looking backward. The whole thing was so foreign to him, because he had seen other instructors on the mountain, and had seen other blind skiers out west, and he said one thing to me with great conviction.

"They just don't do it that way, in front. This is the way they do it, in back."

But I said, "Now wait a minute, something's not right. I keep bashing and smashing into things. After running into a car, a girl and a snow hydrant, would you lean forward when you thought the first thing that you were going to hit was your face?

"I mean, call me crazy — is it just me or is this system not working? I may need to be hit over the head with a two-by-four, but I don't need to keep crashing into animate and inanimate objects to know we have to change something."

I think by then my determination was winning him over and he thought, "By golly, I'll try anything at this stage because this lion's still on the mountain."

I explained why I knew I would be able to hear him and his skis in front of me. I told him about when I was running the 100 meter sprints in track they had a coach with a megaphone in front calling out instructions. So you could run to his voice with confidence.

George felt awkward doing this in the beginning. Then we started locking into each other late on the third day. Suddenly, we were becoming something of a terror. By that third afternoon, we'd skied three-quarters of a run without stopping.

George said, "Geez, I'm gonna have to get an oxygen bottle if I'm gonna keep yelling for that amount of time."

But he had to admit, running in front of me made all the difference in the world in the way I took to skiing. Granted, I was still awkward. We decided it was best to try and maintain a "pocket" of six to eight feet between us and many times that grew to thirty. But it was a heck of an improvement from the first day.

He noticed instantly a change in my form. When he was skiing behind me, I wasn't crouched, I wasn't tucked, I wasn't leaning forward, because then you're leaning straight into the unknown. It's hard to put your nose first. Your mind rebels.

But when he was in front of me, instantly I crouched lower. I leaned forward. Now my body posture said "Let's go!"

To me, my newfound comfort was pretty simple: If he's in front of me, he's going to hit something before I do. So it really played to my strengths and George picked up on that immediately.

All the runs the third day were vast improvements over my previous trips down the mountain and by the last run of the day, we skied clean all the way down.

That was a huge tonic. That one good run made me feel such a surge of confidence; the rib injury wasn't going to dampen my spirits. No way. I was still high on the adrenaline from the three days on the slopes.

Also, I didn't want to go slinking back home to Gordie and say, "I've broken a rib. I can't do this. It's too tough for me."

I was determined to show Gordie and Colleen — and myself — that I was right. That I could succeed at this sport.

When George and I came back to the lodge after the third day, our last day together, he said, "Don't you play the piano?"

I said, "A little bit."

He said, "Hey, play me a tune."

I played a couple of Elton John songs like, "Someone Saved My Life Tonight" and "Yellow Brick Road." And "Let it Be" by the Beatles. I also played a few tunes I had written, some of which remain nameless and lyric-less.

But one of them is called, "I'll Be Waiting in the Wings for You." Another is called "You'll Be Tearing Me Apart." Obviously I had written the second song to a girl, but when you think about it, I guess it was pretty appropriate if you sang it to the ski slopes.

CONQUERING MOUNTAINS

There were some folks gathering around the piano, chiming in, and I felt like part of the fraternity of skiers, which was important to me.

I met Beth, the skier I'd smacked into out on the slopes a day earlier, in the lounge. She was with a group of girls who were students from Boston. She commented on how we went by them that third day. They said we were looking good.

And there was starting to be a lot of chatter by others on the mountain and in the lodge about what a tremendous progression we'd made after only three days. In that short period of time, I'd created a new way for blind people to ski. Other instructors were talking about the change. "Your spirit to move forward was something they had never seen even out of a sighted skier," George said.

By now, there was camaraderie on the slopes. There were people coming up and talking.

"Nice to see you out here."

"Loved your piano playing."

This was affirmation. Welcome to our club. Welcome to our world. You have arrived.

By day four, I ached all over. I could have ripped through ten matches in a row on the mat and not felt this bad. I had muscles hurting I never knew existed. The quads, the hamstrings. My feet were aching from being cramped in those boots. My shoulders ached from the spills.

But when we got up on the mountain, those aches evaporated. I felt much better. I was invigorated by the idea of improving. And George observed how much more relaxed I was skiing. Physically relaxed, not mentally relaxed. I knew what happened when I relaxed my mind going down the hill. But once I relaxed my body, skiing was so much easier.

We skied hard and a lot that last day. We skied more smoothly without some of the previous excitement. When I say the fourth day was uneventful, that's like saying a flight from Los Angeles to New York is uneventful. Think of the alternative.

I had quit crash-landing all over the mountain. In that sense, boring was good. It was one of the great confidence days for me snow-skiing because it seemed like such a quantum leap forward. I came into the lodge that night and said to myself, "I am a skier."

That was also the day the lightbulb really went off over my head.

"George, I'm going for it. I'm going to ski nationals," I said.

He was lukewarm at first: "Oh man, let's worry about next year. You wouldn't be ready this year."

But I wanted so badly to take it to the next level. I wasn't happy just saying, "Ok, this was a nice experience. See ya."

George and I knew our time together was coming to an end. He was a part-time instructor from New Jersey and he had to go back and work. And he wasn't being negative about my chances.

He was just trying to dial in the reality of things.

But by then, by the end of the fourth day, we were going through tougher runs and skiing blacks, those really steep runs.

George could sense my intensity about this challenge. He said he had no idea how good or fast the competition would be at the blind nationals, but, yes, he thought if I kept training, maybe I could compete against the best.

Late the following day, I walked back into the Howes' house. I found Gordie in the kitchen. "So, Bat, you didn't kill yourself," he said, something endearing, as usual.

"Not even close, Chief."

I always called him Chief out of respect — I'm not really sure why, except in my mind he was the head of the entire hockey world. For a boy from Canada, Gordie Howe was it. Mr. Hockey.

Anyway, I refused to tell Gordie or Colleen about the rib and I refused to tell them about hitting the car and the girl and the hydrant and all that. I omitted a few minor details and cut to the chase.

I told Gordie about my vision of trying to get some sponsors together and going for it all. Going to the nationals. At that stage Gordie was pretty supportive. He knew he wasn't going to tame the lion, because I was ready to roar and breathe fire about skiing.

Then I had another Godsend. I was riding on an airplane a week later, flying back to Hartford from New York where I'd given a speech. I was sitting next to a guy named Arnold Kleinfeld. He noticed I was blind and we started talking. Naturally, I told him about skiing competitively. He asked about my goals and I said, "The blind nationals."

He turned to me and said, "I'd love to help." Then he gave me his business card.

Arnold Kleinfeld paid for much of my next phase of training. Someone else had decided to share my inner vision and believe in what I could do. He made it possible for me to ski against the best blind skiers in the country. The rest was up to me.

I pioneered a new way of blind skiing with the guide in front instead of trailing, similar to the way blind sprinters run. My most recent guide, Paul, keeps me on track in a non-competitive run.

CHAPTER TWO
TOTALLY LOST IN SKIING

Kirkwood Meadows, California, in the Tahoe Basin, is mecca for blind skiers, especially for competitive blind skiers. I said my goodbyes to the Howes, thanked them profusely for putting me up, and for putting up with me, then I headed for California. Gordie and Colleen were warm and encouraging, as usual.

I had spoken by telephone with Bob Weber out there, a man who was really connected to the blind skiing world. I explained to him a little about my background wrestling and sprinting, and I told him about my experiences with George Spangler. "I'm looking for the most aggressive ski instructor I can lay my hands on," I told Bob.

Bob put me in touch with Cliff May. Cliff was an instructor at Kirkwood Ski Resort. He was also known as a total go-for-it skier who had raced competitively and seemed to have a personality that would mesh with mine.

I lived in a ski lodge my first week at Kirkwood, then Cliff invited me to come live at his house, which meant for free, a big boost to my finances. Cliff and his wife Christine, lived in a house literally at the base of the mountain. You walked out their door and you were there.

Training with Cliff was a trip from beginning to end. He was funny, kind and patient, but the thing that really hit me was his can-do spirit. He was never-say-die from the first second I met him and his personality blended perfectly with mine.

The first thing we did when we got out to the slopes was to find two bamboo poles about ten feet long. He was on the front end of the two; I was at the back. This was Cliff's idea. It was a horse and carriage concept. What it did was teach me rhythm. It helped teach me the pocket where I should ski. It gave me a feel for how he was going to turn as we went down the mountain.

I needed to get his rhythm before I could get mine. What is it like to make an absolutely proper racing turn? How far am I supposed to come up? Now we were more in race mode. We weren't hooking the turns and looping them as high. We weren't bleeding off speed. We were going for the mental image of cutting a gate and continuing forward.

We also went down sometimes with my two skis between his, with me hanging onto his hips. I'm sure people thought: "Whooo. Look at those two."

But you can stand and tell a blind person what you expect for hours. There's just no greater way to create that mental picture than hands-on. It taught me motion, it taught me the feel, it taught me how it was supposed to be to get into racing position. I learned the runs were wider at Kirkwood than Smugglers Notch. There was not as much ice. California snow was generally a different texture which created a different sound of skiing, as opposed to snow in Vermont. And the trees were much larger than in Vermont which Cliff let me feel. Through Cliff's methods, we were beginning to pick up speed, getting the groove and tempo.

However, it goes without saying that life was not a bed of roses. Cliff and I had some gargantuan wipeouts. I mean, we had some just absolutely spectacular crackups, like some stunts you might see in a Stallone movie. Only we weren't acting.

I'd go straight over the top of Cliff. I was hitting him a lot. I'd speed up, or he wouldn't, or vice-versa. There was just so much that could go wrong in such a short amount of time when you're learning at high speeds.

You are really a team in blind skiing. To get totally in synch with your guide skier requires a lot of persistence on the blind skier's part. But it requires almost unimaginable patience and courage on the part of the guide.

Can you imagine a person willing to go up to the top of a mountain and let someone coming down at, say forty miles-per-hour, smash into him repeatedly?

Cliff takes this stranger into his home and devotes twenty-four hours a day to this project. It takes a unique individual to do this. Unbelievable, really. Cliff never complained about helping me or any of the trouble involved.

Not once.

Cliff was always looking for ways to improve our communication and therefore better my confidence and technique. For instance: He was working on a technique for us coming over a headwall together. A headwall is where the mountain suddenly takes a pitch and falls away, like a roller-coaster. It's the steep part of a mountain. You are either going to be airborne or you are going to increase speed rapidly.

We came up with the one-two-three system of rating them, with three the toughest. Each one we went over, he'd yell out the proper number so I'd know what I was hitting.

When we weren't actually skiing, we lived, breathed and thought skiing, whether it was breakfast, lunch, dinner — that's what we talked about. Composition of the skis, the poles, the boots, the bindings, the wax, the hill, the snow conditions. Or Cliff would read me articles from skiing magazines.

I totally submerged myself in this. I guess it was kind of like going to boot camp in the military. That was my life, twenty-four hours a day, week after week after week.

So naturally, I inhaled more about skiing in two or three months than most people would in several years.

Cliff got completely locked and loaded on this whole wacky idea of mine. We were possessed. We were destined. We were going to win. And by golly if we didn't, we were going to give it a heck of a shot.

Christine was absolutely in my corner and put up with a lot from Cliff and me. Holy buckets, she made pastas, seafood, steaks — whatever we wanted. Unbelievable. It was just like I was part of the family. I had a nice room. A dream come true. I mean, I was right at the mountain. You walked out and it was right there.

I remember one time we had a major snowstorm where the slope was closed a couple of days. When I walked out the snowfall was just enormous. Several feet had fallen.

But Cliff didn't want to waste a day of training. He talked Bob Weber into taking the snow machine up the mountain and then driving us up on the snowmobile when the chairlift was closed, so we could ski down.

Sometimes we'd take snowmobile pleasure tours of the back-country, just to relieve the tension. We ran around, had snowball fights and lived one heck of a lifestyle.

But mostly we were busy pushing ourselves to the limit and beyond. When you do that you're going to win sometimes, and sometimes you're going to lose.

One day we lost, big-time. We took one of those infamous "last runs" where a lot of people get hurt. Not only were we tired, but the wind was howling and biting into us. Going up on the chairlift, we were debating whether I would hang onto his hips and just come down so we could get off this darn mountain. There was no one around; it was the end of the day. We decided, what the heck, let's just try it once without me even hanging on to the poles.

That free skiing was something we liked to do at the end of the day, sort of a reward for hard work earlier.

I was fine about a third of the way down. Then, suddenly, I lost his voice and next thing I knew - wham — I'm into a tree.

Totally Lost in Skiing

It doesn't take long at those speeds to run into something. Some of the corners are near the tree line. I had hit the tree with the tip of one of my skis then hit it with my shoulder. It spun me around so hard it drilled me into the snow like a giant corkscrew. The snow was soft off the trail and the impact and the spinning motion just about buried me.

The impact knocked my helmet off and, of course, both skis. All Cliff could see was my head sticking out of the snow. He skied over and when he first saw me he honestly thought I was dead. If I had been six inches to the left, my face would have hit the tree instead of my shoulder. In that case, I probably would have been dead.

He had a hard time making it over to me because the snow was so powdery. It was all fresh because it had been snowing so hard. Actually, "storming" is a better word for it than snowing. We definitely shouldn't have been up there. But, that powdery snow was probably a blessing; it saved me from a more severe injury. I felt God watching out for me.

In a way the collision put a fear in me that hadn't been there before. But in another way we used it to move forward. We really dissected it that night. While Christine was certain we were nuts — and she was probably right — the comfort we found in all this was that the accident had nothing to do with technique. It had to do with the fact we simply shouldn't have been there. Conditions were bad. It was just sheer stupidity. It wasn't a question of our skiing style or ability. We were a few weeks deep into this by now and we were beginning to really crank down the mountain.

We may not have had the proper judgment. We were both so gung-ho, we needed a stabilizer to say, "You fools, don't go up there."

But the incident made us question what we were doing to this extent: When is enough, enough? It took us to a different level mentally. It allowed us to go at skiing a little more relaxed.

INNER VISION

We skied in the morning, we skied in the afternoon, but we took more breaks from the mountain. We weren't obsessed by it. We didn't let the mountain run us. We ran it.

We'd figured that every minute on the slope was a minute somebody else wasn't practicing. But that's not necessarily true in skiing. We were actually overtraining.

We started doing a lot of work with Bob Weber as the stabilizer. Cliff would ski in front of me and Weber would ski behind me quite a ways, maybe forty feet or fifty even. He was invaluable in critiquing what we were doing. It was a great advantage to have this other set of expert eyes to evaluate us and offer suggestions.

By now we were ready for an actual competition and one, blessedly, came to us in the form of the local Kirkwood Invitational about six weeks after I'd come out West. What was really nice about this competition was that many of the skiers from the nationals were also training periodically at Kirkwood on weekends and were entered in the competition. None of them were there two-and-a-half months straight. But of course, a lot of them didn't need to be there that long. Some of them had been skiing for twenty years.

It was here that I was going to find out how far I'd come and how I stood in the big competitive picture. It was also here that I was to learn just how ostracized I was from the blind skiing community.

I did not yet feel like part of the blind skiing fraternity. I was the new kid on the block and I guess I couldn't blame them. Some of these guys had been skiing for decades. Who did I think I was, that I could come in and even pretend to compete on any kind of equal footing with them?

I was much more than an interloper. I was an intruder. And, hey, it's not like I went out of my way to suck up to them. I was too busy in my own little world with Cliff, trying to absorb as much as I could. It's not like we were on the mountain saying to each other, "Hey, there's a blind skier over there working hard, too." We didn't hang out at the lodge much. We didn't have to. The food was tremendous at home. All the company we needed was Christine. So this wasn't social fun and games.

And maybe, just maybe, they viewed me as a threat.

The Kirkwood Invitational included several previous national champions. They would be good measuring sticks. Cliff wasn't telling me this was too soon to face these kinds of skiers. He wanted to know where we stood, too. The invitational was to be held on the exact same mountain where we'd been training. I was hungry to know if I was in the big leagues or if I was still in the minors.

I was pumped. I was eager to go. It was a one-day competition with the giant slalom in the morning and the downhill in the afternoon.

When it was over, I came in third in the giant slalom and won the downhill. Matter of fact, I won the downhill quite handily. I don't remember the times, but I won by something like six seconds in a field of twenty-three skiers.

Cliff and I thought it was great. I know inside of us, we weren't thrilled about taking third in the giant slalom. We thought we might have done better. But, downhill is known for more speed, more recklessness. That's what I wanted. It put the race into my hands. All I had to do was think about plunging down the mountain faster than anyone else. If it took a willingness to go fast and somehow stay upright, that was a different equation than twisting and turning through a million gates of the giant slalom.

While I had won the downhill this particular day, the victory sharpened our appetites. Cliff and I didn't sit back and say, "Well, we're there." We just got hungrier. We knew this wasn't the big dance; it was a little waltz.

We had two more months to train before Alta and it never got boring. It never got repetitive. That first four months of

1983, I just shut off the world. Matter of fact it was funny: I'm usually a news and sports junkie, but we didn't watch much news or anything. Christine used to keep us in touch with what was going on in the world. At dinnertime after a day on the mountain we were perfectly happy to sit by the fireplace and Cliff would read me articles out of "Skiing Magazine". So when I wasn't on the mountain, I was in school talking and studying about the intricacies of skiing.

We did have one form of entertainment in which we indulged occasionally. A couple of evenings a month, we'd slide into Tahoe for dinner. We'd pull the handles on a few slot machines then catch a show. We saw Frank Sinatra, which I enjoyed. Hey, we Blue Eyes need to stick together, right?

We also played blackjack, just to break up our routine. One night at the blackjack tables, I wound up making about $1,800. The way we did it was simple. Cliff told me what I had and I would just say "Hold" or "Hit." We started at a $5 table because I only had $50 on me. But I put down $100 on the last three hands. I won all three and quit.

With $1,800 on me, you'd have thought I signed a professional contract. I mean, I didn't have any money of my own. I just had the tremendous generosity of Arnold Kleinfeld to depend on. I thought the blackjack windfall was an omen. I was even able to buy Cliff new ski boots and other accessories.

The trip over to Tahoe took forty minutes. One night going back we had another form of adventure in the snow. We were almost buried in an avalanche. It literally happened seconds in front of us. Cliff actually saw the snow coming down. Matter of fact, the after–fall sort of skiffed onto the hood of his car. We were the first car to come upon it from our direction, about 11 p.m.

Cliff stopped then skidded into a bit of snow as it happened. We jumped out…just a natural reaction. When we got out of the car we could hear the snow rumbling and groaning in a sort of distant drone.

"You hear that? That's tons of snow moving," Cliff said. "Jump in. Let's get out of here."

He whipped it into reverse and we took off in the other direction. You don't know if that's all the snow that's coming down. We stopped a couple of cars coming that way and told them to turn around. We spent the night in Tahoe.

That wasn't the first time we had heard the snow move. Several days when Cliff and I were skiing we heard that ominous sound off in the distance, too. You've got to be cognizant of that and take precautions.

As the snow thaws, you have to be even more aware. The temperature rose to about sixty degrees some days when we were skiing. You could ski in a tee-shirt and shorts those days. But you better watch out for the snow.

Nonetheless, I loved the warmth. Just to hear the dripping of water off the trees, to hear the melting of the snow, gave me a homesick feeling, actually. It reminded me of thawing springs in Canada. It brought a whole new array of senses to the scenery. There seemed to be more birds. It was so calm you could hear voices from much farther away.

You take more time to reflect and observe, because it's warm out and your teeth aren't chattering.

Time for a Roadtrip: With a Detour to the Emergency Room

The spring thaws meant something even more significant.

It was time to go to Utah. We flew into Salt Lake City. We went south, down I-15, then over a spur road to the East, up, up, up into the Wasatch Range.

And there is Alta.

The place we stayed was first-class quaint, the Rustler's Lodge. We were the first ones there among the blind skiers. Remember, I had a sponsor. I hadn't spent much money at all living with Cliff and Christine. And I had won $1,800. So we were able to afford to get out there early for the nationals.

We arrived the weekend before the competition, which was scheduled for the next Saturday. Practice went well most of the week. We were getting totally in the groove and finding out about the slope where the race would be held. We were getting a feel for it, big-time.

I loved everything about the place. It was gorgeous. We were having the time of our lives. At night, we'd go out and sit in this big outdoor hot-tub. Being the independent guy I was, I just told Cliff as I walked out of my room one night, "I'll meet you out there."

Of course, I still had my clothes on over my bathing suit. You wore some of your clothes out to the tub because it was still pretty cold. I was walking along nicely when I misjudged the distance and walked right into it, for crying out loud, clothes and all.

It wasn't turned on, so I couldn't hear precisely where it was. It wasn't bubbling. Steam was coming out because it was warm water, but it wasn't cranked, so I couldn't hear the drone of the motor.

I simply underestimated it.

By now, Cliff had come outside. He was maybe fifty feet away. He saw me climbing out, dripping wet with all my clothes on.

"Uh. Here in America we take our clothes off when we get in the hot-tub, ya backwoods bumpkin," he shouted.

"I just wanted to check the water temperature," I said back. "In Canada, we use the immersion method. We don't just dip a toe in like you candy Yanks. We do the whole thing."

Maybe I should have taken the hot-tub incident as a warning. The course for the race was set on Thursday. By Friday, the day before the competition was to begin, we got riskier in our practice runs.

We would have been fine, except we ran afoul again of the

dreaded "One Last Run in Bad Weather" principle. You'd think we would have learned. But we didn't.

It was four in the afternoon. All the other blind skiers had gone in. We thought: Just one last time to wring everything we can out of our preparation.

Again, the weather had taken a turn toward mean and rotten. It was really windy, biting into my face. I was mentally exhausted. Cliff probably was too.

Somehow we chose to ignore the danger signals.

Sure, we'd bought it once before taking that one last run in Kirkwood. But this would be different. I was more experienced. I was a better skier. We'd had four straight awesome days of skiing. That "One Last Run" would be fine this time.

Wrong. We should have closed up shop, gone in and gotten ready for Saturday morning.

Actually, we didn't even go very fast that last run. With the weather acting up, we just wanted to finish. We got near the bottom where Cliff was yelling, "Tuck-tuck-tuck!" The wind was howling, and the cold was biting into my face.

And then some guy started up a snow groomer. "Snow doomer" might have been a better phrase.

That noise proved to be our undoing. When the groomer roared to life, I lost contact with Cliff's voice. The voice is the lifeline with your guide. If it's severed, you are suddenly in a deep blue sea of bewilderment, drowning in uncertainty.

All this happens in a split second. It's not, "Well, why didn't the fool sit down." It's not like I was skiing for thirty seconds not hearing Cliff. I'm in my tuck, nearing the finish line, only a second or two away.

Unfortunately, I didn't know that.

To signify the finish line, they've got a dozen bamboo poles maybe ten feet tall, all shoved in together in two clumps, one on each side. Like a goalpost in football.

When I lost Cliff, I hit smack into the clump of the bamboo

poles on the left side of the finish line. My ski wedged in among them and wrenched my left knee sideways. Some of those bamboo poles sprung back and one of them whacked me right on the right side of the head and about knocked me senseless. It caught me in the ear and in the temple. My head was ringing.

I crumpled in a heap and lay there motionless.

As bad as the blow to the head was, it was nothing compared to what I was feeling in my left knee. The pain just shot through me instantly.

Cliff was there in seconds yelling, "Are you all right, are you all right?"

He was absolutely beside himself. I guess at this point the guy on the snow-cat had shut off the engine and Cliff was furious at the guy. He was freaking. He was just reaming the guy.

"You fool. Why do you think we wear these bibs? Don't you know this is a course where blind people have been training for two or three days? They need to be able to hear."

Cliff was in full cry. His voice was sharp-edged with anger.

The guy on the snow-cat may have botched it for us, but he also helped us next. He had a radio and he asked the rescue people to come with a toboggan.

Lying on the toboggan being towed down by a ski patrol skier, was a humbling experience. I knew the knee was really hurt. The pain washed into my eyes instead of out of them. This was no little tweak; I had been through plenty of those before. This was definitely torn up. No question about it.

The pain shot through me and made me sick to my stomach. It was the paralyzing pain.

This was late Friday afternoon and the races began Saturday morning. Cliff thought the party was over when he saw the knee. No question about it.

But it wasn't over.

I knew already that this wasn't going to be the end for me. Sure, a gnawing feeling crept into my mind that I wouldn't do as well. But I never thought it was over.

TOTALLY LOST IN SKIING

When I arrived back at the ski lodge, they cut my ski pants off. They took a look at my knee and decided I was going to a hospital in Salt Lake City. No messing around with it. My knee was turning weird colors and swelling up huge. It was beginning to look like a balloon. They could tell by looking at my face I was in enormous pain.

The fastest and best thing they could do was to load me up in the back of a half-ton truck. It took four people to get me in the back. I couldn't ride in the cab because I couldn't bend my leg. Cliff and Bill, the driver from the lodge, and a couple of others wrestled me into the back.

I felt like a piece of driftwood being clonked into the back of the truck. Cliff got in with me. They laid down a bunch of blankets in the back. The truck had a cap on it, so we were enclosed from the elements, but it was still cold as heck because we just had the metal bed to lie on. It smelled of gasoline because it was basically a work truck.

It was storming harder by now. Cliff had filled a big plastic bag with snow which he held on my knee as we drove to keep the swelling down best we could. I reassured Cliff I would be racing the next day. He looked at me like I was deluded. "You don't know how bad this is," he said. "You can't see it, my friend."

"Don't worry, don't worry. We're gonna be fine. We'll be there," I said.

"This time I don't think you will be, pal. You're not seeing what I'm seeing. This is ugly and getting worse."

When we got into the hospital, they loaded me into a wheelchair and sent me for X-rays. Suddenly my senses were alerted by the hospital experience. The antiseptic in the air, the sound of the walls and the halls, and bustle of the doctors and nurses, the chatter of a patient or two.

It brought all my previous stays in hospitals rushing back. I remembered the long days I spent in hospitals after being blinded at the age of two. Everything I was hearing and smelling reminded me of defeat. You wouldn't be in a hospital if you hadn't been defeated, my mind told me.

It would have been so easy to throw the towel into the ring and walk away, or limp away, in this case. It would have been so easy to say "There's another day." But I refused to think that way. I didn't want to ski another day. The day was tomorrow.

And then we heard the doctor's prognosis, that it was a badly torn medial collateral ligament. He said I might be able to avoid surgery if I stayed off it for six to eight weeks.

"What do you mean, 'off it?'" I said.

"I mean, off. No weight on it at all," he said.

"You mean no walking?"

"I mean no standing. No weight, period. If you're up, you're on crutches. You're down as much as you can be," he said.

The news almost brought tears to my eyes. I developed the habit over the years of fiercely governing such emotions in public. But inside, quietly, I wept.

Skiing was my life at the moment. Tomorrow, the races would start. I was so close to my dream, I could taste it.

By the time we were finished with the examination, it was about ten o'clock. The doctors thought it best that we stay there overnight and reassess my situation in the morning. Staying overnight, of course, meant missing the race, and, to me, missing the race was out of the question.

When we were alone, I told Cliff, "Look, go have a chat with Bill and tell him we're getting out of here tonight."

By now I had been transferred from Emergency to an official room upstairs. I was on the third floor, dressed in one of those ridiculous gowns open in the back. I turned to Cliff and said, "What I'm saying is, we're leaving."

Cliff said, "What do you mean, leaving? You're nuts."

But remember, Cliff was a free spirit too. I said, "Listen, what are we going to accomplish lying here all night? Nothing. Get Bill and you guys figure out where we're going to leave from. Get a wheelchair up here, load me up in it and wheel me down there. Figure out what exit we can use."

So Bill and Cliff huddled for about twenty minutes and they came back and had their escape route. We couldn't let the nurses or doctors know what we were doing. It was eleven at night and there wasn't a lot of traffic in the halls.

I was having the usual run of nurses come in and check me. One had just come in and said, "If you need any painkillers let me know."

I said, "No, no. I'm fine."

When she was walking out she said, "You have your buzzer there and your buddy will probably be right back."

I said, "Yeah, he went down to get a soda."

She said, "Have a good night's rest. I'll look in on you during the night and see you first thing in the morning."

She had just come on her shift at eleven.

I'm saying, "OK, see you in the morning."

To myself: "I'll be seeing you if you're back up on top of the mountain. Because I'm outta here."

Cliff and Bill came back to my room. Bill said, "Look, what happens if we get caught?"

Cliff and I said something to the effect, "Listen, Bill, if you're worried about the what-ifs in life, you'll never achieve anything."

I said, "Don't worry about it. Just get my butt in that chair and let's get rolling."

We found a service elevator and went down that. We figured it was better than the general elevator, plus it was only three doors down from my room. It had the added advantage that we didn't have to go past the nurses' station.

In football parlance, instead of busting up the middle, we took off on an end run. Or a naked reverse, if you will, considering the hospital gown I still wore.

The service elevator was extremely slow. It seemed to take forever. We finally reached the bottom floor where Bill had his truck waiting at a side door. Again, we thought we probably shouldn't just go tooling out past the front desk in the emergency room.

Meanwhile, I didn't have my clothes; I was wearing the hospital gown. We took the blankets from the bed and wrapped them around me. We were going to need them anyway, I figured. We even took the pillow. I looked like some Arab sheik all bundled up as we walked down the halls.

The joke was, once we got all loaded, Bill asks, "Do you want the wheelchair?"

And I said, "Heck no. We're gonna ski tomorrow. We don't need a wheelchair."

So Bill shoved it back inside the door. He got into his truck and we burned out of there. At which point Cliff said, "God, if he doesn't slow down, you'll hurt the other knee."

By now it was about midnight and we were making the ride back up the mountain. When we got on the outskirts of Salt Lake City, they stopped and got me some ice. The plastic bag we'd been using was full of holes. So it was a good thing we'd brought the hospital pillow with us. We took the pillowcase off and jammed some ice in it.

I only had my underwear on and the hospital gown. I did have my ski jacket which had been left in the back of the truck. So that was slung over me. But my feet were pretty chilly because all I had was my ski boots and I certainly wasn't going to put them on.

Suddenly, I was ravenous. My appetite had pushed through the pain. "God," I said. "I wish I had something to eat."

And Cliff said, "Well, I just happened to raid a juice cart at the hospital." He had about twenty doggone huge chocolate chip cookies and a bunch of juice boxes.

It was one in the morning when we got back to Rustler's Lodge. So much for getting a good night's sleep before the race. But as the altitude rose, so did my spirits. I was getting close to the finish line. Remember, the finish line was down at the bottom of the mountain next to the lodge. Even though my last visit to it ended by crashing into the bamboo poles, I looked over where they were and vowed to myself: This next time I am going to come clean. I am going to ski right between those poles, a winner.

When we got back, Cliff woke Bob Weber, who'd just heard about the injury. He was startled to see us. "I thought you were holed up in the hospital," he said.

"Nope," I told him. "Didn't need to stay. Didn't want to either."

We didn't tell him how we got out of there. We had sworn a pact among the three of us that if anyone asked, we'd just say they sent us home.

So if you're reading this, don't tell anyone how we got out. I'm probably still checked in at Salt Lake City.

Just Give Me a Shot

I hardly slept the rest of that night, partly because of nerves, partly because the knee hurt so much. I was icing it all night. I pretty much spent the hours before dawn in prayer. Not that I wear faith on my sleeve, but I am a person with a deep belief in God. And I believe fervently in the old saying, if the Good Lord gives you lemons, make lemonade.

I had always tried to squeeze the juice, if you will, out of my God-given talents. It's like playing cards. You play the hand that you've been dealt. You can't play a card you're not holding.

So the prayer I was praying was along the lines: "I accept the verdict, whatever it will be. It's in your hands, God. But if it be your will, just give me a shot. That's all I ask."

This was why I went to Kirkwood, California, to train. This was my moment, even though this was my first year of skiing, I didn't want to wait another year. I wanted somehow to find the courage, find the inner strength, to go out and compete. And I know when you're in your darkest hours, when it kind of cuts to the core or the essence of who you are, there's a greater power. So I put it in God's hands.

I also knew it was now up to me to perform. I felt internally that I could do it, although I was experiencing anxiety and fear well beyond anything I had experienced before in my athletic career.

I knew it was a pretty bad injury. I knew when I touched it, it felt hot. The heating sensation wasn't only in my knee. It gnawed and ripped at the pit of my stomach, partly out of fear, partly out of anger at myself — and probably the world at that point.

I knew that if I made it to the top of the mountain in the morning, it would be the biggest challenge I'd faced in athletics. When morning came, my spirits rose.

Running into Tammy, a young lady who worked at Rustler's Lodge, also helped my spirits. As we were leaving the lodge to go over to the chairlift and ride up for the first run of the competition, Tammy saw us. She had heard I'd hurt my knee. She came over and put her arm around me and said, "Gosh, I can't believe you're gonna ski today."

It was really weird. The perfume Tammy wore was similar to one of my serious girl friends in high school, Gail. I used to smell Gail's perfume when I'd run laps at W. Ross MacDonald School for the Blind in Canada. I'd go by the girls' side of the gym and I'd know she was standing there because I could smell her perfume. I'd run a little harder and push a little faster and breathe a little deeper to impress her.

Here I was on the edge of the blind nationals ski championship and I'm thinking about a girl I knew in high school and, from there, about the school for the blind. That wasn't a bad thing at all. I was drawing on a period of my life during which I'd had great success. If you're going to pull from something in your life, pull from a source of strength, a time when you had a tremendous sense of purpose. In those days the purpose for everything I did was crystal clear. To win. To prove myself. To succeed.

The memory gave me a warm, almost overwhelming feeling of confidence.

When Tammy came up to us, Cliff said, "Well, Craig's gonna win today."

"Yeah, right," she said, not being mean, but in a playful voice.

"You'll see," I told her.

And then Cliff — because he was always looking out for my best interests — said, "If Craig brings home the gold medal, he's sitting beside you at dinner tonight."

And she said, "Deal."

I said, "Deal."

And out we went.

Now I'm in my ski boots. I'm kind of hobbling, putting more weight on Cliff's shoulder. Normally I'd be following him, just touching the outside of his elbow. At this point, I had my hand on top of his shoulder. He was my crutch.

From there to the chairlift we didn't talk much. It felt kind of tense between us. Cliff mentioned the sunshine: "Wow...the mountain looks fast today," he said.

He added that it was definitely icy. He said that, I'm sure, because he knew icy slopes are my favorite conditions and it might boost my confidence.

One, ice means speed. Two, on ice I can hear his skis better in front of me. The powder is harder for me to hear, no question. He knew that I lived for the moment of skiing on ice. He used to tease me, saying that it was the Northern Ontario coming out in me.

But, hey, if the iceman cometh right now...I was ready.

Obviously, one thing that inhibits blind people from going fast is fear. When you start really rockin', when you hit thirty, thirty-five miles-per-hour, it can be just downright scary. So what takes you from thirty-five to fifty miles-per-hour? What gives you the extra fifteen miles-per-hour that maybe another blind person doesn't have? Is it because you're a better skier? Maybe not, really.

Is it confidence? Yes. But guts too.

Let's face it. You've got to be willing to push yourself way beyond where you are normally willing to go.

You must write a contract with your soul that says "I'm willing to push. I'm not going to bleed off speed."

So we had perfect conditions for me. Ten degrees fahrenheit. Crisp, cold, with the sun out and little breeze. Weber had waxed the skis for icy conditions. The bottoms of my skis were like rockets. Why? Because Weber and Cliff knew that I was strong enough in the legs that I could cut an edge and I wasn't afraid of the skis getting away from me. Despite my bad leg, we were there to win that day.

When we approached the chair lift, Cliff helped me get my skis on. And we got another tension-breaker there. He crouched over underneath me and said, "OK, click your heel in."

I went to click my heel in and the ski slid sideways and I fell right on top of Cliff's head. We both ended up in a pile.

"Oh. Isn't this a heck of a start?" he said.

I said, "Well, coach, if we're gonna screw up, let's do it now, not later."

Here we are going into this supposedly serious competition and now we're both lying on the ground like two sacks of potatoes and my one ski is going God-knows-where.

Just then, Tammy stuck her head out the lodge door and yelled, "Yeah. Great start guys. Guess I'll be gettin' another date for dinner tonight."

"Not if I can help it," I shouted. "That was just a little Laurel and Hardy routine we've been working on. Now we're ready to rock."

So we finally got the skis on. We started sliding toward the chair lift. Then, Cliff did an interesting thing. He said, "You know, let's just stand here for a minute and slide your skis back and forth."

We were on a little tiny grade — it may have been fifty feet long, going down toward the chair lift. He said, "I want you to get into racing form and follow me."

He pulled in front and hollered, "C'mon. C'mon. Go. Go. Go."

He was saying to me, if you can't envision yourself doing it now, how are you going to do it up there? It was just a little snapshot of the task that lay ahead.

When we got to the chairlift, he kept saying stuff like, "Oh, you look good. You look great. Good form. Good form. That's what I want, from the top down. Stay tight. Stay low. Head up."

"Head up" means you're listening. If you're following a guy in front of you, you want to be honed in on him. Just from that little patch of snow, skiing to the chairlift, not one time did Cliff mention the knee.

The knee, however, was talking to me plenty.

No question, there was an enormous amount of pain because the knee wouldn't really bend the way I wanted it to. It wouldn't let me get as low as I wanted to get on that side. I had two Ace bandages around it. I had iced it and iced it and iced it. Weber came up with some spray and we'd put that on it. I never did ask what it was and I don't know now. Knowing Weber, probably 10-W-30. But it intensified the heat on my knee. The key to it at this stage, we thought, was keeping it warm. When muscles are warm, they perform. When they're cold they don't.

Cliff and I got onto the chairlift. Normally we'd be yakking away at 100 miles an hour. We'd roll through all these scenarios. We'd be like two chatterboxes. That's what made us such a great team. But this time we were very subdued getting on.

Not a lot of back-slapping went on as we started up. I could hear skiers on the mountain. I could hear the excitement, the hustle-and-bustle down by the finish line, of some media folk gathering and others — spectators, parents, and other curious onlookers. After all, blind ski racing is no run-of-the-mill sport. I just sat there and thought to myself: "This is why I'm here. It's time to perform. It's not time to say 'poor-me.'"

And I could have thought a lot about poor me. Just to bend my leg in the normal sitting position hurt like all-get-out. When I put weight on it, the pain shot right to the top of my head.

Those first quiet moments on the lift were a mental healing process. If I was going to win, it was going to be mind over matter. If mentally I wasn't ready to do it, it would never happen.

I think it was halfway up the lift — several minutes — before Cliff broke the ice and said, "How do you feel, champ?"

"I'm almost ready," I replied.

However, I wasn't really prepared for what I had to do. I was still unfocused. Loose. Then, for some weird reason, I entered a place I've come to call the "Grey Zone."

When athletes finds themselves in the grey zone, they experience the same phenomenon that makes Michael Jordan hit a shot at the buzzer. The grey zone is what makes Ken Griffey Jr., hit a home run in the ninth. It's Evander Holyfield in the twelfth round still punching. The grey zone takes champions to a different level. All great champions are not afraid to ask themselves to give a little more than seems humanly possible.

And now the grey zone clicked in for me. I found myself in some place in my mind where I could not be denied.

The tension began collapsing like a stone wall. The next three minutes on the lift, Cliff and I started laughing and chatting about our months of training. By the time we arrived at the top, it was amazing. What started out to be this deathly silent, hold-your-breath, bite-your-lip ordeal, turned into a good feeling.

As I got off, a calm had overcome me, that familiar quiet resolve, the presence every champion knows in the grey zone. I decided to work the stiffness out of my leg first. I rocked back and forth on it. I bounced a little up and down on it. Simple stuff, but even to get my mind to accept simple motions meant a lot at the time.

Most of the athletes waiting their turns were sitting on the hill with their skis off. As the officials went through the line, they'd eventually announce number two or number three in the "hole" — the area around the starting gate. So you had some warning when your turn would be.

The sooner I go, the better, I thought. "Cut my spirit free," is what I was thinking.

My Two Minutes of Living Dangerously

I didn't want to hear much talk anymore. I was in no mood to chit-chat or weigh anything or analyze or speculate on anything. I was ready to race. I was at peace with myself. At the same time, I sensed an air of intrigue from everyone around me. All eyes at the top of the mountain were on me.

It sounds egocentric, I know. But I also knew I'd created a stir on the mountain in practice runs and the competition in Kirkwood. I knew some of the competition was anxious about what I might do.

And now, as word had spread about my injury, I'm sure they were expecting me to come out of the gate and two gates later to be lying in a heap. And eighty percent of the field probably would cheer.

I said, "All eyes on me," didn't I?

Sounds funny, speaking about a bunch of blind competitors. But we all could "see" each other in our special way, and, believe me, we were keeping a vigil on the proceedings.

I also think if I would have crashed and burned, I'd have been covered. People would have said, "Oh, well, he was hurt" But, I wasn't willing to accept that. I wasn't willing to accept, "Oh well, there's next year."

I've never been a next-year type of person. If you're gonna do it, well then, darn well do it now. I'm not here on this planet to put in time. I'm not here to occupy space. I'm here to make a difference.

I was skiing in mid-pack. And in the next ten to fifteen minutes, I was going to make up my mind that no pain in the world would stop me from coming down that mountain.

My high school wrestling coach, John Howe, always said I had a high threshold for pain. That's a God-given trait. And I also thought my leg muscles, built up from thousands of hours of leg presses, would be strong enough to compensate for the damaged ligament in the knee.

As I stood among the forty other skiers and their guide skiers and officials, the conversation I overheard stimulated me. I heard people say, "Oh, he's here." And "There's MacFarlane." My sense of what they were saying was, "Oh, darn, he's here."

But their voices also carried that twinge of sarcasm. I heard someone say, "We don't have to worry about him now."

"Yeah. We'll see," I muttered under my breath.

I felt anger when I heard those things. Absolute anger. It also just plain hurt my feelings. It cut to the bone because I knew a certain contingency of veterans didn't want me there. I was the new hotshot kid and, after all, this race would determine the national team that would compete in the internationals in Switzerland later that year.

I heard a couple of the other instructors talking to Cliff and I loved his optimism. They were trying to cast shadows like, "Gosh, I thought he wasn't supposed to be here." And Cliff said, "Everything's going to be fine."

And one guy said, "Well, we heard this morning that he was done. He was in the hospital in Salt Lake City." I just heard Cliff say, "The doctors let him out. It's a long story."

And then he was back with me. He was rubbing my shoulders. The chemistry between us was always incredible. I never could have done it without him. No doubt.

As we waited our turn, a couple of skiers said encouraging things. One older skier was particularly nice. As we were coming through the hole, his guide skier said, "Eddie, there's Craig MacFarlane on your left."

And he reached out his hand and grabbed my shoulder and said, "God, kid, I can't believe you're here. Go do it."

Eddie, it turned out, was right ahead of me. He wiped out about three gates below the start. He went off the trail, just pulled up stakes and went leisurely skiing down the rest of the mountain.

At this point, it all comes down to what's inside. As I slid into position at the starting line, I didn't have to shift gears mentally. I was already in the grey zone. I was using Eddie's energy. And Cliffs'.

Cliff and I were ready at the starting gate. I say "we" because in blind skiing, the guide skier is allowed to start about ten feet below you. He's going to try to maintain a distance down the mountain of six to eight feet apart. And it's so important in blind skiing that you start together, you start at the right tempo, the right rhythm, the right feel, so he's not sixteen feet, then ten, then twenty-two, then eight feet in front of you. You have to find that pocket to ski in. And you have to find it quick.

The horn sounded.

As soon as it went off, Cliff was on it, yelling out the commands to me.

"Go-go-go. Turrrrrrn right!"

The word, "turn," said like that, means a normal turn.

Then, "Go-go-go, eeeeeeasy left!"

That meant a more gradual turn.

And then, "Harrrrd right! Go-go-go!"

And "hard" meant just what it says — a severe turn.

Then if it's "Go-go-go, three-three-three-three-three-three!" that means we're coming up to a headwall and "three" would be a severe slope.

In other words, "Get ready, pal, because the bottom's going to drop out of your stomach. And you better be with me on it."

I'd never heard the excitement in Cliff's voice the way I

heard it now. I'd never heard that pitch or tone. Nor, the energy. He was half an octave higher than usual. He would have been a great NFL quarterback that day; I don't think a crowd of 100,000 could have drowned him out. It was so important for my confidence that his voice be like that.

As soon as I blasted out of the gates at the top, I immediately found the pocket — I don't know why. But he knew it, I knew it...we were off and running.

As I came around the first corner and I put weight on the leg the first time, I could feel the pain in my knee. It almost paralyzed me for just a moment. That was when my bad leg was the downhill leg for right turns and had to take all the weight.

I just kind of ground my teeth together. I forced my leg down a little further. I crouched a little lower. I snapped my head up maybe another inch so my ears were high.

My ears were my camera lenses. I was seeing the world through them. That's where the winning and losing was going to be decided. I knew I would win or lose this race on how tight I could stay with Cliff.

The pain wanted me to drop my head. I snapped it up even higher. I refused to go where the pain wanted me to go.

Nothing was going to get at me.

I was a time traveler in the grey zone and Cliff and I were hitting those turns like I'd never hit them in my life.

I absolutely decided that after all the hours and months of training that I could endure two minutes of sheer living hell and agony. And that was it. I would have all summer to heal.

I wobbled probably a third of the way down the first run. Cliff and I came over a three headwall and went into a right-hand turn. That's where my knee bobbled. It almost gave out on me.

Which meant I immediately had to shift a lot more weight than I wanted to onto the uphill leg, while I fought to keep the left leg underneath me.

Therefore the pocket evaporated.

Cliff was looking over his shoulder and had to bleed off speed. When he did that, I came up and smacked into him.

Thankfully, we had practiced this maneuver many times before. Weber thought we were crazy when he saw us running into each other on purpose in practice. He thought we were needlessly risking injury. But we needed that practice up here, right now. We pushed off each other and I yelled, "Go-go-go!" We stayed upright and finished the run.

Cliff and Bob were ecstatic.

"Man, you did it," Weber said, rushing up.

I could hardly hear them because I was so upset with my performance. Fifth may have sounded decent under the circumstances, but it was nowhere good enough to do what I'd come to do.

Win.

Somehow, I had to do better the second run. Somehow I had to hold it together. No wobbles. No bobbles. A perfect run. Nothing more, nothing less would do.

I hardly remember getting into the starting gate for the second run. Suddenly, I was flying down the mountain, the butterflies flying in perfect unison with me, the Unknown pulling me down the hill with everything blocked out but just the one single solitary thought riveting my being.

Win.

I plunged down the mountain in the grey zone, Cliff and I, two mirror images of each other, cutting the slope in the same cadence, gate after gate, cutting a couple of them so close they whacked my shoulder in a perfect rhythm. Left, right, go-go-go, tuck. It didn't matter which way the course demanded me to go. The mountain and I were harmonized, singing the same music. We were no longer adversaries. We were confidants, riding the same train of thought, the Grey Train, sharing the same secret.

The mountain and I knew halfway down that I was going to win.

The remaining gates were like a practice run…so easy, so fun, so free. I knew we were headed for the finish line when Cliff started screaming, "Tuck–tuck–tuck."

I knew from the chatter of my skis I had never gone this fast before. Then the finish line arrived. As Cliff started slowing down, he forgot, in his excitement, to tell me. I hit Cliff, did a double-binding release, and started sliding down the mountain on my back. Cliff went another direction. Before I could stop, I took the legs out from under a camerawoman and, for a few seconds, I became a human toboggan for her.

Cliff was on his feet running over to me. So was Weber and a bunch of people.

"Hey, take it easy on the camera person," Weber yelled.

Her named was Laura. She was out of Salt Lake City. She was laughing. And as we began untangling limbs and equipment, I said, "Well, this gives new meaning to the term, 'closeup.'"

Fortunately, it turned out to be mostly a funny thing and no one got really hurt.

As I got up to dust off the snow, I discovered I had snow in my doggone helmet and snow packed in my ears. I must have looked a mess.

When I heard my time, I thought the snow was still plugging up my ears. I couldn't believe what they were saying. Neither could Weber. He went running over to the timekeeper. We thought we heard it wrong.

Weber came back and said I'd skied eleven seconds faster than the leader in the race. At that point we were ecstatic.

Cliff was picking me up and swinging me around and just freaking out. Technically we had to wait a little longer as a few other skiers finished. But two of the last four wiped out. The conditions were almost pure ice by now.

It was ice we'd sculpted into a gold medal.

It brought us all full circle. Cliff and Bob and George and Gordie and Colleen and Arnold and every single person who said he or she thought I could do this came full circle with me.

Totally Lost in Skiing

All the visualization, all the daydreaming, all the wipeouts and the spills melded into one simple sentence. We did it.

Actually, I still didn't know exactly what we'd done until a guy came running over to me and said, "Hey, I run the speed gun. I was on the steepest part of the course, and when you came through the gun, you were in excess of fifty miles an hour."

No one was able to pinpoint what it meant. No official blind skiing speed records are kept by the United States Association for Blind Athletes. But suffice it to say, no one had ever heard of a blind skier going that fast.

I had gone over fifty miles-per-hour downhill and won the competition. That's all I need to know.

The speedgun guy persisted. "Man, you were just flyin' when you went by me." He was a veteran at Alta. He obviously knew how to operate the speed gun.

"That thing must be frozen," I said.

"No. Trust me," he said. "You were just a blur when you went by."

Then he asked me, "How do you hear at that speed?"

I said, "You just do a lot of prayin'."

Not All Victories Are Sweet

The medals were presented next. That was a dream come true. The ceremony was held right at the bottom of the hill after the races. They brought out podiums like the Olympics. I smiled when they called out my name to go up and receive the gold. I was now a national champion.

I insisted that Cliff come up to the podium with me. At first he wasn't going to because he's really very bashful that way. But he had to. No gold medal is given to guide skiers, and there should be. People needed to know I couldn't have done this without him.

After the ceremony, one of my fellow skiers shook my hand and said, "I can't believe how fast you were." Several skiers came up and gave me hugs and high-fives. Tammy was there, too.

"Hey, you did it," she said.

We came off the podiums and glided to the lodge, my team — Cliff and Weber and Tammy — and we were met by a frenzy of media people and others crowding around.

I was not the same guy who hobbled out the lodge in the morning and was standing out there leaning on Cliff like a peg. I was drinking in the moment of emotion. People were congratulating me, people I had never met before and ski officials who had worked the course.

I discovered I was pretty hungry, because I had not eaten lunch. I was ready to eat the leg off a moose. So we went on into the lodge.

Cliff and I went to our room and suddenly, my whole system crashed. I can't tell you how physically whipped I was. I had not slept much the night before after bouncing around in the truck, being in and out of the hospital, riding away into the freezing night air back to the lodge, packing the knee in ice. The needle on the old adrenaline tank nosedived below zero. I was lightheaded. I was jelly. The knee, of course, was throbbing.

We showered and then went down to the restaurant and found a nice quiet spot.

It was a moment of reflection. It was a chance to say "Thank you" to Cliff, small as that was, for the sacrifice he had made for me.

As we mellowed out, I realized that Cliff would go down as truly one of the great heroes in my life. All the attention was on me. No glory is given to the guide skier. But all I could say was, "This is as much your victory as mine. Maybe more."

We hugged each other and it was emotional. I'd been through so much and this was a guy who'd brought me where I wanted to go. He believed in me and I believed in him. We had developed mutual trust and admiration, and when you find that common bond, you can move mountains, or conquer them.

Later that evening, we arrived at the banquet. As we strolled in, I said to Cliff, "Hey, it's you and me in Switzerland next fall for the worlds." How could it not be so?

We were about to find out.

We ate. They handed out some awards. We were sitting there. Tammy had joined us, as promised. Suddenly, they were announcing the team, and I remember Cliff reached over and squeezed my good knee under the table. "Hey, this is our moment, man."

I squeezed his arm.

They began announcing the three-man team that would represent the United States at the blind world snow-skiing championships in Switzerland. I don't even remember the names they called. I just knew mine wasn't one of them.

The people at our table are going, "What? What?" I sunk lower in my chair. It was like someone ripped my heart out. Words can't describe that feeling.

Cliff was on his feet, heading to the front of the room before the last name floated away from the microphone.

Remember, Cliff's a pretty bashful person, but he went straight to some officials, his voice rising higher with each word., "What ...is...GOING ON?"

He was raising hell and said he was lodging a protest right then and there. Which, of course, went nowhere.

Basically, I learned this: Welcome, once again, to the buddy-buddy club. Some members of the selection committee were guide skiers who had other skiers, and some were part of the old boy network. In other words, the team was basically picked before we ever skied nationals.

It turned out my acceptance by the blind skiing establishment lasted a few fleeting seconds at the base of the mountain. Here I was, a new guy in the sport who not only wins the gold medal but just blows the field away. And he does it with one Goodyear tire and one not-so-good.

I was thankful and grateful for the wonderful day I had. But in the same context, how do you climb and conquer a mountain only to fall over the cliff into the valley at the end?

I felt the committee had pushed me off that cliff. It was like they were saying: "You never existed."

They told Cliff my runs today might have been a fluke. I had come so far so fast and that was tremendous, but they had more experienced skiers they wanted to count on for worlds. My time would come, they said.

Cliff's argument was simple: "What do you mean, our time will come? Our time is here. We're here now."

Of course, they weren't persuaded. Cliff kept saying, "Look at what he did hurt. Think when he's healthy. No one can touch him, anywhere in the world."

I never challenged the committee personally. I don't really know why. I'd like to say that, surprisingly enough, maybe some type of maturity had crept in, but I'm not sure that was it at all. I think they did what the knee and the mountain were unable to do.

Whipped me.

Tammy leaned over and said, "I can't believe it. They robbed you." But I was too tired to be angry. I was not riding the adrenaline wave any more.

Several things I would always carry with me from that moment on became evident:

I would forever have compassion for anyone who for political reasons is rendered powerless, despite their best efforts to control their destiny. I understand how that feels. I lived it. I personally went through it.

More importantly, I would always have the love and friendship of the people who helped me become a skiing champion. Those were the thoughts that would linger forever from Alta.

And finally, I also knew that they may have shafted me out of a trip to Switzerland to represent America, a thing that I would have died to do, almost literally. But I knew in my heart and mind that during that particular year, I was the fastest blind skier in the world. No committee could ever take that from me.

The years since have softened how I felt that day. But I still wonder sometimes how I would have done in Switzerland that year. I was so devastated by the committee's decision that I hung up my competitive snow-skis forever. I have never competed in that sport again. But what happened at Alta didn't extinguish my competitive fire. I just needed to find another mountain to conquer.

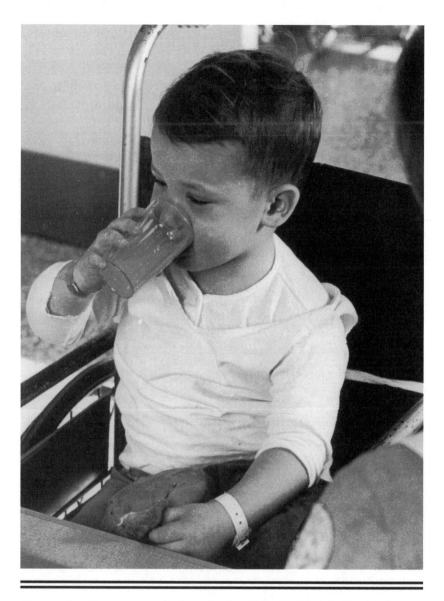

Recovering from my eye injury in the Sick Children's Hospital in Toronto, I had good days and very bad days. I was always known, however, for my liveliness and endless conversation. My parents drove 400 miles to Toronto nineteen times the first year I was there.

CHAPTER THREE
DARKNESS MY NEW FRIEND

Desbarats, the place where I was born and raised, is a wide spot in the Trans-Canada Highway and in my heart.

It is a village of only 400, so tiny that for much of its existence you wouldn't find it in an average atlas. The thriving metropolis of Bruce Mines, nine miles to the east, has a population of 600 and always made the maps. Only recently has Desbarats shown up.

Sault Ste. Marie, thirty-two miles to the west, is a town of just over 80,000 and dwarfs Desbarats to the point that often, when traveling, we just tell people we hail from "The Soo."

Desbarats is where I lost my sight. I lost it to an unintentional act involving the most innocent of activities — child's play. My mother, Joyce, remembers the day precisely: Saturday, October 17, 1964. I was two years, four months and one day old.

In fact, she recalls the event with almost perfect clarity. I had just been inside the house having a bite to eat. She took me down from the high chair, wiped my face and took me outside to play with the older boys — my brother, Ian and some neighborhood kids. They were all about the same age, four. Then she went back inside to get a cup of tea. She planned to come right back out to watch us.

My father, Earl, was moose hunting, which is what most men in the Soo do that time of the year. My mother guesses he was about eighty-five miles away, up the Chapleau Highway with a friend, Tom Bishop. They would be sleeping in a tent that night.

My parents weren't new to medical tragedy. Their first child, a daughter named Bonnie, died at eight-and-a-half months after being diagnosed with a rare form of tracheitis, a disease that causes the throat to swell completely shut. Ian had also given them a scare before I was born with a severe bout of intussusception, where the small intestine telescopes inside the large intestine and creates a complete blockage.

The nurses at the hospital first said Ian wasn't that sick and tried to send them home. My Mom remembers telling them at the time: "I only had one other child and she died in this hospital and I don't intend to lose this one." She insisted they take another look which may have saved Ian's life.

My Mom refers to that hospital as "the scene of our great sadness."

So, when Mom took me out to play that day, she hurried to get her tea. She says she was always nervous and extremely watchful of me. "It's a nice day, he's out there with his older brother and a couple of older kids. He'll be all right for a minute or two," she thought.

While she was in the house, one of the kids reached up on the shed and grabbed a "striker" off the wall. A striker is a metal gadget shaped like a nutcracker about six to eight inches long. It has a flint wheel on it and when you squeeze it together, it makes a spark for lighting arc welders, among other things. The kid stuck his finger in the opening of the striker and twirled it around. Suddenly, it flew off his finger and hit me right square in the center of my left eye.

I don't have much memory of the event. I remember screaming in pain and running into a door, bumping my head as I ran into the house. I remember my Mom picking me up and trying to comfort me.

Mom was talking to a neighbor about a funeral they had just attended. "Suddenly, I wasn't listening to her," she recalls. "All I could see was a tiny little V-shaped cut in the center of Craig's eye. But what alarmed me was that you could see fluid running down his cheek. It didn't seem like just tears. It was a clear fluid but different than tears. There was a tiny bit of blood in it.

"I knew Craig needed immediate medical attention but all the men were gone moose-hunting. Earl had our car. I was stuck. Then I remembered Earl's cousin, Clifford Phillips. He hadn't gone moose-hunting. He was in the barn, milking, over at his place. He had a brand-new truck. He jumped in it and came ripping over to get us."

Mom and Clifford took off for Sault Ste. Marie, thirty-two miles west, in the truck. She remembers I didn't cry much during the drive; I just lay in her arms whimpering. She held a cloth over my eye. "Something deep down inside told me it was serious," she recalls. "But I never dreamed just how serious."

On the way to the hospital, the truck had a flat tire. Fortunately, it happened right in front of the only gas station at Echo Bay. A man came out and changed it in just a few minutes. "We thought we were being smiled on," Mom says.

At Plummer Memorial Hospital in the Soo, our family doctor looked at my eye but said not much could be done about it at that facility. The ophthalmologist on staff was at a convention; he was the only eye specialist in the Soo at the time. Looking back, we would regret this unfortunate timing.

"All they were able to do that night was sedate Craig and put him in a crib with one arm tied to each side so he wouldn't claw at his eye," Mom says. "I slipped into a bit of self-pity that night. Deep in my heart I kept wondering: Why? Why was this happening to Craig? I had tried to watch Craig so carefully because of Bonnie and Ian. I could see people who weren't caring for their kids half as well as I was. Yet these horrible things were happening to our children and Earl and me."

Later that night, Mom called to a hospital in Sault Ste. Marie, Michigan, but the doctor there didn't want to touch the case because he hadn't seen enough like it. She called Sudbury and found an eye specialist who would see us the next day. Sudbury is 180 miles east.

Good fortune gave her a small smile again the next day. Normally, she would not have been able to reach my father hunting. But, uncharacteristically, he had told a clerk in a convenience store where he was camped. A close friend of my parents, Arthur Maitland, had driven to the area looking for Dad and happened into the same convenience store. Arthur found Dad and they raced back down a treacherous river road to the hospital, arriving about five Sunday morning. Mom says she started the night praying for my sight.

The next three weeks were spent in Sudbury where my eye seemed to be getting better, and I could, apparently, still see with my other eye. "Craig's natural live-wire personality was in full force," Mom says. "He would chatter away to anyone and everyone. Nurses would comment on how well he could talk in complete sentences and how he could count at only two years, four months."

When my parents returned with me to Desbarats, I took a turn for the worse. They noticed I was becoming cross, which was not like me. The white of my eye was turning pink. At the same time I caught a head cold. The cold fooled the doctors in Sudbury; they prescribed eye ointment and drops, and said the redness was due to the cold.

Ten days later the cold was better but my eye was worse.

"My fears were confirmed that he was rapidly losing his sight," Mom says. "One Saturday he started walking into furniture. Six weeks to the hour of his injury, we were on our way back to the Soo with Craig. I was filled with fright for the future even more than ever."

From my mother's description, what happened next must have been terribly painful. The ophthalmologist in Sault Ste. Marie put me in a sheet and rolled me over and over so I could not move my arms and legs. Then they held me down and pried my red eye open. They aimed bright lights into the eye to examine it. "He screamed and screamed, and those screams are etched indelibly in my mind," Mom says.

At this time, Dr. Shamess made the diagnosis — Sympathetic Ophthalmia. That's a very rare and complex condition where one eye is injured and the trauma from that injury travels to the other eye. It works like an inflamation eating away at the back of the eye and it doesn't quit until this part is destroyed. In short, the doctors offered little hope I'd see again.

The difficult part is that if the condition is diagnosed right away, the injured eye can be removed and the other eye saved. By the time the diagnosis was made, it was too late. The doctor who finally made the diagnosis was the one from Plummer Memorial who was at a convention the night of the injury.

This disease is so rare few ophthalmologists have seen a case of it. My parents were advised to take me to Sick Children's Hospital in Toronto to see Dr. Jack Crawford who confirmed the diagnosis. He was the premiere ophthalmologist in Canada and would later lecture around the world.

I stayed at Sick Children's four months across the winter of 1964. Doctors treated the disease with massive doses of prednisone. "We're going out on a limb," they said. "We've never given a child such heavy amounts."

My parents were reluctant but they believed they had no choice. "I felt so terrible," Mom recalls. "Here was this little tiny guy, my baby, so small, so helpless, lying there. We had no idea whether what they were trying would work."

My parents drove the 400 miles to Toronto nineteen times in the first year. They'd bring me home and give me the medicine there, but if my eye started getting pink again, they'd rush me back. Many of those trips were in winter; eight hours in the car, singing songs, making up rhymes, learning to count. I was getting medication twenty-three times every twenty-four hours.

The trips and the expenses were rough on the family. My parents began selling things while sliding further in debt. Eventually, they had to sell our home and rent a small house in Desbarats.

Mom remembers the hospital staff at Sick Children's fondly. "Dr. Crawford spent much time just playing with Craig," she says. "Mrs. Irene Hibbins, the desk clerk, was an extra mother to him. They let him wander around on the ninth floor. Once he got into an elevator with a group of people. When he got off, they knew him so well, the nurses brought him right back to nine."

We were back in Desbarats when Mom finally knew I was blind. I was walking along the gravel edge of the road behind Ian. I walked right past our driveway. "Craig, couldn't you see our house?" she asked. "No, Mom," was all I said.

JUST RAISE A KID

Shortly after they realized I would not regain sight, my parents made an important decision. They decided to raise me just like any other kid. It was a decision that would plant me firmly in the soil and the character of the place we lived.

Today, Desbarats is the core and soul of my existence. It may be small, but rooted in the vast Canadian wilderness of Northern Ontario, it is limitless in possibilities, infinite in the power of the land and the people who live there.

It is harsh and demanding in character and nature, once going fifty-seven straight days below zero Fahrenheit; oftentimes a winter will produce in excess of 200 inches of snow.

Yet there is beauty in the ruggedness, empowerment in the roughness and a granite-rock hardiness in its spirit. It asks a lot of you to eke out a living there. It gives back a thousand-fold if you can.

This smudge on the map is really a fingerprint on my soul. The land and the good, decent, hardworking people who can stand up to it, bent me, shaped me and molded me to their contours.

It is unquestionably true that the very ruggedness of my

birthplace also forged me in a completely wonderful way, and gave me insights I might not otherwise have.

"You had to be tough to live up here," my Mom says. "I don't think of it as backward. When I see books written about how 'remote' it is, I don't really think of it as remote. When I think of that, I think of a good day's drive to the Manitoba border. James Bay. That's what I consider remote."

No programs nor books nor classes existed in the Canadian outback for parenting someone like me, blinded so early in life, so my parents, bless them, never tried.

"We didn't know how to raise a blind kid," my Mom says. "So we just raised a kid."

There is incredible, intuitive wisdom in that statement, if you ask me. Being a schoolteacher all her life, I know my Mom is exceptionally bright. A deep-set brilliance shows through what she said, a simple truth that comes from somewhere inside the soul.

Someone in some sophisticated locale may have attacked the challenge of a child blinded at age two with a wide variety of complex protocols and intricate systems. My Mother and Father's way was absolutely crystal clear in its thinking, pure and clean as a Northern Ontario inland lake. This place in the middle of nowhere made a person learn to stand alone. It taught independence and self-reliance. Being products of such a place, self-reliance is what my parents helped me learn.

They didn't teach self-reliance in any sophisticated way; they taught it just by the simple act of living.

Mom, Dad and Ian always included me in everything the family did — no matter what it was. I never remember the word "can't" being spoken in our house. I mean, I never heard it in the context of "we can't do something because of Craig" or "Craig can't do such-and-such because he's blind."

"We took him everywhere with us and we did everything together, same as you would with any boy," my Dad says.

I'd go out trapping, hunting, fishing and canoeing with my

father. I'd pick berries with my Mom and bake pies. I dug
potatoes and shucked corn with her. I baled hay, swam, rode my
bike, had a horse named Rebel and a dog named Blondie. When
we built a house — I was seven at the time — I hammered and
nailed with the older men. In fact, my mother remembers seeing
me up on the roof helping put some of the shingles down.

Nothing in the normal, everyday life of a kid growing up in
my area of Canada, was I not allowed to do.

SOMETIMES I COULD HEAR DEER BEFORE MY FATHER COULD SEE THEM

Some of my fondest memories in life were made in the woods
with my Dad, a rugged, hardy outdoorsman all the way. My Paul
Bunyan. For some reason, Dad would always call me "Bill." It
was just a funny thing to him, an endearment.

So we'd be snowshoeing along his trapline, I'd be about seven
feet behind him, sometimes a little more because snowshoes are
kind of cumbersome, and he'd always say, "Are ya comin', Bill?"
He'd break off branches ahead of me so they wouldn't snap me
in the face. I'm not saying he made it a vanilla environment by
any stretch of the imagination. Let's face it, some of those
branches aren't exactly a picnic hitting people in the eye who
can see.

Trapping may not be politically correct in some circles today,
but growing up in the country in Canada, it was a natural part
of life for some folks. It was a great part for me; very instructive,
very much an example of how my life would work. Everything
was hands-on. When we walked the trapline, my Dad would let
me get down and feel the traps — not when they're set, of
course — but how you'd set them. Before my Dad took the
animals out of the trap, sometimes he'd let me feel them, feel the
otter, muskrat, the mink, the beaver. Before he skinned them, I
would feel their muscles, faces and fur and the shape of them,
learning to tell one from another.

One day we caught a beaver in a muskrat trap, which is a small trap. Dad pulled it up on the bank and I got to feel its silky pelt and flat tail. It was the first live, wild animal I ever touched. Then we let her go. She wasn't hurt.

Dad would let me bring a back pack so I could carry some of the muskrats. Matter of fact, in the spring my Dad would set a few traps out for me and anything we caught in those traps, he'd skin and give me the money. I'd get anywhere from $3 to $8 for a muskrat pelt.

If I could catch a beaver, I might get $80, or so. For a kid, of course, that would be an incredible amount of money. Mostly, I got the $5 muskrats. Once or twice a winter I'd catch a beaver. I guess I never was sure whether we caught it in my trap or my Father just gave it to me.

One time Dad fell through the ice. We were walking along the edge of Desbarats Lake where the water was maybe two-and-a-half feet deep. I was five years old and he was checking some traps along the edge.

Crrrr-ack.

I said, "Where you goin', Dad?"

He said, "I guess to the bottom of the lake."

Thankfully, the water was shallow. When it's that cold, your pant legs freeze like stovepipes. We had to get out of there. When you trap, you're going to fall, you're going to get wet and it might be ten degrees below zero. You knew this. You didn't complain.

My Mom remembers I never had a fear of animals when we went trapping — except skunks. "That must have been because of the odor," she says. "He thought they would bite him. I think he thought a skunk was big and fast. That was one thing we couldn't let him feel, but I would try to tell him how tiny a skunk was. It was just about the only thing I can remember Craig being afraid of. Finally, as he got older, he realized it wouldn't hurt him."

As early as age four, maybe even three, I'd fish with my Dad off Desbarats Dock into Desbarats River. We'd fish for perch, maybe some bass. My Dad had a boat when I was a kid and we'd go out into Lake Huron out into the North Channel.

I'd catch walleye. I'd catch pike. Some nice ones. Eight, nine, ten-pounders on the walleyes sometimes. We'd go out in some of the cold lakes — Diamond Lake for instance — and fish for trout.

My Dad showed me how to put the worm on the hook and how to cast. I felt the fish when we got 'em in. My Dad usually took the fish off the hook, but sometimes I did it. And, again, the whole thing was very hands-on.

When it came to hunting, I'd go with my Dad mostly for partridge. We'd be driving along the road looking for birds and he'd see one. They're kind of a stupid bird and they don't move too well. He'd point the gun and let me pull the trigger.

I actually hit one once in a while.

My Dad would do the dressing of the partridges. When my brother, Ian, had ducks and turkeys to be plucked, I'd sometimes help. I actually got pretty good at it, Ian says. I didn't leave many feathers. My sense of touch came into play. You've got to pluck them right down and get all those little fine feathers, too.

Sometimes Dad and I would go walking through the bush looking for deer. We'd be waiting at the top of a run. More than once, I would tell Dad, "I think there's one coming." There it would be. You've got to remember, when you're deer hunting in November in Canada, a skiff of snow would be on the ground. Even if there's not, the woods can be kind of crunchy with leaves under foot. The air is brisk. Sometimes it's still, sometimes windy. On a calm day, I could hear that stuff.

"Dad, I hear one," I'd say.

"Oh, I doubt it," he'd say. He was kind of teasing me.

"Sometimes Craig did tell me there was a deer coming long before I could tell," Dad remembers. "He could hear a lot greater distance than I could."

For lunch when we were out in the woods, my Dad would build a fire and we would cook pork and beans, eat salami and crackers and just get warm. We'd make hot chocolate. These are fond memories of great times spent with my father. Today, my father still lives essentially the same life.

In the summertime, the family would go out camping on weekends and pitch a tent up the Chapleau Highway, up highway 129. We'd camp by a lake and fish and swim. I would help put up the tent. We'd have a big bonfire at night and roast marshmallows.

One night we had a bonfire and I didn't realize Ian had walked up beside me. I pulled my toasted marshmallow out and stuck it right on his face. He wasn't hurt, but it didn't exactly tickle.

I HAD NO FEAR

I had a family that was in constant motion. It was always going and doing. Snowmobiling, for instance — what a ball of fun. Christmas times, my Dad's side of the family would get together for snowmobiling. You know those little plastic skis that are about two feet long? We used to get a rope out and ski behind the snowmobile on these little skis. When the crust gets really hard, man, you'd get that thing rocking. You'd be going thirty-five miles-per-hour. They were things you wouldn't do as an adult. You look back and you go, wow, that was crazy.

At that age, I had no fear. I'd just get out there and go for it. My cousins, Todd and Jamie, and I, were all being towed behind the snowmobile one time. We ran into each other and absolutely launched ourselves. We wound up on the hard crust where we spun like tops. We thought it was amazing fun.

One time when no one was home, I jumped on a snowmobile myself, revved it up and started to take off across the field. I didn't get very far before running headlong into the side of the barn. It was an abrupt end to a very short ride.

Full-out was just my way. I don't know why, really. Maybe it's just my nature. Maybe it's partly because that's the way my parents made me feel. I could take anything I wanted — to the limit. Nothing could stop me.

Occasionally, my Dad paid the price for helping to cultivate this healthy attitude. He bought a dirt bike for Ian and that sounded like way too much fun for just my brother to enjoy. I jumped on it and got it around to where my Dad was.

"Hop on, Dad. I'll take you for a ride," I said.

What was he going to say, after teaching me I could do anything?

He climbed aboard and we peeled out as hard as I could crank the thing. We were going like a blur when I just missed a big old telephone pole by about three inches.

"That was the end of my passenger days with Craig on the dirt bike," recalls Dad. Hey, I didn't hit the thing, did I?

I wasn't always so lucky on my bicycle. I rode it all over town constantly. "Actually, he wore two bikes out, riding all over the place," says Dad.

I'd cruise all over with Blake Marcel and Matthew Hunter, two friends of mine. We were like the Three Musketeers, never very far from each other.

One day Blake was riding double with me. I was doing the pedaling; Blake was supposed to be steering. We ran straight into a telephone pole beside Stella Moore's house and I was absolutely cold-cocked.

Another day we hooked a rope between my bike and Blake's and went blasting down a hill where the road makes a hard right. Blake put on the brakes to turn right, but I didn't. I kept right on going and when the rope jerked, I went flying and so did Blake. We both came out of the ditch, muddy and bloody from head to toe.

My refusal to back away from anything almost did do me in one day. I was out on the road riding along with Matthew and a dump truck came along, so we pulled over. I heard it go by, then pulled back into the road. I was not aware a second dump truck was following. Matt jumped off his bike and, in a flash, shoved me and my bike into the ditch. Thanks, Matt, for saving my life.

We loved to rip and run. We'd get up on this bluff in back of our house and play cowboys and Indians. In the summertime, we'd play up there morning, noon and evening. Mom knew that was a pretty safe place for me.

Except one day.

"He was just over three," says Joyce. "I looked out and I couldn't believe it. He was in this tree about twenty-five feet high — way, way up at the top." Ian came out.

"Do you know how to get down?" he asked.

"No," I said.

"Together," says Joyce, "we told him, 'Put your foot here. Now put it there.' Somehow he made it down."

It scared my Mom, but she had a theory about raising me: "If you don't let a child develop normally, how does he develop?"

No doubt the absolute highlight of my childhood, though, was getting Rebel, my pony. When I was six years old, we'd go down to Southern Ontario to visit a man named Jack Manders. He owned and raced horses. He had a sulky racer named Rebel.

Rebel was an Ontario champion. He was an awesome sulky racer and Jack used to take me on sulky rides behind Rebel. I would always ask Jack how much he wanted for Rebel.

He'd always tell me, "$11."

I decided to save my money. Finally, I amassed $11.50, which was a pretty hefty fortune for a kid my age. We went back to Jack's and I told him I was ready to buy Rebel.

"How much will you give me for him?" he asks.

"I've got $11.50 saved," I tell him.

"I don't know. He's a pretty fine horse," Jack says.

"It's all the money I've got, but I could get you more later," I'd say.

"Well, I guess since he's retired, $11.50 will do," Jack says.

"Will you sell him, then?" I ask.

"He's yours," Jack says.

Later my Dad told me that Jack gave him the $11.50 back and told him to put it into an account for my future. I'm kind of glad he didn't tell me at the time. I was too proud of buying my own horse.

Rebel was my friend, as much as my human mates. To me, he was like a dog following me around. I spent hours currying him, brushing him, feeding him, cleaning his stall. I'd stand on his back and jump off. I'd hang from a tree and jump on his back like I heard they did in the movies. Rebel let me do anything with him.

When I went to the fence he would come to see me. I spent hours with him. He was my salvation, my life, my tranquility, my peace of mind. So gentle, yet so quiet.

I discovered that if I tied a pole on a twenty-foot rope and dragged it behind him, the instant he heard it, he took off. He thought it was a sulky. He'd tear off through the bush, up over rocks — sometimes the pole would get caught on a tree and send me flying.

Another time Rebel went under a low-hanging branch. Needless to say, that was a quick exit for me.

Another time I didn't realize I was riding us straight into a barbwire fence. Rebel stopped. I didn't. I sailed over his head into the fence and got ten stitches for the trip.

Despite a handful of incidents like those, Rebel and I had a special communication which worked almost without fail. I always rode him bareback. Usually I rode with no reins. He'd let me pat his head to make any turn I wanted. If I carried a little grain in a can and rattled it, he knew to take me back to the barn.

A Hearty Land, a Hearty Child

Long winters remind me that we didn't have an indoor toilet in those first few years growing up. It was the old outhouse routine. They were just a part of the landscape in Desbarats. Let me tell you, when it's twenty below zero Fahrenheit in the outhouse, a person wouldn't sit around and read the sports section or daydream about what he was going to do tomorrow.

In those early years, I spent a lot of time with my Mother also, time that I really loved. Later, when I lived 500 miles away at the school for the blind, I would crave times like those.

When my mother made jam, when my Mother made pickles, when my mother baked pies — which she did every Saturday — I was right in there with her. I baked my own pies. I put so much stuff in them, the whole bloody mess boiled over. Raspberries, blueberries, raisins — I had a heck of a mixture in my pies. I always ate them, too. Hey, when you're five years old, even if it didn't taste good, you pretended so she'd let you do it again.

I helped my Mom plant the garden, corn, beans, peas, radishes, onions and carrots. She taught me how to tell the difference between raspberries, blueberries and strawberries, how to tell they were ripe and just right for picking. I helped pick the green and yellow beans and the peas. I helped dig the carrots and pull the onions.

I loved to pull a carrot right out of the garden, break the top off, wipe the dirt off a little bit and start chowing. I never washed it. Now that's a real carrot. Yes, you might get the odd grain of sand or dirt, but the freshness compensated.

I was eating a green apple one time. I had it about three-quarters gone when Ian looked over and said, "Craig, there's a worm crawling out of it." God knows how many worms I'd eaten up to that point. I was always eating apples off the trees.

In the fall, Ian and I would always make huge mountains of leaves and jump in them. When you've got as many trees around as we did, you take advantage of them.

My Mom got me into swimming lessons at the age of seven. She took me to learn swimming at Caribou Lake. My teacher, Nellie, was wonderful. She was an older lady with only one arm who was a dynamite swimmer herself.

They had two weeks of swimming lessons for kids every summer. It was $10 for ten lessons. What a deal. It was great for me because Nellie only had one arm and yet she was a fabulous example, teaching me what can be accomplished if you put your mind to it.

I remember her saying, "Trust me."

I said, "OK. I will."

She won my confidence and when you trust — and believe in — a teacher, you learn so much more. One thing I learned was simple: Here was someone with a physical problem and that problem could have stopped her, but in no way did it slow her down.

I liked swimming, but I preferred the lake frozen. My favorite sport was not for the fragile. Hockey was huge in my upbringing. Hey, I'm a Canadian. What else am I going to breathe, but hockey, eh? Oxygen ranks just below ice as a necessity to every Canadian, and I'm no exception.

I was probably three when I started to ice skate. It wasn't a great achievement where I come from; this is just what everyone did. When I was a kid we used to shovel off a spot on the Desbarats River, right across from Bud Mill's Gas Station, across the TransCanada Highway. The Desbarats River stretches out quite a ways before it connects with Lake Huron. We would clear an area sixty feet wide and maybe 150 feet long. Now that was a workout before you even started to skate. In those days, Desbarats also had an outdoor skating rink where the kids would play hockey. That's been replaced by an indoor hockey arena with artificial ice.

Think about it. How many towns in America with 400 people can boast an indoor arena?

Some of my best memories as a kid are listening to hockey

games on the radio. I could listen to three radios at once — three games at a time. Mom and Dad were amazed that I could follow it all. Ask me anything about those games, I could tell you every detail. Who scored the goals. Who got the assists and who was winning. I would know the answers.

I guess I was beginning to learn that other senses compensate when you lose the use of one of them.

Hockey also was a direct link to one of my very favorite people in life, Grandpa Jefferies, my Mom's father. We'd argue endlessly about strategy; which players were best for the Soo Greyhounds, our local junior team, or the Toronto Maple Leafs and what players the teams should trade to be better.

One of the things that definitely made me better was going to kindergarten when I was five. It was at Bruce Mines. Mom and Dad and the school officials thought it would be a good idea for socialization purposes.

I pretty much loved the whole experience of kindergarten and I truly loved Mrs. Martens, who was my teacher. "Craig was intelligent, active, and asked many questions along the way," she recalls. "His mother said to show him no favoritism and undue attention. So the other children accepted him as an equal and he entered their world of friendliness.

"He was a leader, an idea person, always offering suggestions. He preferred to be with people, to play with people rather than being alone. He soon learned other kids' voices and called them by name. Other children responded well.

"He had a sense of direction and a sense of humor. He played jokes and teased, but he was never hurtful. He had a sense of fun and others could laugh with him.

"He talked a great deal, maybe because he didn't want to feel alone. He could listen, too.

"He could put on winter outdoor clothing by himself. He could help others. There was a sickly girl from Desbarats and Craig would always help her get ready for the bus — help her put her boots on, put her snowsuit on. Another little boy had

Downs Syndrome and Craig always watched out for him when it came time to get on the bus. The children would line up and Craig would call out, 'Howard, where are you?' That loving child would reply, 'Here I am, Craigie.' Craig would take his hand and lead him out to the bus.

"I'll never forget that little sickly girl. He would make sure she was on the bus, too."

I did love Howard and the little girl. It's been pretty easy to feel that way about others because so many people in Desbarats and other places have been so nice and supportive of me. But, if Mrs. Martens makes me sound like a saint, I wasn't. Let it be said I could be ornery as all-get-out.

One day, Dad was having fun squirting me with a garden hose. I hauled off and cracked him right in the shins with a baseball bat. Another time, a few years later, I was kicking a soccer ball in the back yard, I tripped over a wheelbarrow. In a flash of anger, I threw the wheelbarrow on the garage roof. I guess that was after I started doing pushups.

Then there was the infamous Mrs. Marshall's Candy Store Incident.

We were living in a two-story house. I was four or five. My parents had moved from the house where the accident was, to a larger house downtown. Next door was Mrs. Marshall's Candy Store. We'd walk next door and get little bags of penny candy. I knew my way there myself. Mrs. Marshall always gave me candy, even if I didn't have money. Bubble gum and jelly beans and ju-jubes and jawbreakers and all that good stuff.

One day I asked Mom if we could go to Mrs. Marshall's and she was down on her hands and knees scrubbing the kitchen floor.

"Craig, I'll go with you when I finish the floor," she said.

That wasn't good enough for me. I started whining about wanting to go now.

Again she said, "Be patient. We'll go when I'm done."

I slammed the door and stalked out of the house. I picked up a big old rock and threw it at the side of the house and smashed the kitchen window above the sink.

"I was down on my knees for about five minutes," Mom says. "When I stood up, here comes this rock flying through the window. It's almost like he could 'see' when I stood up and threw it then.

"I was so mad at him, I can't even begin to tell you."

Needless to say I got a warm fanny for that performance. She spanked me good and sat me down and scolded me for a long time. When I got spanked, it was usually the hand on the butt. Once in awhile, you might get the fly-swatter. Of course when you heard Mom heading for the flyswatter, you were immediately heading the other way. That's when you kicked in your Carl Lewis steps or your Donovan Bailey. You turned on the afterburners and you were history.

One day I was loading the hay wagon with Dad and Ian. Ian tossed a bale and clocked me right in the side of the head and knocked me off the hay wagon. I didn't care, really. The job still was fun and made me believe I was capable of contributing to the family.

The economy of all Northern Ontario is not good; Desbarats doesn't stand alone on that front. It used to thrive on lumber, steel and copper mines. Algoma Steel once employed thousands. Now, it employs a fraction of that. The Algoma Central Railway employed thousands, too. Now, only hundreds work there. My Dad worked a lot of years on that railroad.

Through all the years and changes, Desbarats has retained a strong spirit and sense of community. When I look back on those times, I'm grateful I was allowed to make my own mistakes. My parents gave me my wings and let me fly. The place I grew up in instilled independence, helped me gain confidence in myself and helped me develop self-esteem. Most importantly, it let me be a normal kid. For other parents with children who have physical challenges, let this be a guide to raising them so they can be champions in life.

One of the original buildings at the Ontario School for the Blind. It was torn down on its 100th birthday in 1972 and the new complex became known as W. Ross MacDonald. I spent 10 years of my life here. Many times I wanted to escape; later I realized what a wonderful facility it was for a blind student.

CHAPTER FOUR
BRAVE LITTLE SOLDIER

I don't think I actually admitted to myself I was blind until I was five.

Somewhere in some distant compartment of my child's mind I had stored this general idea that I had lost my sight. I had stored it like some foreign, uninteresting, vaguely harmful object. I had taken the information that I couldn't see, tossed it into a dark mental closet and covered it up with my toys and friends and endless days of happy play.

At five, I persisted in asking the nurses in the hospital if I was ever going to see again.

Until then they'd always answered, "Yes," I might still see.

They were afraid to tell me the truth. Either that, or I hadn't heard them when they told me. On occasion, doctors had indicated my condition was permanent, but I didn't know what permanent meant.

"Craig, you'll never be able to see again," I was told.

So for the first time those words sank in, yet even then, not really. Even then, I don't remember feeling sad.

I was too busy trapping and fishing with my Dad, climbing trees and playing cowboys and Indians with my friends on the bluff, and riding my bike and my horse and running with my dog and picking berries and baking pies and learning to swim and going to kindergarten with other kids.

Blindness had hardly intruded on my life at all.

I mean, when the kids started learning to write and I couldn't back at Bruce Mines — that made an impression on me. Mrs. Martens, my teacher, kept saying, "Well, next year you'll have your own special way to read and write. You'll learn Braille, where you can read with your fingers."

As for Mom and Dad, they waited until the summer to broach the subject of me going to a different school. When they did tell me, their words had no special meaning. When you just turn six, it's like, "Ok, so I've gotta go away. Hey, I've got the summer holidays to go. Who gives a rip?" I still had a summer of tearing through the countryside with my buddies.

As the time drew closer, my Mom was busy sewing name tags on every piece of clothing I had so they wouldn't get mixed up with other kids' stuff.

Still the fall season and this other school were a million miles away. They weren't part of my world. I couldn't conceive that they ever would be. Until the day they became real.

Reality was the Ontario School for the Blind, which a few years later became W. Ross MacDonald School for the Blind in Brantford, Ontario. It would become my home for many years.

Before I knew what was happening, I was in a car with my Dad, headed for my new school. Mom said her goodbyes to me in Desbarats. She had to stay behind with Ian and start her own new school year teaching a new class. Looking back, maybe it was just too hard for her to go and drop me off — even for someone as tough as my Mom.

So I rode with Dad. It was September 1968, the day after Labor Day, which was the first Tuesday of the month. I had turned six on June 16. We took off on the 465-mile, eight-hour trip to Brantford, sixty-six miles southwest of Toronto.

Actually, the trip was pretty pleasant — as all car trips were with my Dad. My Dad was fun. He was pretty good at conversation. We kibitzed a lot. Matter of fact, those were some of the memories I cherished with my Father, those long rides to and from Brantford.

We chattered endlessly about hockey, especially the upcoming National Hockey League season. The Boston Bruins were my team.

They had Phil Esposito — from the Soo — as an All-Star centerman.

They had the best player in hockey, I thought, Bobby Orr, who grew up not that far down the road from me in Parry Sound, which we would pass through on the way to Brantford.

On the ride over, we stopped at my Grandma and Grandpa Jefferies — Hazel and Ed. They were two hours away from home, towards Sudbury, along the way. They were in Nairn Centre, where my Mom grew up.

We stopped there after a couple of hours to say "Hi." As we rang the doorbell and went in, Grandpa greeted me with the way he always did: "Oh, there's my little dumpling. Come on in!" he'd say.

Grandpa was from England and in his seventies by then. He was a big sports fan and a huge hockey fan. So we talked some more about the NHL.

We had a quick bite to eat — hardboiled eggs and toast — with Grandma and Grandpa. From there, Dad and I had about six more hours to go. We talked about the scenery. We were seeing a lot of rock and a lot of bush, then a lot of bush and a lot of rock, especially that 100-mile stretch of nothing between Sudbury and Parry Sound.

What did it matter? Let's face it, when you're blind, the scenery never changes.

We talked about trapping and hunting and fishing and things at home. Despite Dad's best efforts, it was a long trip for me.

Travel by car is just that way when you can't see.

Then we were there. Brantford.

I remember being overcome by the strangeness of the school

because it was so big. It was an endless campus, it seemed through my child's ears. I was right W. Ross MacDonald was bigger than some colleges.

We walked onto the playground and it sounded like the entire town of Desbarats was out there. The noise was deafening at first because there were tons of kids. You had kids running into kids.

All of us six-year-olds were new. None of us knew where the heck we were. We were all excited. When you're six, you have a certain spirit of adventure about you.

However, my heart was also heavy because I knew that I had been under the careful wing and guidance of my parents and I was getting ready to leave the nest and say goodbye to my Father.

I was starting to remember what my parents had said about going to Brantford and staying there by myself. "Son, you have to be a brave little soldier."

I didn't know very much about soldiers. All I knew was that I was sitting on the swing at W. Ross MacDonald when my Dad left for home that first day. He'd stayed there a couple of hours to help get me settled. We'd been up to my room at the junior school and now, as we were walking outside to the playground, my Dad said, "Well, I guess I should be going soon. It's a long drive home again."

I knew this was the time to say goodbye.

I felt sad that he had to drive home alone. Also, I wanted so badly to go home with him, to be with him. Life was so beautiful at home. I had my dog, I had my brother and my friends, my family. I missed Rebel. I wanted to go to school with them.

I guess I have a tendency to ignore the low points in my life or to steamroll over them. I believe that's one reason I've been successful, because I don't dwell on the bad things in life.

But, I couldn't gloss over this. No doubt one of the lowest of the low moments in my life was the day my Dad had to walk away and head out for home, leaving me behind at the school for the blind.

Suddenly, I was devastated. I felt lost. A tear rolled down my cheek. I sat there thinking, "Am I ever going to see my Dad again?

"What if something happens to him on the way home?

"If I do get to see him, how long is it going to be?"

These questions were boiling around in my six-year-old mind, brewing an emptiness in my belly. I knew in my heart he wouldn't be gone just a day. It wasn't going to be a week. I knew it wasn't going to be a month. It could be two months.

Standing there at my age, I just couldn't even begin to imagine what two months might actually feel like. Would it feel like a million years? Would it be like forever?

My Dad was my last link to my home. That link was about to break. He walked me over to a swing. I got on the swing and he pushed me a bit and tried to help me feel a part of my new place, to kind of break it in. Then, the shock and the finality of it engulfed me.

Geez...when he's gone, he's not a mile away or twenty miles away. He's eight hours away. In that moment I experienced what that would be like. My Dad gently touched my shoulder and I felt the rough hand that had set steel traps and skinned moose and felled trees and built a log cabin...now that hand grew soft as he squeezed me.

"Brave soldiers don't cry," he said, his voice calm but choked.

"Ok, Dad. I'll try to be brave," I said.

I tried not to let any more tears come into my eyes.

"I hope you're safe going home," I said. "I'll be talking to you soon. Ok?" I hoped that sounded brave.

He said, "Have fun, son."

He was off. His words hung empty in the air.

Fun? How could I have fun, all alone, stranded, away from home, with so many people I knew nothing about?

The ironic thing is, my Dad couldn't have left me a better

parting line. Before long, I was very busy discovering ways to have fun.

In the first few moments after he left, I was feeling sorry for myself. I was angry at my blindness. If I wasn't blind, I wouldn't be there. But, within the first hour of being at Brantford, I caught a huge break. I met Eric.

Eric Lambier was my dear partner in crime for ten of the next twelve years. We really clicked. We were roommates. Each room had six roommates, actually, but Eric was the one who mattered most.

He was from up past Bowmanville and Oshawa, by Port Hope, northeast of Toronto, maybe 150 miles away from Brantford. He was a rough one just like I was. He lived on a tobacco farm and I was from rural Canada. We chatted a couple minutes out on the playground. Then we got down to the business of playing. Playing with Eric was weird. That was the first time in my life I'd ever played with a blind kid. I remember I wanted to show Eric my radio in my room — the one I'd keep under my pillow to listen to Bruins games on WBZ when I was supposed to be sleeping.

We were going to our room and a kid ran into me. I was going in and he was coming out and I said, "Watch where you're going, will you?"

Eric laughed and said, "He's blind, you dummy. He can't watch where he's going."

I said something like, "Well, he better open his eyes a little bit wider."

I was used to other people seeing me coming and adjusting their course or making some allowance. Now here I had to do it for some other kid.

The guy I ran into turned out to be Roger St. Louis, one of our classmates. I remember when I ran into him, he felt a little pudgy. I said, "Geez, you got a large belly."

He said, "Who is that?"

I said, "It's Eric."

BRAVE LITTLE SOLDIER

So already I was at it. Stirring up mischief. Causing havoc.

You think kids pull pranks on each other in regular school? It seems like that's all we ever did in blind school. If we could scuttle someone or take the wind out of their sails, we never hesitated to do so.

I had a lot of chutzpa so I became a ringleader of pranks.

I also had a lot of guts. My years on the farm and in the woods made me tough. I was always a rugged, aggressive kid. I wasn't timid. I wasn't hesitant.

Eric was much the same. When you put us together, the combination was deadly. We started with little things. In Grade One, I locked the teacher out of the classroom. When she went out for something, I just sneaked up to the door, closed it and turned the lock.

She knocked on the door for someone to let her in. Someone did.

"All right, who did that? I want to know this instant," she said.

Well, it might have been the right thing to say in a sighted school, but wholly ineffective at a school for the blind. I mean, think about it for a second. Who was gonna know? I could slip up to the front, close the door and get back to my seat and no one else in the room could see me.

The teacher I did this to was Miss Mannings who was a dynamite teacher. I wasn't doing it because I disliked her; I thought she was terrific. I was just doing it because I was mischievous. I was always looking for some prank to pull.

We had other pranks. When we were walking into a class threading our way between the desks, we'd just kind of reach over and give a guy a smack on the old head. We might not know exactly where he was, so it might be a glancing blow, but other times it would be home run, a full palm.

Some of these guys had a little sight, so they knew it was me. Even if they couldn't see, they'd have a pretty good idea it was me. Who else was better known for causing trouble?

Sometimes we'd move another student's book from the right-hand side of their desk to the left-hand side and they'd be looking for it.

Some of this was to get under people's skin. Some was pure rebellion. At W. Ross MacDonald, we were taught table manners, so we didn't eat with our fingers. I was up on that because my parents raised me like any other kid. They taught me how to hold the fork and cut the food from an early age. At school, sometimes the meat wasn't that tasty. They always wanted us to try a few bites. "Take a bite..." they'd say.

Naturally, that set me off. "You've got to take two bites of meat," they'd always say. I used to throw it under the table. I could cut it; I just didn't want to eat it. I didn't like the way it tasted. You could have put a new sole on my father's work boots with that meat sometimes.

I'd hide it on the ledge underneath the table. Hey, after about a month I had a heckuva wad of meat under there. Then I'd sneak a dried out hunk of it onto another kid's plate.

My Parents Make a Move to Be Near

Pranks kept me busy, but I still had a hole in my heart for my family. Early in my stay at Brantford, Mom and Dad tried to be close to me. They sold their house in Desbarats and moved to Brantford. This was a huge sacrifice for them.

It was hard for Dad to find steady work there. He got a job with a refrigerator company, but, he said, "This job won't last.

By Christmas, they'll be cutting way back and I don't see anything else here. If I was home, I'd be trapping and other odd jobs. We'd have a little something to fall back on."

Mom was a teacher and couldn't get a job that quickly in a new school system in a new town. "I just don't see getting a job here," she said.

Besides, they weren't really "city people." The move was

hardly good for Ian, leaving his classmates and friends back in Desbarats. "I hate it here," Ian said. "The kids at school aren't interested in anything I am, and there's nowhere around here to do anything we did back home."

So, actually, the move turned into just a two-month experiment. I remember coming home one day and saying, "I think it's best you folks go back home and I'll be all right here."

I was just six. I don't know why I said this. I just somehow sensed they would be happier if they went back to Desbarats — and so would I. If they went back, then when I did come home from school, I would be coming home to the place where I grew up, and it would feel more like home. When they lived in Brantford, I was staying at the Brantford school Monday through Thursday anyway, and just coming home on weekends.

My parents were torn. That's a heck of a move to uproot your family. My Dad was born and raised in Desbarats. That was probably the only two months of his life he hasn't lived in the Desbarats area. They were willing to try to tough it out for me, but, financially, it just proved to be impossible. I have a lot of respect for my parents. They were always willing to go the extra mile — or, in this case, 465 miles.

KEEPING FOLKS LOOSE: GOOD TIMES IN HIGH GEAR

When Eric and I entered seventh grade, our adventures became more mature. I discovered I could time the night watchman's rounds down to the second. I knew once he came by our room, we wouldn't see him for another forty-five minutes. We'd slip out of the boys residence, go over to the girls dorm and climb up the side of their building to talk to them.

Whoever the genius was who designed the building, couldn't have played into our hands better. The corners had bricks jutting out in a criss-crossing pattern which made for natural steps.

Once we got up to the second story, we felt our way along a convenient ledge where we'd tap on the girl's windows and flirt with them and tease them until we knew forty minutes were about up.

That gave us just enough time to scoot down the corner of the building, whisk back over to ours and be back in bed by the time the watchman came around again.

One time I remember we were making too much noise outside the girls residence. A counselor came out to investigate. It was 1 a.m. I picked up an apple and cranked it as hard as I could. It connected.

"Urk," we heard her grunt.

She couldn't speak for awhile and her eyes must have been watering, too, because we escaped.

The next day, everyone got a major lecture.

"I know it had to be someone who can see, because he hit me right in the throat," the counselor said. That took us off the suspects list. Even though a lot of the kids at MacDonald could actually see quite a bit, Eric and I are totally blind.

I showed a cerebral side, too. We had a music wing with twenty-one individual practice rooms for whatever instrument you played. I actually liked playing the piano and I seemed to have an aptitude for it. That didn't save the piano as an object of sabotage.

One night, before our music teacher, Mrs. Black, could get down to the practice rooms, I went in and turned down all the wing nuts on the damper pedals. Practice was canceled for the night. I saw myself as something of an orchestral Spartacus, freeing slaves from the chains of piano practice.

In the dining room, if dinner was horrible, which it was more than once, I could trip the latch of the home-economics room with a comb. We'd raid the fridge and help ourselves to the cookies and pies that had been made during the day by loving student hands. Not that we always gained gastronomical ground in doing so. Learning to bake for a sighted youngster is difficult, but for a blind kid, it's worse. There were a lot of burned cookies in there, a lot of pies with all the filling on one side and a smidgen or two on the other. They certainly didn't taste like Mom's pies. Even if they weren't perfectly made, we were getting away with something and the sense of adventure heightened our sense of taste, which made them seem better than they were.

Another favorite trick: The "stylus" you use for punching out the dots in Braille paper to make Braille writing is a long sharp object. Where do you think we put them for unsuspecting fellow students?

Yep. You got it. In their seats, sticking straight up.

Ouch! I've had it happen to me.

Sometimes I think the school for the blind was rougher than the average sighted school.

I developed my own way of navigating during my years at Brantford. I had a trick where I clicked my tongue to get echoes off objects — trees and posts and stuff like that. Kind of like a bat's radar, I guess. Not everybody had this "facial perception" that told them where immovable, inanimate objects were, and where they weren't. So we'd tease someone — especially some of the older kids, get them really steamed up, get them chasing. Then I'd duck around a tree and the guy who was in hot pursuit would smash into it. I'd run away laughing hysterically.

I was the unchallenged champion at dealing this kind of misery.

Some people couldn't do the tongue-clicking thing and get it to work for them. In fact, they even kind of made fun of me for doing it because it sounded weird. I could do it even when I was running and it developed into a kind of unerring sonar for me.

After my classmates kept crashing into things, they asked me to teach them how to do it.

I'm not saying I was perfect at it. I took my fair share of lumps and bumps crashing into things, too. But, my "facial perception" and acute hearing developed to a pretty high degree.

One incident brought this home to me indelibly.

With all the trouble I was getting into, my Dad decided to pay me a surprise visit to try and straighten me out.

I had no idea he was coming. He wanted it that way. So he hopped into his car and drove the eight hours to Brantford. He walked up the sidewalk, into my residence hall, up three flights of stairs...and saw me.

I was walking down the hall towards him, chattering away — as always — to friends on either side. Dad walked right past us and on down the hall and he didn't say a word.

Without skipping a beat or breaking stride, I turned my head and said, "So, when did you get here?" It freaked him out.

He hadn't called anyone to say he was coming, much less me.

He comes almost 500 miles, walks into the building, buzzes past me without uttering a peep and I greet him.

He was spooked.

That move wasn't as hard as it appears. I knew the sound of my Dad's boots on a floor almost as well as I knew my own voice.

I knew his cologne. I even knew the way the keys jangled in his pockets. Even talking to my buddies, I could tell he was coming down the hall almost the minute he entered it.

I guess God just blessed me with these kind of senses to compensate for my blindness.

My vaunted facial perception and radar system didn't always work. Especially on low-lying park benches scattered around the grounds where people could sit to catch some fresh air. To me, they were a daily nightmare, since I was always taking one in the shins.

I'll never forget the day in seventh grade when Mr. Adams took one on the chin from me. Mr. Adams taught piano tuning and music appreciation. He was totally blind, our only blind teacher.

He was teaching one day when Eric and I weren't in his class. We were roaming the halls, looking for something to stir up. I opened the door and could hear Mr. Adams talking. I guessed where he was and hit him right in the face with a big, soft snowball.

He wasn't as mobile as us, or as fast, and he couldn't catch us. He went running over to the door and roared, "Who was that? Get back here right now."

Then, we were gone.

I admit it was mean, but we did it because we thought it was funny. You can say we took advantage of him. You're right. At the time we didn't see it that way. Heck, he was blind and we were blind, so that put us on even footing.

It didn't mean we disliked the guy either. He was actually a very nice person. It was just a prank you do when you're in junior high school, even if it's a pretty nasty one.

Later that year when the weather warmed, we'd take turns going to class. When roll was called and it came to my name, I'd say, "Here, sir."

Then when he'd call Eric's name, I'd scootch my head over a few feet and say, "Here, sir." Then I'd crawl out the open window at the back of the class.

One time Eric and I planned an escapade on a kid named Arthur, who could see some — and he was fast. He was about four years older than us. My job was to go downstairs and sneak into this big playroom where the upperclassmen were playing ball using a soccer ball with a bell inside. When the ball got by them, I stole it and ran like heck.

I streaked up four flights of stairs. As I passed Eric on the third landing with Arthur on my tail Eric let go a whole bag of one-hundred marbles. When Arthur hit the marbles, he went ass-over-teakettle. He went for a loop. We definitely did not wait around to hear what Arthur was saying.

If only we'd put as much time, energy and thought into our studies or worthwhile pursuits...no telling what we could have accomplished. We were just too bad, too wild and untamed to care at the time.

INDEPENDENCE BECOMES MY CAUSE

During my years at Ross MacDonald, I developed a passion for independence. It came out as a sort of rebellion against some of the rules designed to make life easier for blind kids at the school. An example is the rule that everybody was supposed to walk down the hall on the right side keeping a hand on the wall.

No way. I'd always cruise down the middle of the hall. I could hear kids coming toward me, and for the most part, I'd just step around them. I hated following the wall. That was not me.

We used to play a game called tin-can hockey where we'd hit a can instead of a puck. You had to wear a mask because as the can got beat up, it developed sharp edges and you could get dinged up good. We didn't wear full face masks; these were more like a T-Bar with a bar up and down and two across. Still, if the can got little enough, it could even go through the openings.

You think there's slashing and tripping and hooking in the big leagues. You oughtta see the blind league. Holy buckets! You were constantly fighting the lumber.

During some of those games, parents would yell, "Careful, you're going to put an eye out." What did we care? I broke a kid named Johnny's leg once like that, by accident. I was going in behind the net after the tin-can at full speed. I absolutely crunched him and broke his leg. It was completely accidental and I felt horrible. I didn't even know he was there.

The roughhousing was a tradition at Ross MacDonald. Even the superintendent took part. One time, the superintendent paid rather dearly for his willingness to be one of the boys.

We were playing the annual student-staff tin-can ice hockey game. I accidentally sticked the super in the face and gave him four stitches. Since I was always in his office for pranks, why did it have to be me who nicked him? As it turned out, he was getting off light that year. Another year, the superintendent accidentally slapped me with his glove. I hauled off to hit him back just as he stepped away and I punched him right in the crotch.

"Ooof," was all I heard him say.

He doubled over on the ice and stayed there quite awhile.

I'm not sure there's a tougher job anywhere than administrator at a blind school.

One day at dinner I was spreading butter that felt about as thick as axle grease on a piece of bread. I got the bright idea of winging it at Eric.

I gauged his voice pretty well, let fly and scored a bulls-eye. It hit Eric right in the back of the head — and stuck there, this gooey mess. He turned around. He didn't need to guess where it came from.

"MacFarlane, you dirty little..." he yelled. He scooped up a handful of mashed potatoes and flung them at me. The mashed potatoes barely grazed my right ear and smooshed someone right next to me. I hollered, "That was Eric. Get him!" Soon, you could hear and feel food flying everywhere. It must have been a pretty good blizzard. I didn't get off Scot free. Especially when the corn cob came whizzing in and caught me flush in the cheek.

The only thing I could find by that time was a grape. It was a big juicy grape. I slung it as hard as I could, and caught Mr. Stout, one of the residence counselors, square in the ear. I couldn't have gotten him any better if I'd walked up, taken him by the head and squashed the grape in there.

It exploded in all kinds of pieces and they went inside his ear. He had to go to the hospital; it was quite a scene. One-hundred blind kids in a food fight. No such thing as an innocent bystander.

ROUGHHOUSING BY THE RULES REDIRECTS MY LIFE:
A SPORT MADE FOR ME

Clearly I needed something to siphon off the high octane
running through my veins. It came early in my life at Brantford.
Wrestling. I started wrestling in the fall of Grade Two.
John Howe, the wrestling coach at Ross MacDonald, brought
Eric, another friend Doug Poirier and me from our grade to
wrestling practice.

He also brought one kid from Grade Three...Kenny Burgess.
We were the only kids that young asked to join the junior
wrestling program.

And, for one of the few times in my life, I felt a little
intimidated. We were leaving the junior school and going over
to the gymnasium, which was in the senior school. The big kids
were there. It was some of our first contact with them. Those
first three years at Ross MacDonald, you're pretty isolated from
the rest of the school. Even our cafeteria was in our own junior
building. We ate just up the hall from the infirmary. We did
everything under that one roof. This is going from the warm,
cozy environment of the junior school to the big leagues.

At first, I wasn't sure I liked wrestling. I mean, I liked
roughhousing but here we were roughhousing with kids bigger
and stronger than us. Suddenly, I wasn't able to pick on other kids.

Other kids were picking on me.

In practice you'd get bullied around by kids up to eight years
older. You'd be doing your situps and two guys would start
horsing around and you'd get a foot in the face. It was not for
the light of heart. You have a mat full of blind guys and it was
like a demolition derby. You get a body that lands on you and it's
forty pounds heavier and it's like, "Hey, I'm not supposed to
bend this way."

The lightest weight class in junior wrestling was sixty pounds.
I weighed fifty two. I had to wrestle eight pounds under the
lowest class. My first competition was the Brant County Junior

Invitational held at the YMCA, and I was seven. It was February 1970. The night before, I was so excited. The tournament was on a Saturday and I had started wrestling just two months before in December. But, John Howe said, "I think you're ready to try this tournament."

One reason I was both excited and nervous was because this meet would be against sighted kids. To be able to compete against them was important. I was still a little annoyed about being at Ross MacDonald. It was a fine facility, but that didn't compensate for the fact I didn't think I should be at a school for the blind, anyway.

In my young mind, if I hadn't been played a mean trick being blinded, I wouldn't be there. Now this wrestling was a way to lash out against my blindness. It was a way to get back at the sighted world for putting me where I was, a long way from home.

Even more, it was a way to gain acceptance to the sighted world I so resented, and yet, wanted to join. I finally went to sleep really late.

We had to get up early to go down and weigh in. It was all foreign to me. We got on a little bus at the school. John Howe drove. We arrived, walked up some steps and went into the YMCA. Inside, it was full of commotion. A lot of parents and kids were there — imagine your eyes being flooded with an array of flashing lights. That's what filled my ears — indistinguishable noise.

We went to the change room. You're supposed to strip down to your underwear to weigh in. Heck, I could have weighed in with my shoes and still made it under sixty pounds. John Howe took me by the hand and led me up there. Confident as I normally was, I was scared this time.

There was no way you were going to make it to the scales on your own, much as I wanted to. Shoot, there were probably 100 people there in the room between me and the scales. I didn't know the space or configuration of the room and it was a sea of people brimming with confusion. There was too much noise for me to "hear" my way around as I was used to doing.

For once I wasn't so certain of myself. I wasn't so full-speed ahead. Maybe afraid is a better word.

I got on the scale and the guy said, "Fifty-two pounds." I walked off.

Off-stride as I was, electricity filled the room which jolted me in a good way. We got our stuff back on and grabbed a bite to eat. I was so nervous I didn't want anything, but Coach Howe said, "Well, you have to. You won't have any strength."

I had a bowl of cereal. I hardly tasted it as it went down.

My weight class was up first in the competition. We came back changed into our wrestling shoes and uniform, a singlet, they called it.

I didn't know if I was any good, but I guess I looked the part anyway.

We went out to the mat and sat on the bench. The place smelled of old sweat. There was a lot of kidding and laughter on our bench. When they announced the first matches, Coach Howe came over and rubbed my shoulders, loosening me up, telling me to do some jumping jacks.

These kids in my weight class were all fifty-eight, fifty-nine, sixty pounds. In those days, we shook hands and then locked arms. When I felt my first opponent's arm, I thought, "God, how much bigger this guy is than me."

It was frightening, but I wasn't psyched out. I had butterflies. Even though I was so young, I felt I had something to prove. I thought if I ever was going to get out of that school for the blind, this would be the springboard.

I guess you'd think such thoughts wouldn't cross the mind of someone so young. I promise you they did. It wasn't that I was so mature for my age or had any great understanding or insight. It was just a longing and a hunger to get out of the school for the blind. I sensed, on some deep down level I didn't even understand, this was a way to escape it.

Before I wrestled, I had gotten a word of advice from one of the people who mattered most in my life — Grandpa Jefferies.

At Christmas, he told me, "Craig, give 'em hell from the start. That's the secret to winning." I took his words to heart. The match took twenty-four seconds. I pinned my opponent.

I had been losing to that point. He got an escape and a reversal, so he was up on me by a point. Then we went off the mat. He just kind of walked into a move and I wound up pinning him.

It was a very short match, but a ton of action. It was spirited from the first whistle and, somehow, I had won. I was flushed with pleasure. A rush of deep satisfaction swept through me. Give 'em hell. Grandpa, you were right.

At the end of that first match I turned and said to John Howe, "Coach, someday I'm going to be a champion."

WINNING AND BUILDING, WINNING AND BUILDING, I BECOME A WRESTLING JUGGERNAUT

I remember hearing some adult sitting in the bleachers behind coach kind of snickering when I said I would be a champion some day. Maybe he wasn't making fun of me, but just chuckling because I was so little saying this.

Coach Howe ignored him and said, "Craig, you keep working hard and someday you will be."

Little did we know that day was already here. That afternoon, I was a champion.

It took four more matches working through my bracket to do it. One was memorable because the guy I wrestled, Richie Dawson, bit me. His Dad was a referee. Richie got suspended.

I was pinning Richie and he bit me on the arm. I slugged him right in the face. It was just a reaction, part of my rough-and-tumble nature. I didn't know what they would do to us.

The whistle blew then the refs ripped us apart. I showed the bite marks and Richie was disqualified. That first tournament helped establish my habits on the mat. I wouldn't take anything from anybody. That was the start of the mental toughness that would define the rest of my athletic career.

So did winning.

Winning that first gold medal was spectacular. When I went to bed that night I clutched my medal tight in my hand until I'm sure my knuckles were white. I slept with it in my hand. I slept with it under my pillow. I tried it both ways, seeing where I liked it the best, where it seemed most comforting or prolonged the sense of satisfaction I had felt on the mat.

That medal was my link to the outside world. It represented hope. It stood for something I had achieved against sighted opponents. It touched the core of me, into my soul.

Winning that medal clearly was a turning point in my life. It catapulted my spirits into thinking I really could be competitive in a sighted environment.

I couldn't wait to tell my parents the next day on the phone. So I didn't. I phoned them that night. Collect. They were thrilled. They couldn't wait to hear how I had done.

My Mom answered and I said, "I won first place."

My Mom said, "Oh, that's terrific."

I could hear her voice choke up. "Really, how many matches did you have?" I said, "I had five matches."

I talked to my Dad and I told him I had pinned four of them. He said, "Well, what happened to the other guy?" I said, "That's the guy who bit me. He got disqualified."

When I went to school on Monday, I got called into the office of Mr. Armstrong, the superintendent. Oh no. What had I done this time? Although my pranks and misbehavior were almost daily occurrences, I couldn't remember any current crimes. I couldn't imagine I was in trouble, but it wouldn't have surprised me. Maybe I was doing so much wrong I couldn't keep track of it.

All I knew was that I had never been to the Super's office. I mean, he was the head of the entire school, and I was only seven. Mr. Armstrong was the Big Kahuna. I was going to see him. I was pretty nervous. I was thinking, "How does he even know who I am?" I went down, I walked in and, instead of lecturing, he congratulated me. "Hey, that's truly terrific what you did in the wrestling tournament. We're so proud of you," he said.

Not only that, I was invited to eat with Mr. Armstrong that night. In his house! He lived on the grounds in a big house. No cafeteria food that night. It was a home-cooked meal. I'm talking real potatoes. Just like home. When you're away from home, a meal like that means everything.

Mr. Armstrong was to become like a second father to me. Two years later, he died of a massive heart attack. I learned of it in an all-school assembly. I was devastated. I sat frozen in my seat, his congratulatory words reverberating in my head.

After the dinner with Mr. Armstrong, I sort of fell in love with both wrestling and winning. I thought, "Gosh. This is great. People are really all for you when you do this wrestling thing. When you win."

I was determined never to lose a match.

I did open my career by winning my first twenty-seven matches. I was in the third grade before I lost — to a sixth grader who was about ten pounds heavier.

I was wrestling him in an exhibition match. Even though wrestling went by weight class, often in dual meets, John Howe would have me wrestle an extra match in addition to my normal match. The extra match would be against someone ten pounds heavier, just to gain experience.

It was an excellent strategy for improvement but on the day I lost my first match, I wasn't so pleased. Inside I was really boiling. I mean, I guess you're not really supposed to think you're invincible, but tell that to an eight-year-old kid who has won twenty-seven in a row. Part of me was angry at having to wrestle someone so much heavier.

Coach Howe explained that it was making me a better wrestler and a better person. It was making me work harder.

Eventually, what athletics did for me was to teach me to win with humility, to lose with dignity and to always give my best shot in every situation.

That first taste of losing was terrible. If that's what failure tasted like, then I didn't want to eat failure at all.

I think the expectation that I would win all the time, this perpetual victory machine, was first started among my classmates. Maybe, to a certain degree, I became a beacon of hope to them. I'm not saying I became a hero — because I don't think that's true — but I had gone out and won something against the sighted world and I was one of them.

I think I succeeded early on because I had that enormous fear of losing and I was always willing to put in a little extra to do better. That was far from being a braggart. The arrogance people saw was just a facade I tacked up over the uncertainty and fright I had of failing.

In fact, I started building myself up to the point that at nine years old, a lot of days I was doing five-hundred situps and five-hundred pushups. Not all at once, but, during the course of a day, I would do 500 of each.

I was partly driven from that level of anxiety that I didn't want to lose. I also didn't want to use my blindness as an excuse if I lost. Also, I had a hunger, a thirst, for being the absolute best I could be; to compete against sighted kids was certainly something that fueled my fire at an early age.

By age nine, I had probably built myself up to eighty pounds. When I was eleven or twelve, I could do 500 situps in a row, no problem. Pushups? I could do a couple of hundred straight.

You grind your teeth together, you make a few faces, you grunt a little, you pull from areas you didn't think you had. I found that I wasn't afraid to ask myself for a little more, to push a little harder, to dig a little deeper.

I would get up at four a.m. and run and be back in bed by five, so no one knew I'd been up. I didn't want people to know how hard I was training. I was a maniac. I was fighting for an opportunity to be treated as an equal. In my mind, I think I was fighting to get back home. I was fighting to be accepted in a sighted world.

Wrestling at other schools was like you were out on furlough for a day. I'd travel across town to compete, people would be yelling for me, I'd be slapped on the back when I won. But then I'd travel back to school. When the applause faded and the lights went down at night, I was back in my bed at W. Ross MacDonald. I was not with my parents. Winning was the best thing I had to hold in my arms at night.

Between meets, I still drove myself to prepare for that fleeting moment of competition. I never did weights to build myself up at the time; just pushups and situps. The only exception were my legs. As I began to mature, I could do 600 pounds on the leg press machine. My legs were the main source of my strength. I was blessed naturally by God to have that. By nine years old, I'd hear the whispers whenever I went onto the mat: "Hey, look at that blind kid. There's that blind kid. Hey, the blind kid's here today. Hey, Sam, you've gotta fight that blind kid today. He's here."

Wrestling is an individualized sport. You don't phone home for help. Your teammates and your coaches can't help you — not much, once you're out on the mat, anyway. Wrestling develops tremendous character, tremendous individualism.

Let's face it. How many sports do you know that can be that humiliating, where one guy goes out and wrestles the other guy and one guy is gonna get whipped? Ok. Boxing. That's just about the only thing that compares.

Love Enters the Picture

As I got older, I was fighting in front of my girlfriend. You have the potential for being embarrassed on a major scale when that happens. I don't think I was aware of girls coming to watch me until age ten. Even in a sighted school, not many girls came out to watch a wrestling meet. But, at the school for the blind, wrestling was the only sport where blind people could compete on an equal basis with sighted people.

Everything changed about fifth grade. Until then, I had been a pure athlete, fighting to win for the sake of winning. But in fifth grade I met Jane. Suddenly I had another reason to win. Better said, I had another reason to fear losing.

It seemed like I fell in love with her at first "sight."

I guess you'd say "first listen" or "first touch" since those are the ways blind people see. We often speak of "seeing" and "watching" in conversation just like most people. I got that from my Mom and Dad. We would say, "I saw so-and-so at the store the other day." Or we would talk about "watching" a television program. I'd be listening, but getting images of sorts through my ears and so "watching" was just the language we used.

So, I fell in love at first sight.

She was slim and athletic. I loved her long hair, three-quarters of the way down her back. She had a sexy voice, though she was relatively quiet and very shy — qualities that were the opposite of me. At least on the outside we were opposites. Inside, we were very similar. When it came to girls, I was painfully shy inside. I just covered it up with swagger and bluster, acting confident even though I wasn't actually feeling that way.

Jane was sensitive and intelligent and she saw the real me, the tentative person inside, and she cared for me anyway.

As much as I loved the touch of her and the smell of her and the sound of her voice, I loved her heart and spirit more. We had great conversations.

Jane was a cheerleader, so she was always there to see me wrestle. I think she motivated me as much as anything or anyone ever did

— whether it is Coach Howe, my parents, my grandpa or myself.

Over the next four years, I believe she helped bring my athletic career to a higher level. Maybe it was partly a self-imposed pressure to win in front of her. When I was really down, she lifted me up. She ignited a flame inside me. I didn't want to fail in her eyes.

And, incidentally, when I say "eyes" here I mean that more literally than figuratively. Jane could actually see quite a bit. She could read the large print in some books. She could see me coming fifty feet away.

She was like a lot of kids at the school for the blind. Many of them who had a considerable measure of sight. In fact, I wasn't even sure why some of them were there, as much as they could see. They fit a legal definition of blindness and had somehow elected to go to Ross MacDonald, or their families had decided for them.

I was glad Jane could see as much as she could. It made me think maybe I was cool, if a beautiful girl like her could actually tell what I looked like and she was attracted to me.

Of course, she may have also been attracted to my full-out attitude for life, which put us in tight spots more than once.

Ross MacDonald had a gorgeous auditorium with a big pipe organ. I used to sneak into it by using my old friend, the pocket comb, to trip the latch. In the beginning, Eric and I would climb up on a catwalk around the organ pipes and explore.

Well, one day Jane and I were up there, poking around and joking and kissing. Darned if when we got up there, one of the music teachers didn't come in and start practicing on the pipe organ. The sound was deafening; some of the pipes were inches from our heads. We thought if we ran, we'd be seen or heard and get in trouble. So we hid up there with the catwalks shaking from the vibration of the pipes, covering our ears as best we could.

It's a wonder both of us didn't come out of it deaf as well as blind.

That was just one of my many adventures. During my eighth

grade year, I probably set a school record by being sent to the principal's office three times in one day for my adventures.

I remember the last time going there and the principal said, "You know where your chair is."

I said, "I'm surprised you didn't move it."

He said, "I didn't have time."

Later that year, in English, Eric and I were sent to a supply room as punishment for our behavior. Not a terribly good move, actually, on our teacher's part. We closed the door back there and in our explorations I found a number of pieces of indoor-outdoor carpeting that were cut out in the shape of the provinces. They all fit together to show blind people how Canada is formed.

So Eric and I got to playing Frisbee with Manitoba. Don't ask me why not Saskatchewan or Alberta. Manitoba just seemed to sail nicely. Well, one of us ended up winging Manitoba behind a four-foot-high filing cabinet. The top of it was loaded with stuff. No way one person, much less an eighth-grader, was going to budge that puppy.

So Eric, crouched low and was pulling on the bottom and I was pulling on the top. That worked out pretty good for me. Eric? Well...the top was lighter so it came forward, the bottom didn't move. I didn't know what was on top of the cabinet, but we found out all too soon.

An entire gallon jar of Bond-Fast Glue, smucked Eric right on the head. It knocked him stiff. Mrs. Tinkus heard this ferocious crash and came running in, only to find Eric in a puddle of glue and glass, looking quite dead. My pants were splattered and I had this look of terror on my face.

Eric came to not long after that and we scraped him up off the floor, but the same couldn't be said for the glue. I think they're still trying to pry some of it off the floor today. Eric was sporting one heck of a goose egg for days to come.

Once wrestling and girls began to kick in full force, my classwork took a back-seat to everything at school. I knew I was bright enough to do well in class, but there were days I hardly applied myself at all. At first, Braille seemed so incredibly complex to me, I thought I'd never master it. Braille is a system of dot patterns you use to create letters and numbers. The Braille alphabet has twenty-six letters, just like the sighted one. After you learn your letters, which is called Grade One Braille, you must master 198 contractions, known as Grade Two Braille, kind of like a form of shorthand. As you probably know, a blind person "reads" by passing his or her fingertips over the raised dots.

What a sighted person may not realize is how cumbersome the system can be. You can pack a Reader's Digest in your pocket. In Braille, it's four volumes in a box.

Braille seemed an unbelievable thing to grasp when I first got to Ross MacDonald. By the time I got out, I was able to take dictation of teachers' lectures, using a "slate and stylus", with which you punch Braille letters onto a piece of rather stiff Braille paper.

Even though I loved learning new things in life, I just wasn't ready to do the type of work I needed to do to get all A's.

My best efforts still were reserved for athletics, pranks and girls. I'd daydream in class — just like a sighted kid, I think. I could sleep by resting an elbow on the desk and my chin in my palm. I'd dream about new wrestling moves and I'd dream about Jane and I'd take her over to the gym later and try these new wrestling moves on her. I invented moves and would test them. Ok, maybe some of it was just to feel Jane next to me. Some of it actually was strictly because of wrestling.

I was consumed by it. It seemed to drive my every waking minute; when I wasn't thinking of girls or thinking of pranks, I dreamed about gold medals. My quickest pin in wrestling was ten seconds and that was against a sighted opponent. I lived for victories with losses haunting me between. I learned to never take winning for granted. One time I was out there and quickly found myself down 8-0 in the first of three rounds. Coach Howe gave me hell. "You look out of control out there," he said.

"You're here in body, not spirit. What are you thinking about? Get your head into it!" I went out and quickly pinned the guy.

THINKING ABOUT HOME

I appeared to be on top of my world. Actually, there was a huge void in my insides. That was on weekends. My main link to my parents was the telephone. I usually got one weekly call from them — on Sunday.

If that phone call was a minute late, I would think that something happened to them. If the call was supposed to come in at 10 a.m. on Sunday and the circuit might be busy, our line might be busy on our end, it just crushed me. I always waited down the hall for that phone to ring and I was always hoping it was ringing for me. When it got near 10 a.m., I'd always be anticipating that phone ringing. They'd come and get you if the call was for you, but I always kept an ear cocked on my own, just to make sure.

Of course, when summer holidays rolled around and I did get to go home like everyone else...well, that was heaven.

Rebel. Blondie. Ian. My friends, Matthew Hunter, Blake Marcel, Randy Barber — -all those people. Glen Moore, Scott Hatton. We were back playing cowboys and Indians up on the rock. Swimming and ripping. Playing with my cousins, Todd and Jamie, Kim, Bonita, Cathy and Paul — playing in the hay mow. Every fall, I'd return to W. Ross MacDonald. At first, each return was like torture. But, as I got more used to it and the school became my "domain," I began to appreciate what a fantastic place it was.

If you had to be sent away to a school by yourself, this definitely was the place to be. In fact, there is little doubt W. Ross MacDonald is the finest school for the blind in the world. As an adult, I traveled to all kinds of blind facilities all over Canada and in America. Nothing holds a candle.

Yet, I was getting awfully antsy staying there. In fact, I began to feel the urge to leave this "blind world." I felt that I had to go test myself in the sighted world.

That was really what I had been striving for, ever since age six, the second I hit the place. I was straining in every way I knew how to leave. Or to prepare myself to go. Times came when I'd get terribly frustrated with my blindness and its supposed limitations. I was struck sometimes by the way blindness imprisoned so many of my friends. I think that's why I developed such a frontal personality, always pushing, always striving. It was just a great need to infuse myself with confidence, to use confidence as a jackhammer to break out of that prison.

I felt I was meant to be able to move and live among the "real" world, the sighted one. Before I was through with wrestling, I would win more than ninety percent of some 500 matches against sighted opponents. Just winning wasn't my yardstick. How I did against the "normal" world was.

My name started to spread outside W. Ross MacDonald and outside Brantford.

Between my eighth and ninth grade years in 1976, I was picked to compete in Canada's first National Games for the Physically Disabled and the first International Games for the Physically Disabled.

By then, my athletic ability had extended to track, where I began to excel in the sprints — the 60-, 100- and 200-meter dashes. I was winning or placing in at least the top three in almost every race I entered. So I was brimming with confidence now.

I truly thought I was ready to handle anything any sighted person could do. I didn't have any idea how difficult it was going to be to leave W. Ross MacDonald.

By the time my eighth-grade year rolled around, several of the biggest incidents in my life were about to unfold.

First, we lost my grandma MacFarlane. That in September

1975. She lived next door to us in Desbarats and I was close to her. Eight months later we lost Grandpa Jefferies.

I was at a three-day regional competition in wrestling and track and field, which qualified you for the Ontario provincial championships. I had won a gold in sprinting and my Mom and Dad went to see Grandpa Jefferies in the hospital.

They handed him the medal and Grandpa grabbed it so hard that he wrinkled the ribbon and scrunched it up in his hand. They said he wouldn't let go of it.

I was extremely torn about what to do. I wanted very badly to go see him because we were all pretty sure he wasn't going to make it.

Mom and Grandma insisted that I stay in the competition, because if you didn't win here, you couldn't go to the provincials. They said that Grandpa wanted me to stay and compete and win for him.

I took them at their word. I did stay and I won the gold medal in wrestling and sprinting.

After I won, Ian and I jumped on a train for Nairn Centre. By the time we got there, Grandpa had died.

A few days later, we held his funeral. It was the day before the provincial wrestling championships for the blind in Southern Ontario, so I had to hop onto a plane right after the funeral because weigh-ins were being held the next morning, followed by the competitions.

It was extremely tough.

I was thirteen. I felt badly about not being there before Grandpa died. I had a huge lump in my throat as I weighed in. For the first time since I could remember, I didn't want to compete. I had lost the fire.

During the first match, which should have been easy, I was floundering. At the end of the first round, I was losing to someone I had easily defeated many times before.

In the split second between rounds, I questioned whether I really wanted to be a champion that day.

Coach Howe had his arm around me. He knew I wasn't myself. He wasn't yelling at me this time. He knew what was going on inside. Then, to my amazement, something clicked as I walked out for the second round.

It hit me.

That old saying Grandpa used to give me all the time.

"Give 'em hell on the start, Craigie."

Suddenly, I felt I was really letting my grandpa down by not trying my best the first round. I figured he would be watching me from wherever he was, and how disappointed he must have been with my effort so far. I felt a warm, tingling sensation come over my body. My muscles got tight. I found that eye of the tiger I had been missing.

I went out for the second round and I pinned the guy midway.

"Good going, my little dumpling," I could hear Grandpa whisper in my ear.

I believe I have fought with the eye of the tiger — and the ear of my grandpa — ever since.

I was even more convinced that I was to take the lessons I had learned from Grandpa and Mom and Dad and Coach Howe and Mr. Armstrong — and all the others who had helped me and meant so much to me...and try them full-time in the sighted world.

I told administrators at Ross MacDonald that in ninth grade I would be transferring to Central Algoma Secondary School. It was the huge public school right in my own home town, Desbarats.

I was going home! I would be with Mom and Dad and my horse and dog and Ian and all my friends. I would escape the limiting world of the blind at W. Ross MacDonald. I was finally going to break the shackles of blindness. Not just a little during wrestling and track and field competitions. Always.

I could scarcely contain myself, but there was only one major drawback. Jane.

I didn't really know how I was going to be able to break this news to her or talk to her about it. We had been inseparable the last few years. She lived inside me as much as my own heart and soul. She was an extension of me and, I believe I was the same for her.

I went over to get her at the girls' residence. We joined hands and walked down Center Boys Walk, a place we had strolled so many times before. This time was different.

I told her my plans. I told her I would be leaving.

For a moment I thought our hearts collapsed and the world stopped whirling, like some toy top that had run out of spin and toppled on its side.

We kissed.

Then I stood there, holding her as the long breezy moment began to sweep over my body and engulf my soul. I smelled her perfume. My knees got weak. My eyes swelled up with tears.

Could a thirteen-year-old have this kind of emotion for someone? I bit hard on my lip as I felt a knot come from my stomach into my throat.

She was crying on my shoulder.

"Please don't leave," she said. As I choked back the tears, a faint voice came from my mouth. "I have to," I murmured.

Did I really? Why? What was I trying to prove? And, to whom?

I thought the big bad sighted world was beckoning to me. But, in my heart, I knew the right decision was to stay here, with Jane.

As Jane and I slowly strolled back up Center Boys Walk, I could feel the dampness on my shoulder from her tears. My arm was around her. I was grateful for the sight that she had because my senses were certainly on autopilot and I was letting her lead me, oblivious to the trees and lampposts that we were passing.

It felt so natural. It felt so right. I wanted this moment to never end. This was my comfort zone, here at W. Ross MacDonald.

I was about to take a bold step. As we reached the bottom of the steps at the senior girls' residence, Jane and I stopped and embraced one last time.

I was coming to realize I was not that tough, macho kid who roamed the halls like the Lone Ranger. On this particular day and in this Moment, I was humbled in Jane's presence.

On the way back to the senior boys' residence, I stopped and sat on a cement wall at the end of the field where we had played football so many times at noon hour — Doug, Roger, Eric and I.

That field represented great times. Laughter. Bloody noses. Skinned knees. Blind kids running full speed. Horrendous crashes into each other.

It was a field of independence. It was a place where you didn't need anyone to lead you around. You didn't have to hold someone's arm.

I thought about these things for a long while as I sat on that cement wall, my feet dangling over the edge. I wondered if life would be as independent back in Desbarats, back at Central Algoma Secondary School. How would kids treat me?

I knew if it wasn't now, it would be four years from now that I would enter the world of the sighted, never to return to this sheltered environment of the school for the blind.

Tomorrow morning I would be going home to the beautiful things and my perfect world in Desbarats, but so far away from Jane and this safe world of the school for the blind.

For a split second, I didn't even want to go home.

I pushed with my hands off the wall and jumped down that eight feet or so.

I landed upright.

I stood there for a minute.

Then I slowly started jogging for the last time across the friendly, familiar grass that served so many years as my field of dreams.

My friend Gordon Hope was also one of my toughest competitors. Wrestling - and the competition involved - helped me win a place in the mainstream.

CHAPTER FIVE
MY PRIDE IS SHOWING

Mainstreaming.

The word contained almost mythical power for me.

Now that I was leaving W. Ross MacDonald and going to Central Algoma Secondary Public School, I believed I was headed home, where I was always meant to be. I had always considered myself a mainstream person. I was raised to be a mainstream person.

One of the great ironies, I suppose, is that some at MacDonald were busy looking down on me for my departure.

One teacher called me "stupid" and told me that I would be a dropout if I left MacDonald. This person told me that I would never succeed in a sighted school and would miss the support system at MacDonald, a place on which I was turning my back.

To some I was a traitor for leaving. They probably wished I'd fall flat on my face at Central Algoma. Their doubts made me all the more determined to succeed in a sighted school.

"You SOB," I thought, when the teacher called me stupid. "I am going to have the last laugh. I will make sure I prove you wrong."

I was full of vim and vigor, anyway, as I entered Central Algoma. After my uncertain moments leaving Jane in the spring, I'd had a pretty big summer.

At age fourteen, I carried the Canadian flag in the Olympiad for the Physically Disabled in the Toronto suburb of Etobicoke. I was the youngest member of the team. I took representing my country seriously; I saw it as a deep honor. Perhaps I took it too seriously. We got into a couple of scuffles in the change room with kids from the U.S. They were fairly minor scuffles, really, shoving matches, a few wild punches thrown without real damage. The atmosphere was intense.

It was also at the training camp one week prior to the Olympiad where I got a little comeuppance for my sense of invincibility. We went on a tour of the Blind Olympics facilities, including a lake where the diving would be conducted. The guide explained how high the ten-meter diving tower was, which is almost thirty-three feet. I had been listening to the Montreal Olympic Games on TV, and I'd heard them talk about Greg Louganis doing a "double back flip with a twist in the pike position."

That sounded like fun.

"Hey, coach, watch this," I shouted. I ran up the tower. I took a huge leap backwards off the top and started trying to flip through the air. I had no problem with flipping. I had big trouble not flipping. After I got into the air it occurred to me, I didn't exactly know what a pike position was. I wound up twisting around and over-rotating into about two and three-quarters flips — landing square on my back.

They say even when an elite diver executes perfect form, hitting the water from the ten-meter tower is like diving through a sidewalk. I now believe them. I thought I had split myself in two when I hit the water. I could barely walk the rest of the day. My back was red for a solid week.

But I won a wrestling silver and I planned to ride that international victory into my new life at Central Algoma Secondary School. I had represented my country in international competition and brought back a medal, so my confidence was high. But, back at home, I had a bigger challenge waiting than I thought. To tell the truth, breaking in at Central Algoma was no piece of cake.

True, I was thrilled to be back home in Desbarats. I was

overjoyed to be with my old running buddies, my horse, dog, mom, dad, brother — the works.

That part I knew would be great. I was less sure of how I would do at a new school, a sighted school, though I didn't let on that I was apprehensive.

The first day at Central Algoma, I was equally nervous and excited. Ian and I were at the same school for the first time. I was excited about that. But I was nervous about how I would appear to my new classmates and about how I would fit into their world.

I spent what seemed like a century getting ready for school that first day. I've always been particular about my clothes and hair; I once counted forty tee-shirts in my drawers and closets. I may have tried on every one of them that day. I also brushed my hair about a thousand times, all the while dogging Ian to death about how I looked.

I wanted to make a major first impression. People at Central Algoma had heard about me in the media. I'd started to have some athletic success beyond Brant County, where W. Ross MacDonald was located. I'd been on television a few times. I'd been written up in the papers. So I thought I'd have a lot of eyes on me and I wanted to look just right.

I knew I would encounter more than a thin veil of jealousy at my hometown school. The only blind athlete in a place with 700 kids has nowhere to hide. People will know if you're as good as you've been portrayed. They'll know if you can cut it or you can't. And, they're bound to test you first chance they get. No doubt about it, I was coming in with a highly touted athletic background and that caused some animosity among my would-be teammates in wrestling.

Some of the kids were just splendid, enormously helpful. And my new wrestling coach, Mel Prodan, was my biggest supporter. He believed in me. He was excited about my past record and thought I'd be a good addition to his team. I told him I appreciated that — and I did. But I also told him I didn't want special favors.

So Coach Prodan and I got off on the right foot. The same, unfortunately, couldn't be said about my new teammates. I couldn't have botched the first step much more.

It turned out some of the guys didn't want me on the team. At the very least, they wanted to test my abilities. It didn't take me long to find this out first-hand. My first day in the cafeteria, I sat down at the table where the other wrestlers were.

"Pretty clever how you cut your food like a normal guy," one of them said. "When did you learn to feed yourself?"

Maybe I could have taken this as a joke, but it didn't sound like one and I didn't feel like putting up with his crap if it wasn't.

"Been doing it as long as I can remember," I said. "How long have you been a jerk?"

Absolute silence.

The real challenge came right from the top, in the person of Tim Golick, the captain of the Central Algoma wrestling team. The first day of wrestling practice, he walked into the lunchroom and got right in my face.

"You and me," he said. "We got to get it on."

"Sure," I said. "You want it right here, right now, in the cafeteria?"

"Practice, today," he said.

"Anytime, buddy," I said. "Anytime at all."

The question was simple. Stay and fight or run and hide? Anyone who knew me at Brantford could have guessed my answer. Eric Lambier could certainly have guessed my answer. I've never dodged a challenge.

Frankly, by the time he challenged me, I was ready. For one thing, I was growing tired of all the banter. It was getting on my nerves. But instead of making me jittery, it only hardened my jaw.

I mean, I had worked my tail off for eight long years, since I first arrived at the school for the blind, to prove I was able to operate the same as any sighted athlete — and to do it on his own turf, if need be. I longed for this opportunity and no one was going to take it from me.

I went to practice knowing that I wasn't trying to win a match or a medal. I was fighting to prove my worth and identity, both as an athlete and as a person.

Word had gotten around about Golick and me because a pretty good crowd had gathered around the stage in the cafeteria, where wrestling practices were held. I got my wrestling stuff on and climbed the stairs to the stage, ready to go.

"Hey blind boy. Let's see what you're made of," someone yelled out of the crowd.

So that's how it was going to be. Not only with the team, but with everyone else.

Well, now this was my game. I'd spent a lot of years feeding off people's taunts or their ideas that I was limited because I was sightless. I heard girls' laughter in the crowd and that also worked in my favor. I hated losing in front of girls more than losing itself. It was a major part of my self-worth. Right now that was working to my advantage. There was no way I would let this guy beat me, no matter who or how good he was, in front of girls. I had the same mind set I'd had for championship matches.

Then it turned out I didn't even square off with Tim Golick first. Another kid on the team, Jack MacIntire, jumped in. Maybe he was trying to lessen the tension. I didn't know. But if he was just kidding around, I wasn't. I found out right away I could beat him and I did. And then I kind of followed his lead, acting like pinning him was some kind of joke.

That was all the final goading Golick needed. No sooner did I pin Jack, than Tim walked onto the mat. I knew I'd pricked his pride by dispatching Jack so easily. Now the team's honor, not just Tim's, was at stake.

It barely mattered. Tim was a good wrestler, quick and tough. But on this particular day I was a little hungrier, I guess. I pinned him quickly, too.

"Enough," said Coach Prodan.

Now the same guys who'd been giving me so much static

crowded around. They pounded me on the back, laughing and joking and roughing my hair. The first two guys to do it were Tim and Jack.

Now I was officially welcomed to the team. I was fully accepted and not only as a wrestler. I started hanging with my teammates and became good friends with many of them. They were part of the cool crowd at school so, naturally, my social standing improved.

Guess who became my roommate for road trips. Golick. And, later, he became a guy I really liked.

Mike Busque was another guy I grew close to. He was a dynamite wrestler and we became pretty inseparable on and off the mat. He was a lot like me. He was a free spirit and a real handful. But with me he was always courteous and quick to come to my defense. A good friend in a pinch.

The rest of my swan dive into the mainstream had varying degrees of difficulty and success. Just the sheer size of Central Algoma Secondary School was not a significant difference.

In my age group at W. Ross MacDonald, I was an unquestioned ringleader, even for many kids older and younger. That was mostly because of wrestling. I occupied a high-profile position among my peers — at least the ones I hadn't alienated with my pranks. But at Central Algoma I was less revered. It was just plain strange to walk into a place where everyone else could see and you couldn't.

And since Central Algoma Secondary School wasn't built with blind people in mind, negotiating the facility wasn't exactly a breeze. Visually, they say, Central Algoma is very impressive. It won numerous architectural awards for high-school design in Ontario and North America. But it was designed with benches in a magnificent indoor courtyard and I was constantly running into those benches. Some of the steps were designed in a way that offered no warning to a blind person. Potted plants, benches in the patio, trash cans, chairs moved around here and there made walking sometimes quite treacherous for me. It was a lot easier to run into something at Central Algoma. Because of the "facial perception" I've described before, I could tell after a fairly short time where the doors and steps were. Still, the building had juts and angles that took a long time to master.

I often was forced to take a classmate's elbow, just lightly to get from one place to the next. This was something I'd have cut off my arm before doing at Ross MacDonald. With 700 kids changing class helter-skelter the halls were incredibly crowded. Worse, kids at the sighted school walked down the halls anywhere they wanted, not keeping to their right as they did at MacDonald. My disdain for that rule softened in the chaos of the halls at Central Algoma.

One time I was late for class, hurrying through the courtyard under some fig trees and a girl and guy were sitting on the stairs. I was carrying my Brailler, which weighs a ton, and I smacked her right square in the noggin. The school bell and her bell rang at about the same time. Thankfully, she was pretty understanding about it. Another time I was sprinting late into class and a desk had been shoved out into the aisle. I went over it like a full-back diving over the pile for the goal line. I smashed down, face and chest-first, feeling totally foolish.

The best I could do was spring to my feet, hold both hands over my head and yell, "Touchdown." I got a rousing ovation out of it anyway.

Despite the difficulty of maneuvering in a sighted school, I lived a normal social life. I dated a few girls but nothing as serious as I'd felt for Jane at Ross MacDonald. In fact, getting to know anyone well was harder at Central Algoma. Everyone went home after school, or extra-curricular activities, unlike MacDonald, where you could still see your buddies or your girl friend in the evenings. They were right there with you. Everyone ate together and played games in the student lounge together after dinner. We were more like a family.

At Central Algoma you might be interested in a girl who lived one mile away or thirty miles. So, almost anybody I went out with wound up being pretty casual. And sometimes those experiences were pretty funny, too. My buddies liked to set me up with blind dates. Yes, that's right. They'd ask girls who didn't know me at Central Algoma if they'd be willing to go out with me on a blind date. That's all they knew, that they were going out with this wrestler named Craig MacFarlane. It wasn't until we picked the girl up that she discovered this was the first real blind date of her life.

Academically, I wasn't setting the world on fire. I have to admit, it was a bigger struggle than I thought it would be to succeed as a student in a sighted school. My Mother was a tremendous help to me with my homework. Because of her, I was able to get my share of 'B's at Central Algoma. I found out then what a wonderful teacher she has been to all her students over the years.

Almost all the teachers tried to help me as much as they could, except for one math teacher I didn't really get along with there. A good example was in art classes, where you'd think finding projects for a blind student would be difficult. When the other students did dot portraits with shading, I did mine with pin dots. When students were painting, I'd be throwing pots on the potter's wheel.

Periodically, while I was molding a bowl on the potter's wheel in art class, I'd accidentally get a little too much water on the wheel. Next thing you know, pieces of the bowl were hurtling toward some innocent bystander several feet away. Of course, those flying pots weren't always accidental. Maybe I overloaded the wheel once or twice to see how far it'd spray.

Once, after a wrestling match at Central Algoma, I was walking to the change room near the gym and Tim Golick yelled, "I'll tell you when to turn...

"Turn now!"

I wound up not walking into the boys' change room, but into the girls'. They shrieked and freaked out of course, until they saw it was me and realized I couldn't see a thing.

"Nice seeing you ladies," I said. "You're all beautiful. I'll be leaving now."

"Well, stop by again...since you can't see," one said.

"You know, you're turning beet red," said another. "Are you sure you can't see?"

"Unfortunately, no," I said with a laugh.

To myself, I said, "Nice one, Tim. You'll pay dearly for this."

Tim became my Eric at Central Algoma. Playing pranks on each other became a way of life for the next two years.

Things were progressing just fair, actually, on the athletic side. I held my own, winning most of my wrestling matches at Central Algoma. On the outside it was hard to see I'd lost my edge, but inside, I knew. The social life of a typical teenager distracted me. New surroundings were also a distraction. Maybe it was a matter of wanting to hang out and just be a normal guy, rather than this person always defined by his athletic prowess that caused me to lose a degree of interest.

I FIND MEANING IN OTHERS

The trophies and medals began to lose their meaning for me. I had been winning them since I was seven. They didn't shine as much any more. One day at Central Algoma I tried to inject usefulness back into them, and I learned a great lesson in the process. In the ninth grade I had won this big wrestling tournament in the States and was given a large marble trophy. I gave it to a ten-year-old polio victim who'd been watching me loyally for five matches. I felt that his loyalty should be rewarded. This boy would never be able to win such a trophy and to me it was just one of many. I hope that it made him feel as good recieving it as it made me feel giving it.

I'm not trying to pass myself off as a great humanitarian at that point. As I said, I was still very much a work in progress. But I can't tell you how good it felt to give that trophy away.

And one of the things I dearly loved at Central Algoma was coaching junior hockey. Matt's father, Hughie, allowed me to help coach the bantam team in Desbarats. During games he would let me make up the lines, send them out, change them up. We won the championship that year. I won a better understanding of what you get when you give.

In fact, I think you could see a lot of my pranks in this light, as well. Sure, my pranks were always for laughs. But they were also a way I could loosen people up who took themselves or their blindness too seriously. And they were part of the whole atmosphere at Ross MacDonald of making people independent. Sighted people played pranks on each other. Why shouldn't blind people? I think I was keeping life real for us, the way my life had always been. I was breaking down this idea that blind people were somehow fragile. If you were charitable, you might see all my pranks as my contribution to a normal social life at Ross MacDonald.

Anyway, it was important for me to realize how good it felt to help others. I'd spent my whole life struggling to be independent, avoiding help from others when I could. It did me good to feel what it was like to be a helper for a change. It helps you get out of yourself.

If I wasn't exactly burning up the wrestling mat that year, I was on a fast-track in other national blind competition. In the summer of 1977 I was a big favorite to win the 200- and 400-meters at the blind nationals. I overcame my little competitive swoon to get cranked up for those games.

Here's how sprinting works for a blind athlete. A coach stands with a megaphone at the end of the 60- or 100-meter dashes. He calls out "five-five-five-five" if you are dead-center in your lane. If you drift left, he yells, "four-four-four-four" and if you veer right it's "six-six-six-six." In sprints only one blind person runs at a time so there's no such thing as a photo finish.

Running the curves of the 200 and 400 were tricky. Here, you need a guide, like in snow skiing. You need someone as fast as you, who can also have rhythm and anticipation enough to get his arm swing and leg drive synchronized with yours.

The 400 was the nastiest race of all. It also was the scene of some of my major battles.

MY PRIDE IS SHOWING

The Ontario provincial championships came first in the summer of 1977. The weather was rare for Canada — 107 degrees. Why they didn't cancel the race, I don't know. But I do know I let it psyche me out, something that doesn't usually happen.

My strategy normally was to hang back the first 250 meters, then kick the last 150 — which is normally where the race is won, anyway. Sometimes I'd turn on the jets so late I'd pass people in the last five meters. That was my style and I was very successful with it.

But on this day, I decided to change because of the heat. I took the lead early but I couldn't hold it at the end. I lost in a photo finish by one-hundredth of a second. I'd fallen behind by 20 meters and I'd fought back, but I just didn't have enough at the end to be first at the tape.

At nationals, the temperature was 85 degrees. I ran my normal race. I blew away the guy who beat me at Provincials snapping the tape fifteen meters ahead.

I wasn't as successful when I wasn't running. I broke curfew. The team manager was waiting for me when I got back to my room. It was the last night of the competition, so I really didn't have anything to rest up for. All the same, I'd broken the rules.

"MacFarlane," the manager said, "I'm taking your medals and your uniform. You're suspended from the team."

I blew up. The uniform was a souvenir for competing and I thought I'd earned both that and my medals.

"Fine," I said. "Take your stupid medals and your damn uniform. But don't ever ask me to do anything for you again."

I was steamed. My parents had driven all the way to Edmonton — 2,500 miles away — to watch me wrestle and run in these games. It showed their dedication and love to me and here this jerk was taking my stuff from me and denying me an opportunity to parade them in front of my parents.

Of course, I had the wrong slant on things. I had broken team rules. I was the one messing it up for Mom and Dad, not the team manager. I could have learned a valuable lesson then, but I didn't. I was still the fastest blind 200-meter sprinter in Canada at the time, regardless of age. My coach relented and gave my uniform and medals back. I competed and won.

Instead of learning a lesson, I learned I had a little power, even at age fourteen. I was the best and I found out I could use it to my advantage, which is hardly the healthiest thing for a teenager to know.

Aside from school and sports, I was reveling in being home. It was true that Desbarats was boring compared to Brantford. Desbarats is a village of 400; Brantford is a town of 70,000. Brantford had so much more to do than Desbarats. But just being at my home was fabulous and I had all the room I needed to make my own fun.

I rode endlessly on Rebel. I spent time with all my old pals. Even work was fun — if sometimes dangerous for all concerned. One time I was hired with David Stobie and Blake Marcel to pitchfork manure out of a barn owned by Ed Karhi, a local farmer. The manure had gotten crusty. And I jabbed the pitchfork down hard on a hardened patch, only to discover it wasn't a cowpie, but shoe leather. With David's foot inside. I drove the fork right through his boot. He needed stitches, but he's lucky he's still walking today.

Me too, I guess. One day Ian and I were up in our hay mow at home. We were working up top, taking loads of hay off an elevator all day. I thought the elevator was up instead of down, stepped out onto it and discovered it wasn't there. I stepped into twelve feet of nothing straight down to the ground. Fortunately, I landed in a pile of hay. No real damage done, except to my pride.

"Hey, Craig, babe. You gotta watch that first step," Ian crowed.

We had such wonderful, easy-going, days and nights. I couldn't have asked for more.

And then, as happens sometimes in life, just when you think things are going too good to be true — they are.

Tragedy struck. It was February 26, 1978, a day that will forever be embedded in my memory. It was about 10 p.m. We were all sitting around the house, watching television and reading.

Ian looked out and shouted,"The barn's on fire!"

I jumped up, got dressed and threw on my coat. It was extremely cold, snow was on the ground. The fire siren, the Desbarats volunteer fire department, sounded three times. The volunteer crew came rushing over. They were there in no time at all, actually. They did a really great job.

But the barn was old weathered wood, an absolute tinderbox and it was full of hay. No one could have come quick enough to save it.

Or anything that was in it.

Rebel was trapped in the burning barn. My heart dropped right through my shoes, onto the frozen ground. I couldn't believe what was happening and it was no better for Ian. No better at all. He was raising his prize Appaloosa colt and she was in there too.

Ian dashed into the barn trying to free both horses, with Mom and Dad, screaming, "Ian...NO!"

But he couldn't hear them or wouldn't listen. He plunged into the barn. A beam fell down on him and almost trapped him. He barely got out alive before the barn came down with a tremendous crash.

I honestly don't know how the family could have gone on, after all the other difficulties Mom and Dad had to deal with, if Ian had been seriously hurt. We were spared that, thank God.

But that didn't diminish the heartache for the rest of us. We could only stand there helplessly as the barn went up in flames that were leaping into the arctic air. By now a good share of the village of Desbarats had turned out to hold us and watch the thing go down to the ground.

We lost all the chickens, the rabbits, the hay and the tools. But losing the horses devastated us. I'm not sure which of us was more heartbroken, Ian or me. Quite possibly, Ian. He had saved and saved to get that colt. She meant everything to him.

He was just inconsolable. No one could get hardly a word out of Ian for days.

The only time I remember him speaking was when Mom and Dad said, "Son, I know it's hard, but we'll get another horse for you, OK?"

"No," said Ian. And that was all he said.

He put his heart and soul into getting the Appaloosa. Nothing else could replace it just then.

As for me, well, everyone knew what Rebel meant to me. Rebel my constant companion. We had done everything together for nine years. When I'd gone away to Brantford at 6 years old, the very first thing I said in my first letter home was, "How are Rebel and Blondie?"

I realized the hardest pill to swallow was the way Rebel died. It wasn't from natural causes, but of smoke inhalation. It was the realization that he suffered which dug a hole in the pit of my stomach.

More than anything, I felt like I had just lost my best friend. For much of my childhood, in fact, I never had a better friend — close as many of my childhood buddies had been. I knew I'd lost something I just couldn't replace in Rebel. And, in truth, I never did replace that friend. A country kid and his horse create a bond unlike any other you will find in life.

BE CAREFUL WHAT YOU WISH FOR...

I don't know whether it was losing Rebel or not — I really don't think so — but later in 1978 I found myself wanting to leave my new life in Desbarats, my newfound freedom at Central Algoma, my hard-won superstar status among the sighted.

Of all things...and it astounded me at first...I longed to go back to Brantford.

The idea began to sink in with me that spring. W. Ross

MacDonald was where I had been truly the most free. I had carved out a life for myself there where I could roam at will. I knew every nook and cranny of the place. I'd learned and achieved things that I hadn't at Central Algoma — I was a better student, for one thing, in a school set up for blind students. Ross MacDonald had things likes raised maps for learning geography. Academically, that kind of help really makes a difference. I'd thought I was going to find independence in a sighted school but many of the methods set up at Brantford actually gave me more freedom to learn.

I hated to admit it, but the teachers who'd said I'd miss the place were right. Hey, maybe I also missed the attention I received at MacDonald. I had popularity and acceptance enough at Central Algoma. But that wasn't like being king of the hill. Not even close.

More than anything, I missed the special closeness of my former classmates at Brantford. I missed the feeling of family that came from staying together day and night. I especially missed my best pals — Eric and Doug and Roger and the others. And all of them seemed to miss me as well including the faculty, my coach, John Howe, the administration, the campus, as I would come to learn.

I was not slinking back to Ross MacDonald a failure. I had done what I set out to do at Central Algoma. I'd won acceptance. I'd demonstrated I could operate in a sighted environment with a high degree of proficiency. I had blended in socially, mentally and, needless to say, athletically.

When I told Coach Prodan that I was thinking of going back to Brantford he was, as always, extremely kind and understanding, wanting only the best for my welfare. He said I'd been a big part of the team's success. He said I'd be missed.

But then he turned to me and said, "You don't have anything to prove to anybody anymore. You did what you came here to do. Now do what makes you happiest."

It was simple, direct and eloquent.

I knew then it was time to get back to my other "home." My

return was triumphant. I was welcomed with open arms, well, maybe not by every last person. But at least I hadn't burned any bridges.

In fact, I was elected student council president two years in a row, my junior and senior years. I was putting to work what I had begun to learn about giving to others. My platform had wide appeal. I didn't smoke, but I thought blind folks should be treated like human beings, and I wanted the smokers who were there to have a decent place to gather outdoors. I got us two juke boxes. I fought to have times without chaperons.

We weren't calling for sin, but trust, and seeing us as kids with normal needs. We wanted the same flexibility other fifteen, sixteen and seventeen year old kids had. In sighted high schools you could wear a tee-shirt with a saying on it. Not here.

Also, most of us resented the constant tour of outsiders that always seemed to be in progress at W. Ross MacDonald. It felt like we were animals in a zoo. We'd be in history or typing class and another group of people would walk by to see the little blind kids on display.

When I was younger, I made animal noises when those groups came through. Or I'd raise my hand and ask some totally stupid question: "Was that blind chef on duty last night? The meat tasted a little burnt." Other kids did the same thing. It was our way of rebelling against these "sightseers." Now, as a high school junior, I knew such tours helped raise interest and money in the school. But I was hoping we could curtail it somewhat, so kids didn't feel like such a freak show, which the administration did try to do.

Independence was a theme of my campaigns, just as it had always been in my life. Coach Howe allowed me to be a little more independent as a wrestler. I'd learned a lot from Coach Prodan and I added that to what I'd leaned from Coach Howe. Coach Howe let me take the best of both and mesh them together. He let me decide what would make me the best athlete I could be.

One snag to returning was Jane. As earth-shattering and as

life-as-we-know-it-ending as my goodbye with Jane had been, things just weren't the same between us when I got back.

We'd only been able to get in touch with each other half a dozen times a year over the last two years. I say "able." I guess that's really all we wanted to do.

What I found out is that I had loved the Jane of my grade-school years with a love I hadn't known up to then. And it was a true, heart-and-soul love. But I also discovered that a great deal of my love had been as a friend. We continued to have good, strong feelings for each other. But we didn't have the heat we had earlier.

The hot sauce in my life came from two other sources. First, Sylvia. She was a lean, longhaired, beautiful sweet Asian girl, with a very sensitive, gentle touch. She had the softest soft skin I'd ever touched. She was very romantic and I was intoxicated with her. I inhaled her with every breath and I thought about her every time I breathed out.

After her was Gail. Gail was also willowy, had a beautiful voice and was soft to touch. In addition, her personality was the most like mine of all my girl friends up to then. She was full of gremlins in a good way. And she didn't go home on weekends like me. She was from Quebec and couldn't make the long trip, just as I couldn't go home to Desbarats.

So we spent all our free time together on weekends, as well as evenings. We went into town to movies, took walks, went to dinner. We sat and talked for hours. We kissed, of course. Lots of kissing. I was almost uncontrollably attracted to Gail. In fact, it got to be a little too much attraction for awhile.

I was so wrapped up in her that I actually dropped out of wrestling for a few weeks. I was torn. I wanted more and more time with her; it was the classic high-school romance.

One day I was sitting in the upstairs student lounge with Gail. As much as I loved being with her, I felt guilty about missing practice. I hadn't missed many practices unless I was ill, since I was seven years of age. All along I'd believed every extra minute I could train, every pushup, every situp, every mile I ran, was just one more the competition wasn't doing. In the late rounds, in a close match, I counted on that dedication, that drive, that hunger, to pay off. And it did.

But here I was tossing all that down the drain.

Then, as I sat there, I heard those familiar footsteps climbing the stairs to the lounge.

"Craig, are you up there?"

It was John Howe.

"Where are you supposed to be right now?" he said.

"Practice," I said sheepishly.

"Then why aren't you there?"

"I'm confused, coach," I said. "Maybe a little burned out."

"Let's talk," he said.

To his office we went, the old familiar room where he'd been such a friend, father figure, brother. I guess in a strange sense, it was the living room of my soul for so many years.

We talked at length. He realized that at sixteen it was natural that I'd be interested in girls. He also realized I didn't have much time for girls with my typical training schedule. I usually worked out in the morning, did some kind of physical activity at noon and practiced after school for two-and-a-half hours every day, I really didn't have any time for Gail until after supper.

By that time I was physically and emotionally exhausted, and I still had homework ahead.

Coach Howe talked about how I'd let my teammates down. How I was a leader and they looked up to me. He talked about the example I was setting for the younger wrestlers. I had no idea they cared what I was all about until Coach Howe told me.

"My door's open when you're ready to walk through it again," he said.

Those next two weeks were difficult. Coach Howe was my physical education teacher as well. But never once in that time did he pressure me in any way.

I figured that out on my own. For those two weeks, if I was intoxicated with Gail's love and affection for me, I was sobered by the reality of knowing something that made me complete was missing.

Wrestling.

After one week away, I started secretly getting up at five a.m. and doing my situps, pushups and running, just like I did in my earlier years. I didn't tell anyone. Not even Gail. But I didn't want to lose that step. My edge. I didn't want to fall behind my teammates. I thought I was making up my mind but, in reality, my mind had already been made up by the second week.

I would enjoy a few more four p.m. meetings in the student center with Gail. And then it would be back to the grind. The sweat. The smell of the locker room.

In essence, my home.

I prayed a lot that week. I prayed that God would help me find the balance between athletics, academics and my social life. I know not all prayers are answered in the timely fashion we would like. But the greater power delivered in this case with perfect timing.

I learned from Eric later that John Howe had told the team that when I made my decision to come back there wouldn't be any questions. They gave me my space and I respected them immensely for it. I guess that's what teamwork and camaraderie are about.

I was still feeling for my athletic moorings, though. The year wasn't perfectly smooth from there. For one thing I got into a bad habit of toying with opponents. If the guy had a sister or his family or a girl friend there, I wouldn't pin him right away, even if I knew I could. I'd rack up a lot of points first, to show off how good I was.

Not a very flattering picture, huh? I was not always the nicest guy you'd want to run into on the mat.

In fact, we once had a bet among team members to see who could run up the highest score on an opponent. We each put up two bucks. I beat this guy 54-0. I kept getting him down, letting him go, then scoring on him again.

When Coach Howe figured what was going on, he was livid. And he should have been. It was a terrible thing to do.

At the same time, I started feeling there was an enormous amount of pressure on me to win. If I lost, the only question I got was, "How'd that happen?" Like I was just never supposed to lose. My enemies, the ones who thought I was too confident, would be saying, "Serves him right." And when I lost, I felt I also lost face with my friends.

I was driven to win. What's more, I was driven to win the biggest challenges. In the spring of 1979, at the blind national wrestling championships, I found out three national champions would be wrestling in the 125-pound class. I wrestled at 136 pounds.

I could have won pretty easily in the 136-pound class that year. Instead, I decided to lose enough weight to wrestle at 125 pounds. I said to Gail, "I'm checking out for the next couple of days. You won't see much of me. I have a mission."

Across the next fifty-two hours, I dropped eleven pounds by not eating, drinking only enough water to stay alive, and exercising to near exhaustion. At the weigh-in, I let Gordy, Pat and Eddie take the scales first. Then I stepped on. A hundred and twenty-five even. Everyone in the room was shocked that I had lost the weight. But the biggest challenge was still ahead.

Gordie had been undefeated over the last two years in blind competition. I was fortunate to pin him in the second round. Next up was Pat. In a hard fight, I outpointed him fifteen to nine, which setup the showdown for the gold with Eddie. Four national champions in one weight class; only one would walk away victorious.

At the end of the first round I was leading Eddie five to four. Then, with just a few seconds to go in the match, we were tied at ten. At this point, I was literally tasting my own hunger from the loss of weight I'd put myself through, and I could also taste blood in my throat. I was dizzy, weak and faint. The whistle blew and by the grace of God, I scored a one-point takedown on Eddie as time expired.

I had done it, but at a cost. I had to be helped to my feet. I was exhausted. Wearing one of the most special gold medals of my career, I spent the next three days in the hospital hooked to an IV.

My most memorable match upon returning to Brantford was one I lost. My arch-rival in town was Jeff Nunn. He was from North Park High School. He had never beaten me, although we had some major wars.

One day I was uncharacteristically whipping him pretty thoroughly. I was leading 14-0. I was so far ahead, I got lackadaisical and wound up pinning myself.

I tried a new move that I'd dreamed up in English class that day. Not such a good idea against someone like Jeff. And especially in competition where the shoulder blades only have to touch the mat for one second. The ref's hand slapped the mat and I had in essence pinned myself with my new move. Not a pretty picture.

Technically, Jeff pinned me, but it was such a nonchalant move on my part — totally contradicting my usual habits on the mat — that gave him the opening.

He went ballistic. You'd have thought he won the Stanley Cup. He ran around and around the mat hooting and hollering and inciting the crowd to higher and higher cheers.

I went on into the change room then headed dejectedly into the shower. A few minutes later, Jeff Nunn came into the shower, too.

"Well, I finally beat you, you blind son-of-a-bitch!" he crowed.

I didn't say a word. I just went to whaling. I swung with everything I had as many times as I could. I wanted to tear his head off. The feeling was mutual.

There we were, buck naked, toe-to-toe, neither giving an inch, blasting away at each other. Several coaches and other people heard the commotion and finally dragged us apart.

No. I still hadn't lost the fire for winning.

INNER VISION

SHARING WHAT I'VE LEARNED

In 1980, I left W. Ross MacDonald one-half credit shy of
graduation to travel to Arnham, Holland, with the Canadian
team to compete in the worldwide Olympics for the Disabled.
The night before I left, I couldn't resist one last prank.

This one came at the expense of my old buddy Darold. He
had a report to turn in the next day for astronomy. He hated
typing and I was good at it, so I volunteered.

He began dictating. The report was pretty good; I just
decided to help him with it.

When he came to the part about the Dog Star, I added, "Yes,
the Dog Star wanders around the heavens, licking at people's
hands and dumping on their lawns." I also added: "Pisces, the
fish star, has wings that it can use to fly to Mars and swim down
Orion's pants."

"All done," I said at the end.

"Thanks, my man," Darold said. "How can I thank you?"

I got my thanks on the way to the airport early the next
morning. Eric and I had one last great laugh together.

In Holland, I competed in wrestling, sprinting and "goalball."
Goalball is a game developed for the blind in Europe. It uses a
ball that's bigger than a soccer ball with bells in it. A goal area is
signified by a piece of indoor-outdoor carpet. Three players are
on each team. Each player is blindfolded — even those who are
totally blind. That's to ensure a level playing field with some
athletes who may be partially sighted — as many are in blind
competitions.

The object of the game is to get the ball into a goal, just as in
soccer. It's a heck of a sport. When I was younger, that ball
would knock me down sometimes. A good thrower could rocket
it more than twenty miles per hour. Unlike soccer, you rolled
the ball back and forth; you don't kick it.

When we went to Europe, I knocked myself down a few
times with incidents that had little to do with the fierce
competition that distinguished the games.

MY PRIDE IS SHOWING

First, I went wandering out in downtown Amsterdam, by myself. I wanted to buy some wooden shoes. Mission accomplished. I had them slung over my shoulder in a sack. I was walking by myself. No cane, no dog. I was using the canal as my guide, because I knew it led right back to our hotel, and I could tell by the sounds of the water and the cruise boats and the general conversation around me where I was.

How clever of me.

Until I cleverly misjudged where I was and walked right off the sidewalk, straight into the canal, wooden shoes and all.

Later, we were wrestling an exhibition against a local Dutch club. It included some of their blind Olympians, including the Dutch champ, who was thirty years old. The matches were right next to a strip of bars and the matches drew sizable crowds of rather liberally lubricated Amsterdammers. Also on hand were all the Dutch wrestlers sweeties. You know how I hate to lose in front of girls.

I pinned the guy in two minutes.

Then, feeling rather pleased about the whole thing, I took off for the change room, got undressed and I headed for the sauna. The Dutch coach said, "Second door on the right." It was not the first time this trick had been played on the trickster.

Instead of the sauna, I opened a door and strode right out into a hallway full of the same folks who'd just seen me wrestle. Well, not quite as much as they were seeing now. I was stark naked.

My finest move in cementing international relations, however, came during a side trip to East Germany. The Berlin Wall still stood between East and West Germany at the time. So we were briefed about what we could expect and all the things we should and should not do. Included was a rather pointed reminder that we were in a Communist country now and surveillance was a big deal. Be careful how you talk in your hotel room because it could be bugged, we were told.

Bugged?

Now you're talkin'. I was determined no Commie was going

to listen in on my vital conversations. I was all over this bugging business. I combed my room, running my hands all over the walls, climbing up on chairs to feel the ceiling, feeling behind furniture.

Then I found it! The bug!

I ran my hands over a bumpy place in the carpet. I got down on all fours and began peeling back the rug. I felt a steel plate. The bug had to be in there. I had a Swiss Army knife and I started loosening all the nuts. I worked and worked until I finally got the last one all undone...

...Just in time to hear an absolutely thunderous crash down below.

Seems I had loosened the plate that held the chandelier in the room beneath me. It was a room occupied by a honeymoon couple, a honeymoon couple engaged in the most serious business of a honeymoon.

Did the earth move for you, too, darling?

Well, needless to say, hotel security was up there in a flash. Fortunately, the fact we were an official party representing the Canadian government worked in my favor.

We were more successful in the Olympics than I had been in that Berlin hotel room. I won a silver medal in wrestling and, as our team came in fifth out of twenty-seven countries in goalball, which was a new sport for Canada.

By now, my name and so-called fame had spread around fairly decently throughout my native land. I'd been the subject three times of documentaries on Canadian national television. And I had taken up a new pursuit, one that would become lifetime sport for me. I was finding a new way to express all the fire and energy I had inside. It was a new way to harness the ten-thousand butterflies in my stomach. I was constantly being asked to speak to groups about my life and my accomplishments. Doing that, I was finding a new way to get the pleasure of giving.

MY PRIDE IS SHOWING

I DISCOVER THE POWER OF PRIDE

During one of the first speeches I gave, I came up with some ideas which have continued to guide me since. I hadn't planned these thoughts. They came from the heart and have remained there.

I call them PRIDE. They go something like this:

P. The "P" stands for perseverance. It is the backbone of everything we do in life. It's the intestinal fortitude you need to be able to do what you have to do today to accomplish goals, dreams and aspirations you have set for tomorrow. If you don't have a purpose in mind, I don't believe you ever wholeheartedly throw yourself into something. In wrestling my purpose was to mainstream into a regular school. I had to ask myself, "Do I go to the gym to work four days and then, ah, it's raining...slide on the fifth?" Or do I have the mental strength to push past the moment of decision and keep making myself the best I can be?

For almost eleven years, I built myself up by doing several hundred situps and pushups a day, not because I enjoyed them, but because I never wanted to give people the opportunity to say I lost because I was blind. I never wanted people to look at me as handicapped, but to look on my loss of sight as a minor inconvenience. We all have inconveniences, regardless of what stage and age we may be, and how you overcome these inconveniences will ultimately determine how successful you are. Not just monetarily, but in attitude, spirit and overall outlook on life.

R. The "R" stands for respect. If you don't have a sense of belief in yourself, how can you expect others to believe in you? It's also about respecting all the unsung heroes who don't necessarily receive the recognition — parents, grandparents, coaches, teachers, the people who take time out of their lives to make ours just a little better. And I'm sure if you think about it, you won't have to go back very far to come up with your own unsung heroes who've touched your life.

It's also about respect for authority and respect for those in need. I encourage everyone to never be too busy or too complacent to extend a helping hand. Because somewhere, someday, you are going to hope that someone is kind enough to come along and help you — even if you think you're invincible, which a lot of us do. I could not have made anything of myself without the helping hands of others and I need to pass that along to someone else.

I. The "I" stands for individuality. This is my favorite. Blindness never gave me a chance at team sports on an interscholastic-competition basis. I was part of a team, but always in an individualized sport — wrestling, track, skiing. But it's OK to stand alone on some things in life. The peer pressure and the decisions we make today could potentially have an enormous impact on the person you become tomorrow. It takes a much stronger person to walk away from a negative situation, than to stay and participate. The question is, are you going to be a leader? And, if you choose to follow, will you follow the right person? That takes as much strength of character as leading.

You can let other people set the odds for you. They can say you're not good enough or fast enough or smart enough or good-looking enough. They may say you come from too limiting a background to succeed. If you're looking for someone to doubt your ability, you won't have to look far. Be your own individual. Stand on your own two feet. Make your own decisions. And when you draw the bottom line for whatever you do, ask yourself if you could have done a little more. Did you leave any cards on the table unplayed? When I got finished with a wrestling match, I often barely had enough energy to walk off the mat. I let it all hang out. I left nothing to chance. If I lost, a better person won that day. I didn't want excuses to be made for me. I wanted the deciding moment to come down to me, alone.

D. The "D" is for desire. Desire is that constant burning drive that needs to exist inside us all. It is that eye of the tiger that we need to live life to the fullest. It's that stick-to-it attitude, that longing. It's how willing you are to pay the price and ultimately achieve your goals or dreams. Live your dreams! In wrestling, I tasted my own hunger sometimes making weight. If you want something badly enough, you have to almost be willing to taste your own hunger, to feel that fire burning in the pit of your stomach. Desire is the spark plug of life.

E. The "E" is for enthusiasm. It is that spirit, that zest, that passionate attitude we need to live life every day. The flame you feel in your heart is reflected by the spark in your smile. No one likes to be around people who are always complaining, negative, looking down on life. I found that a smile can carry you a long way, not only in business, but in personal life. You want to be that breath of fresh air walking into any room. You want to always bring energy and life to the table.

This is how I close every one of my speeches today.

I can honestly say that, given the opportunity I would gladly trade all those gold medals and championships that I fought so long and hard to win — I'd gladly give every single one of them just to be able to have my eyesight.

To be able to see how beautiful the colors must be in a rainbow, to see what my parents faces or what my son or daughter look like — or the things you take for granted each day...the trees in the fall, a gorgeous sunset.

But as I travel around, I understand there are people who are less fortunate than I, who have not been blessed as I have been. It is a responsibility for every one of us to make someone else's life better along life's highway.

I will always hope and pray to do that. Because I have always had so many people pick me up and give me a lift as I take my own hike down that trail.

I had started to find myself with these speeches I was making. I felt good knowing I could share what I'd learned. I'd decided to go to college, and I thought my athletic career might be over. Little did I know, it was just beginning.

In 1982, Gordie Howe brought me to America to live with him and work for the Whalers in the NHL. After practices, I'd skate with Gordie. I can always say I scored on one of the Whaler goalies; of course the goalie was tired and Gordie got me lined up for the shot. The goalie took some teasing from Gordie, as you can imagine.

CHAPTER SIX
HOWE I CAME TO AMERICA

It is good to live next to The King. Especially if The King is Wayne Gretzky.

I got to experience this entirely wonderful turn of events because a fellow classmate at North Park Collegiate invited me home to dinner one night. I guess I had this starved puppy look about me.

Maybe it was also because I looked like I'd burned myself at the stake. I had moved into an apartment by myself in my thirteenth year of school. In Ontario, you take a thirteenth year if you plan to go to a university, and I had that goal in mind. Ironically, I took the second semester of my thirteenth year at arch-rival North Park Collegiate. I loved living in an apartment but I found it's tougher than I thought for a blind person to do it the first time.

One day I was whomping up my house specialty. Hot dogs. I usually did OK on the dogs. Hey, how can you foul up boiling water? But when it came to the intricate part of the meal — the hot dog bun — the plot thickened.

Or blackened in this case.

I always toasted the buns in the oven. I reached down to get them when they smelled right, grabbing them with a hand wrapped in a bath towel — my theory being, the bigger the towel, the less chance of burning myself. Another one of my brilliant theories that worked better hypothetically than in actuality.

As I pulled the buns out, I noticed how nice and warm they were. Too nice and warm. I thought they'd caught fire because a pungent smell was now permeating the kitchen. Only then did it dawn on me. It's not the buns that are on fire. It's me.

At least it's the part of you connected to the bath towel. The bath towel had caught on fire. The flames spread from the towel to my sleeve which now was beginning to set a nice blaze.

I flung everything into the sink and plunged my arm under the tap. Luckily, that stopped the fire. If it had gotten just a smidgen more out of control, I could have been really hurt.

As it was, the apartment was choked with smoke. My next-door-neighbor smelled it and came over to see if she could help. Everything was under control by the time she got there. Even better, I realized it was the girl everyone had told me was so good-looking next door, Marg Levchuk. Heck, if I'd known all I had to do to meet her was set myself on fire, I might have done it earlier.

Later, Marg invited me home for dinner. Marg, her family and I had a great time laughing about the fire incident. We also laughed about the time I came home from wrestling, grabbed a can of beans and popped it in a pot to cook for dinner. I went to shower, came out and smelled this foul odor filling the apartment.

I'd heated up a saucepan full of pineapples instead of beans.

We also kicked around some of my mysterious misadventures of Blind Man's Buff. That's where I had to run around half-naked all the time trying to keep up with the laundry. I could master the washing and the drying and all that fairly easily. What threw me for a loop was telling what the heck I had afterwards in sorting it all out. So many shirts seemed the same to my touch, I had to memorize tag sizes and other characteristics of the shirts to tell what color I had.

Marg's folks were very generous, kind and friendly. We did so much laughing. I thought, what great people to be around all the time. Marg was a lucky girl, being in a family like that.

I soon was almost as fortunate. The Levschuks asked me to live with them and their other daughter, Cheryl, for the final three months of the year at North Park.

I accepted with an enormous amount of relief and enthusiasm. I had to admit living by myself was more than I bargained for at the time. I could save money living with them, too. I had hit the jackpot, thanks to these wonderful people.

And then I discovered the best reason for moving in with them. They lived right next to Walter and Phyllis Gretzky, whose children just happened to be named Kim, Brent, Glenn and Keith and Wayne.

Wayne was only twenty at the time, but he was already a genuine legend in the making. He was the hero of every Canadian kid, almost from the moment he stepped on the ice for the Edmonton Oilers. He still came home a lot at that stage of his career and I got to hang out with him quite a bit.

One night I sat behind the wheel of his Ferrari and he let me peel rubber in an empty parking lot. He was even brave enough to sit in the passenger seat — or smart enough, thinking he might grab the wheel if need be and save tens of thousands of dollars worth of sports car.

Actually, that wasn't the first time I'd been behind the wheel of an automobile, believe it or not. I had driven my own car, in a similar manner. I actually did own a car. When friends would say they couldn't get a car to go somewhere, I'd say, "Let's take mine." I could hear their jaws drop. One night at a mall, they let me drive quite a bit. I was laying rubber like Mario Andretti — and getting the hang of it, I believe, when the cops came up.

They asked me for my driver's license. They thought I was getting smart because I wasn't looking at them. Then the cop recognized me and said, "Craig, you son-of-a-gun, get out of that car."

And then he saw that one of the kids in the car with me was the police chief's son.

I liked having this car, even though, obviously, these were the only couple of times I drove it. It made me more normal. A friend and I could take it on double dates. Other kids had cars. Why couldn't I have one?

Also, on the subject of driver's licenses, I actually did go so far as to get a learner's permit. A friend used my ID and took the eye test. I once whipped my permit out for an ID at a hotel and floored 'em.

But the Gretzky Grand Prix still was my best racing performance. And our friendship didn't end there. I felt like I really got to know Wayne because he came home to his Mom and Dad's after the National Hockey League season. We sometimes skated together or sat on his front porch and talked long into the night.

I told him I was planning on going to Carleton University and study law. In fact, I was the subject of a documentary on Canadian national television titled, "I Want to Be a Lawyer." This was one of three times television crews would do documentaries about me and this one covered my entire life, not just athletics.

Wayne admired my goal of furthering my education. But he was still very interested in my life as an athlete, and he told me he thought that was something I ought to somehow cultivate to the maximum before letting go. Carleton didn't have a wrestling team, so going there meant an end, of sorts, to my sports career. I'd be concentrating solely on academics.

As much as I thought of Wayne and thanked him for his direction, I still thought education was the key to my future. So I enrolled in Carleton pre-law in the fall of 1981. I had a ball there. Carleton is nestled alongside the Rideau Canal, which offers pleasant boating in the summer and "The world's longest outdoor skating rink" in winter. It runs several miles so I don't doubt the claim.

I had plenty to do there. I lived the typical college party life. I stayed up late night after night. We had a wake-a-thon once and I stayed up 107 straight hours and won.

My dating life took a sharply different turn, also. Gail and I had grown apart after two-and-a-half years of extreme closeness. I think moving to an apartment originally had something to do with it. It was perhaps something of a declaration of my increasing independence. Maybe it was my cooking, or lack thereof.

I had started to date a few sighted girls at North Park. By that time, I think my blindness was actually working to my advantage. In addition to a little bit of notoriety in athletics, I represented something of a curiosity to some girls. I was no longer different from other guys. I was unique. A fine line exists between those different and unique, the best side of the line is unique.

Then, when I got to Carleton, my dorm presented a wide open sea of endless opportunity. I lived on the sixth floor of a coed dorm, Glengarry House. Our floor had thirty-three guys and thirty-four girls. I went out on dates with many of those coeds.

Dorm life also set up one of my wackier experiences with women. I'd been out late and when I came home I was surprised to find the door wasn't locked. I thought I'd forgotten my key. I took my shoes off, took my pants off and sat on the edge of the bed only to discover that, like The Three Bears, someone was sleeping in it.

I heard a tremendous squeal and a girl came out from under the covers saying she was going to call the cops.

"What are you doing in my bed?" I asked, bewildered.

"Excuse me. You mean mine, don't you?" she asked.

"Isn't this the sixth floor?" I said.

"Don't give me that crap," she said.

It was only then she discovered the blind guy she'd been hearing about was in fact a reality. Me.

One of the things at work here was that the floors were all

identically shaped and I'd just gotten off on the wrong floor. That was the beginning and the end of the episode for me. Not necessarily for her. For weeks, she took a teasing — and good-naturedly at that. Someone was always walking by her saying, "Hey, Sweetie, I'll be the blind guy up there tonight."

Another time I was demonstrating how cool I was to a date, trying to get some catsup out of a bottle. I steadfastly refused help. I was suave. I could do it.

"Hit the bottom of the bottle," my date said.

Maybe she shouldn't have. Or maybe I should have known better.

I gave it a good thump. Then I heard her gasp.

"What's wrong?" I said.

"You just hit me square in the face with a big glob of catsup," she said.

STRETCHING FOR INDEPENDENCE

I was one of the few freshmen who got to enjoy living in a dorm suite. I don't really know why for sure, but I think my athletic reputation may have had something to do with it. It wasn't the blind thing. I knew that.

We had a living room, two bathrooms, four bedrooms and I had some really great suite-mates, Mick, Richard, Len and Dale. And my roommate was Rob Podreciks. Rob and his girlfriend Evelyn both helped me tremendously. Today they are married and living in Toronto; Rob is a successful architect and Evelyn a lawyer. They'd help me get to class sometimes. Help me with lunch.

I made good friends. They took me along to concerts — Journey, Foreigner. We went to Syracuse, New York, which was a few hours away, to catch the Rolling Stones.

And I did OK on my grades. I had devised a method of note-taking with the slate and stylus in which I could actually

This is a picture of the actual striker that caused my blindness. Some people might say, "Why do you still have it?" But it is kind of a deep part of my history. It's certainly not something we display on the wall, but I do have it. I'm grateful that my parents kept it. I know that when my mother sees it, she still gets kind of choked up.

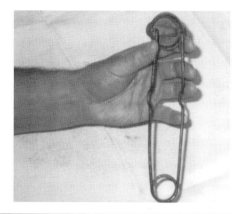

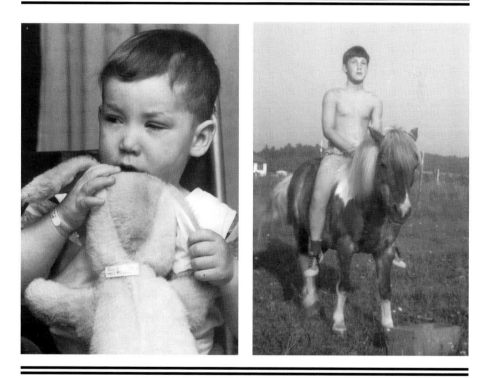

My bunny brought a bit of home during one of my long stays in the hospital during the year after my injury. I was five before I knew for sure I was blind. I asked one of the nurses, and she told me the truth.

Rebel was the pony that I got when I was just a kid, probably about six years of age and I had him all the way up to when I was 14 years old when he died in our barn fire. When I came home from the School for the Blind, I would ride him bareback, stand on him and jump off. He was an Ontario Salky race champion before he was retired, and then the owner gave him to me.

I was about two years old when we got Blondie. He was part of our family for about 14 years. Blondie was wonderful. He was awfully forgiving. I would step on him and trip over him and never, ever would he bite me. He was a wonderful companion and a great source of entertainment.

My brother, Ian never treated me like I was blind. Even as a very small child, he always included me in activities and things. My parents and Ian treated me as an equal and it helped me tremendously in my attitude and my outlook. We've had a close relationship. I think we understand each other. Certainly, if two brothers could be opposites, we are definitely that, but I think we have a great amount of mutual respect and admiration for one another.

At the School for the Blind, they would take us out on school outings to have hands-on experience with various things. I got to sit in the cockpit of this helicopter, got a chance to feel the controls and hear the pilot talk back to the tower and sense how the whole thing was done. We always looked forward to these outings to learn more of what was out there in the world.

I was a Program Director for Living Well Fitness Centers, based out of the Houstonian Club in Houston, Texas. I was living at the Houstonian Club and I would participate in many different things. How I shot a free throw: I would have someone stand underneath the basket, I'd listen to their voice. Then, "muscle memory," would kick in. It told me how far and how high to shoot. If it's too far left or right, I'd have to readjust for the next shot.

When I ran individually in blind sprinting competitions my coach would stand at the finish line with a megaphone. He would repeatedly say the number five if you were running straight, four if you went to your left or the number six if you went to your right. This picture was on the new track at the Queen Elizabeth field in Sault St. Marie. That was the night, just after the opening ceremonies, that I set a Canadian 60-meter sprinting record for the blind.

What more could any Canadian kid dream than to carry the Olympic Torch beside hockey legend Gordie Howe? Here we are on the streets of Washington, D.C., in the summer of 1984 as the torch continued its journey to Los Angeles.

When I play golf, I find myself quite frequently in amongst sand and other obstructions. So I feel very much at home, just another day on the beach coming out of this sand trap. I've always said when I play golf I don't worry about the hazards unless you tell me they're there. If I have 100 yards of water to carry before I get to the pin, I'm not going to think about the water if you haven't told me about it.

Flying on skis can be dangerous, as I found out after a particularly ugly crash at Cypress Gardens. But the feeling of flight behind the churning motors of a speed boat, can't be matched. At Cypress Gardens, I became one of the crew, earning a paycheck like everybody else, which was important to me at the time.

I'm just out for fun here, but imagine me like this at fifty miles-per-hour downhill on Alta, a breakneck speed for anyone, let alone a skier who knows where he is by the sound of the voice of the guy flying down the mountain in front of him.

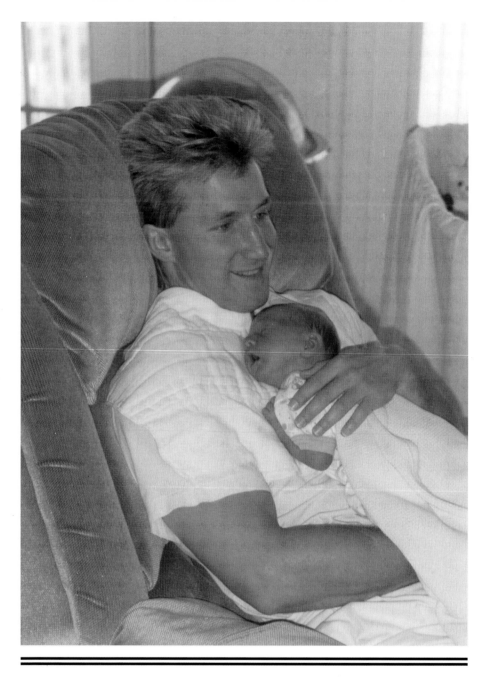

When Dalton came home from the hospital, I worked very little in those first few months just so I could be with him, even though he was very young. If that's part of the bonding process, maybe that's why we're so close today. He used to sleep for hours on me as I watched baseball games and hockey games. I used to carry him around and he just spent hours and hours each day camped out on me.

I lace hundreds and hundreds of pairs of skates throughout the course of a winter, Dalton's and other kids as well who may need help in the dressing room, so I'm definitely a hands on Dad.

Hunting and fishing were a big part of growing up in rural Canada. My brother Ian was the marksman, I was along for the adventure!

When Dalton and I go out bike riding I listen to his voice. I listen to the wheels of his bicycle on the gravel road to give me a sense of direction and a point of reference. It's no problem following him for the most part because he never stops talking.

At home in Debarats with my mother Joyce and father Earl. They made a conscious decision to raise me just like any other kid, and that decision is responsible for the exciting life I've lived since then. They could have wrapped me in cotton, but I wouldn't have learned to be bold, resilient and, always, as self-sufficient as possible. I'm sure that decision gave them some gray hairs, but I'm glad they did it that way.

With Mario and Michael Andretti. Believe it or not, auto racing is one of my favorite spectator sports. Maybe that goes back to my college days when I actually had a car of my own and enjoyed driving it around large parking lots late at night. I even had the pleasure of wheeling through Indianapolis with Mario at the wheel in a rush to catch a plane. Auto racing is where I met Paul Newman and Tim Allen.

I met Evander Holyfield through a dear friend of mine, Shelley Finkel, who was Evander's manager at the time. We just hit it off. I went to Vegas to some of his fights and when I was in Atlanta I went over to his house to visit him and hang out. The picture was taken in his gymnasium where he has his ring set up.

This was shot at the Detroit Grand Prix race back in '95. Tim Allen and I were shooting some video for my documentary. Of course, it took us several takes because of all the clowning around. I think we had more great outtakes than actual takes.

This picture of Don Cherry and I was taken in 1982 in the Memorial Gardens in Sault Ste. Marie, home of the Soo Greyhounds. There were over 40 celebrities that came in to play tennis and raise money for charities. The event was called the Craig MacFarlane Molson Celebrity Tennis Classic. Don Cherry was one of the folks that came in. He has been very good to me over the years. We've done a few appearances together and I certainly admire him. He is a voice, that when you hear it, you don't need to see the face.

Joe Thornton was the 1997 number one overall first round draft pick in the National Hockey League draft to the Boston Bruins. Lucky for me it's always been my favorite NHL team.

This picture was taken at The Palace in Auburn Hills after a concert in '94. I got to know Steve Tyler through various events. We've had a few laughs, I love his music — it's been a neat friendship.

Through Mario Andretti, I've met numerous people and Paul Newman has been one of those. He's been very good to me. He's a gracious person, very humble, very caring and does an enormous amount for charity. He's certainly an unsung hero.

This is Governor George Bush Jr. and I at the capitol building in Austin, Tx. He was honoring me for my work with the youth of America.

I first met Joe Theismann when I was a teenager. Joe was playing for the Toronto Argonauts football team in the Canadian Football League. I sat beside Joe at a head table of a banquet. We became very dear friends. When Joe came to the NFL, I became a big Redskins fan, which I still am today. Joe and I bumped into each other at President Clinton's '93 inaugural ball.

This picture with Carlos Delgado was taken in the summer of '96. It was during one of my many visits to Skydome. I actually met Carlos in '94 during some guest appearances on behalf of Wal-Mart. They were just moving into Canada then. We really connected. He is, without questions, one of the most kind-hearted guys that I've ever met and always has time for his fans.

I actually lived next door to Wayne Gretzky at one point in my young life. For a kid who grew up with hockey games playing on the transistor radio hidden under his pillow, knowing Gretzky is a dream come true. He was only twenty when I lived next door and he actually let me peel rubber in his Ferrari one time.

My closest friend and confidant Dick Schultz and I always find the time to share a few laughs. Dick understands me better than anyone.

Over the past 12 years, I have spoken at over 1,600 schools in eight different countries. This picture was taken in Lewiston, Idaho during one of my many appearances on behalf of Edward Jones Co.

follow along and take dictation from my lecture classes. Basically, it involved a lot of finger nimbleness and quickness.

I was able to post a 'B' average at Carleton. I should have been satisfied but I wasn't. At the end of a semester I was increasingly restless. I had time to think at Carleton and what kept coming back to me were my conversations with Wayne Gretzky about maximizing my marketable worth as an athlete, not wasting all the years and effort I'd put into sports, but somehow wresting some kind of living from them.

I also found that talking about becoming a lawyer sounded a lot better on a documentary than in real life. I'd been thinking more and more about an eventual career in politics or being a sports agent, and I thought a law degree would be good for either of those. But I just wasn't ready to knuckle down and do all the enormous work, frankly, that would be required to make it through law school. I think if it had really been my calling, the academics wouldn't have stopped me. Nothing would. But I was still just a little too action-oriented in those days.

Maybe I just wasn't ready to hang it up as an athlete.

Given time to reflect at college, I thought back to a car accident that had happened the summer before I entered Carleton. A friend of mine named Dave Tickner and I were driving from my house in Desbarats back to Brantford and a drunk-driver hit us head-on in Parry Sound. My knee smashed into the dashboard, racking it up pretty well.

The incident got wide play in the Canadian media. Paul Hendrick was a good friend of mine and a popular sportscaster from Hamilton, Ontario. He played it up big and a lot of others followed suit.

The question was: Did this knee injury knock me out of the wrestling blind nationals in August? After I got out of the hospital, I stayed for a couple of days with Doug and Arva Orr, the parents of hockey legend Bobby Orr, who lived in Parry Sound. I'd met Bobby at a couple of banquets where we'd both done some speaking. We'd become friends, and his parents were kind enough to take me in while I was waiting for Dave Tickner to get out of the hospital.

Then we were going to continue on to Brantford, as originally planned, where I'd try to do some training for the nationals.

But, I couldn't really work out until about five days before the competition because of the knee. But I did end up wrestling and, despite all that had happened, I won the gold medal.

That layoff during the summer after the competition and the time spent with the Orrs made me think how much I missed sports. But where was I actually going to pursue anything that would promise athletic rewards? I really didn't know. Carleton didn't offer an outlet. The only thing I knew was that I wanted to carve out my own living and stand on my own two feet.

The Canadian government starts sending you checks when you turn eighteen if you're blind or disabled. The whole idea incensed me to no end. I almost can't tell you how mad it made me. What got me the most was that they just fired these things off without any real knowledge of an individual's capabilities. If someone really needs the money and legitimately can't work, then more power to them.

I actually could have used the money because I was just starting at Carleton when the checks began coming. But I sent them back. The government kept sending them to me. I kept sending them back. It took innumerable calls and letters but I finally got them to turn off the dole.

For me, it was a matter of principle. I didn't want that kind of money. I didn't take it because I didn't earn it. I didn't want a government handout or government assistance. But I did want income. How to get it? Again, Wayne Gretzky loomed large in an answer.

In 1981, when Wayne held his annual Wayne Gretzky Celebrity Tennis Tournament, he asked me to be honorary chairman. I was stunned, but extremely pleased. It gave me the idea of hosting my own event, so in 1982 I held the Craig MacFarlane Celebrity Tennis Tournament. A lot of people thought putting a thing like this together was beyond me. I was just nineteen. But I made up my mind I would throw every ounce of energy I had into it and make it a success.

We held it at The Soo in the Memorial Gardens, with Algoma Steel donating the frames for the netting. I wanted a major sponsor and shot for Molson Brewery. I was fortunate enough to arrange a meeting with Bill Juke, a Molson executive. He agreed to meet at one of my friend's apartments in Toronto.

I had just stepped out of the shower when Bill knocked at the door. I quickly threw a towel around me and with water dripping out of my hair — not the ideal way to meet an executive you're going to pitch for thousands of dollars — I opened the door and welcomed him in.

I went to the refrigerator, knowing that my friend, Peter, would have a few beers on hand. I offered one to Bill.

As I handed it to him, he laughed.

"You really do have a sense of humor, don't you?" he said.

"That's what I've been told," I said. "Why?"

"This," he said, "is a LaBatts."

And I said, "Oh, try it, you might like it."

I went off to dry my hair.

"Yeah," he said as I retreated, "Maybe you can get your buddy to convert to Molson's."

I found Bill not only to be funny and fun, but generous. He pledged a whopping $250,000 for the tournament. Not bad for my first sales call as a nineteen-year-old. We were off and running.

Next I wanted a huge name to go with our huge sponsor. I decided to go with the biggest name in Canada. Hey, if you're going to shoot for the moon, go by way of the biggest star. I wanted Gordie Howe.

Of course, to me he was our country's biggest sports idol. Like every other kid growing up, I'd have given anything to meet him. And in fact, in third grade, I'd written him a letter in Braille which a teacher underlined with penned words, so he could read.

"Dear Mr. Howe," I'd written, "I think you are one of the greatest hockey players in the NHL. Can I have an autographed picture of you? I am a pretty good hockey player myself. Sincerely, Craig MacFarlane."

Of course, growing up I fervently believed I was going to be the first blind hockey player in the NHL. So I'd put some of my young heart and soul into that little letter. Obviously, it's one dream I didn't realize. But my next Gordie fantasy did play out.

When I asked him to be the main celebrity for my tennis tournament, he remembered this letter from the little blind boy so many years ago. In fact, he'd kept it. And he wasn't going to have any trouble remembering me at nineteen either. His wife, Colleen, says, "Craig used to bombard me with phone calls — call after call — trying to get Gordie to be honorary chairman of that tournament. I just finally said to Gordie, 'You know, that guy isn't going to give up so we might as well just do it. It might actually be kind of fun."

I think in large measure because of Colleen — but also because Gordie has a warm, kind, considerate heart — the Howes said Yes to my tournament. Of course, after they came aboard, so did everyone. Restaurants and hotels and other businesses made donations. We ran into a huge hitch when Air Canada went on strike the day before many of the forty celebrities were to fly to The Soo. We had to arrange charters, which cost us dearly and cut down the amount we could give to charity.

That was extremely frustrating, but the tournament was one of the turning points in my life. The night after it ended, Colleen and Gordie and I sat up until about 3 a.m. talking. Colleen asked me what I wanted to do with my life. I told her that somehow I wanted to take my athletic experience into some form of business path. I said I didn't know how because opportunities were limited for blind athletes.

Later that month, the Howes asked me to their cabin at Bear Lake outside Traverse City, Mich.

"My wife was very impressed with Craig," Gordie said. "She talked to him, talked to his parents and asked a lot of questions. The kid was concerned about his future. By the time I sat down with him, Colleen and I had already decided that we should assist him. She wanted to take him back home to Connecticut and virtually adopt him for a period of time. So she helped him get a green card, the work permit and helped him get a job. Colleen did most of the work at that point. When she decides something, the project is already half-way done."

Actually, the green card, normally like pulling eye teeth to obtain, would be little more than a formality, because my Mom was born in Detroit.

The Howes made an amazing offer during that visit to Bear Lake. They asked me to come and live with them in their home in Glastonbury, Conn., a suburb of Hartford. Gordie was a Hartford Whaler executive and said he'd get me a job in promotions with the Whalers. In this capacity, I could learn more about sports marketing and perhaps that would be my field for the future.

Talk about dreams come true. In the span of a few short months, I had the Babe Ruth and Ty Cobb of Canadian sports — Wayne Gretzky and Gordie Howe — at work in my life. They literally changed the course of it.

BRIDGING THESE GAPS BETWEEN US

On September 19, 1982, I found myself on an airplane, leaving Canada to live in the United States.

It is hard to describe what I felt as the plane took off. My heart would forever be, as long as it was able to beat, Canadian. But I was also being called forth by the love of a new adventure in a new country, the U.S., and all the opportunity that it represented and offered. I had been in the athletic trenches for my country, I had proudly worn the maple leaf on my chest, waved the flag, sang the patriotic songs at international competitions and, quite frankly, poured out a lot of blood, sweat and tears over the years for Canada. Now I was leaving. Little did I know I would be competing for America very soon. Right now, I thought my athletic career was over. I had only a few bucks and the clothes I took with me. I was just a trace apprehensive leaving behind the enormous support system which all my network of acquaintances and friends had afforded in Canada. But I also felt a surge of excitement of the unknown. The unknown has always had this mystique, this romance, for me.

My fears were calmed when I got off the plane and heard the words, "Welcome to America, Craig."

It was Gordie, there to pick me up at the airport.

When I went to sign my papers at immigration and one of those bureaucrats whose sense of humor had been surgically removed at birth, was manning a desk. The papers mentioned something about my now being eligible for the military draft.

And Gordie said, "What's he gonna do, drive the night fighter?"

Not even a sound from the guy. Gordie said not a flicker of a smile. Whew, I thought, what a tough room. That was a funny line.

Gordie was undeniably one of the roughest, toughest — some would say meanest — players ever in any professional sport. But he also was one of the biggest-hearted pussycats I've ever met in my life. He was a mentor, a role model and one of the most humble human beings I've met. He and Colleen constantly counseled me about the ways that I could make the transition from successful amateur athlete into the business world.

They both said I had a gift of gab and that public speaking could be my bread and butter. They introduced me to some corporate people, working with me on my speaking presentation. Gordie and Colleen both felt I had a great ease with people and a genuine love of meeting them. They said I was comfortable getting up in front of people and talking. And, since I had drawn a lot of attention from my early athletic days, I was at home dealing with the media.

The Whalers gave me some real work, not just busy work, but still we all viewed it as a temporary job while I looked for the real future I'd map out. While our time together had a serious side, life with the Howes was always full of wacky fun and nutty moments.

Colleen found it funny that I'd tell her to turn off the light when she went to bed, even if I was up.

"Hey, how's it going to matter to me?" I said.

But she couldn't get used to shutting them off while I was still up fiddling with something, getting a late-night snack or "watching" television.

Gordie could always make me laugh, and, I guess vice-versa, which is a nice thing to have in any friendship. We were driving along once in Washington, D.C., looking for an address.

"I'll look on the right side, you look on the left," he said. We both cracked up.

But actually, he wasn't being intentionally funny in this case. It was just a sign of how natural we were together and how he'd forgotten I was blind. Which I liked.

One time in a bank, he forgot a little too much for his own good. We were standing in line and he took out the money clip the NHL had given him for twenty-five years service. I tried to close it and I broke it.

He was standing there chewing me out. "Hey, you goofball, you broke my money clip..."

Several women at the bank jumped all over his case for picking on me. Hey, Gordie, give him a break. It was only an accident.

Gordie's presence and name were magic in public. His fame once saved our bacon, I believe. We were setting out from New York to Glastonbury. Gordie and I ran out of gas in a pretty rough neighborhood. We're in Gordie's lo-o-ong Lincoln, two white dudes, broken down in the ghetto.

I was genuinely nervous and Gordie, tough as he is, said later,

"I thought it might be Taps."

Then one guy stepped up and said, "Hey, ain't you Gordie Howe?"

They couldn't do enough to help us get back on the road.

We drove away with me thinking: Somehow, we have got to tap into the common feelings that can bridge gaps. Just the power of a star athlete's name can make people treat each other OK. Isn't there some hope to break through our barriers?

That supplied me with another piece of my puzzle. It added meaning to my desire to be public speaker, a motivator. I thought I might be able to use my experiences to show people how we're all the same under the skin. If I could build bridges between blind people and sighted people, I could also build bridges between people separated by color or gender.

Another time I saved Gordie. We were driving back from yet another late-night speaking engagement. Suddenly, I sensed something wasn't right. I punched Gordie in the shoulder.

"Hey, Chief. Wake up!" I said.

He had dozed off at the wheel and I caught him before he veered off the road.

I loved working for the Whalers, and I loved getting to know Howard Baldwin, the owner, who was my boss. He's a terrific guy who today is major owner of the Pittsburgh Penguins and a movie producer, with numerous films to his credit. "Sudden Death," an action-thriller starring Jean-Claude Van Damme, was set at the Pittsburgh Civic Arena, during a hockey game.

I also enjoyed skating with the Whalers after practice and to skate and shoot with Gordie. I can always say I did that. I actually scored on one of the Whaler goalies, although admittedly in one of those ragtag after-practice sessions. The guy was in goal when Gordie said, "Hey, why don't you let the Bat here take a couple shots on you?"

So Gordie lined me up and the first one, the goalie saved easily.

"Put some oomph in it, for cryin' out loud," Gordie said.

I skated in a few strides, let a wrist shot go and it sailed over the goalie's right shoulder into the top corner of the net.

Gordie howled.

"God, you're so bad, even a blind guy can beat ya," he said.

STRAINING FOR THE TAPE, A LIFE LESSON

The Howes, in the midst of the jokes and good times, were always seeking ways to encourage me and challenge me to reach my fullest potential. One day, Gordie said to me, "If you don't want to be just another blind athlete, if you really want to be the best ever, why don't you win 100 gold medals? Why stop now?"

When he said that, I had ninety-three gold medals and, frankly, I was satisfied, or so I thought. I thought I had all I needed. But Gordie is always looking for the kind of excellence in others which he requires of himself — the kind that saw him play effective major league hockey into his fifties and actually take the ice again in a professional game at the age of sixty-nine for the Detroit Vipers of the IHL. Now he saw a goal worth reaching for me. He inspired me to go for more gold.

I decided the quickest route would be through track and field. Aside from sprinting, I'd actually learned to high jump, throw the javelin, discus and shot-put.

Bob Lucas, the president of the Whaler booster club, and his wife, Bev, invited me to live with them and their daughter, Sue, and son, B.J. — more names to be added to my list of unsung heroes who touched my life. They helped host dinners to raise money for me to travel to competitions. The same month Gordie encouraged me to go back to competition, I entered the U.S. Blind National Track and Field Championships in Long Beach, California I won four gold medals, beating a blind All-American sprinter, Doug Rose.

I needed three more golds for the century mark. I entered the New Jersey Blind Invitational in November. The first event was the 60-meters held indoors. The guy running right before me ran off course and right into a steel post knocking himself out. As I was loading up in the starting blocks, I could have sworn I still heard that steel post ringing. This is not the way to get a confident start. I lost by three one-hundredths-of-a-second.

Mentally, that created a hurdle for me to get over. I wasn't used to losing a sprint right off the bat and I had to give my confidence a booster shot. That would prove tough to do in my next race, the 400 meters.

I got a great start and was well ahead coming into the last 100 meters. I heard steps on my left, but I was bagged. For some reason, the tank was not full that day. Plus, the Jersey competition was outstanding, and a very good sprinter was running me down in the stretch.

We got into one of those prolonged stretch duels that happens every now and then. I could hear both of us grunting and wheezing as we came toward the tape. I started to cramp. I thought I was going to throw up. One leg went numb. Suddenly, I went from asking myself, `Will I win?' to, `Will I finish?'

At 40 meters, the guy passed me. I fought hard to keep him right here, just in front. I went into my Grey Zone and really had this kind of out-of-body finish where I almost didn't know it was me running. Somehow, I lunged right at the very last moment, pulling my guide runner with me. By then I had no earthly idea where the finish line was and I kept on lunging and sprinting. Someone said I kept running a good twenty yards past. After I collapsed, I learned I had won by two feet.

Gold medal number ninety-eight.

Number ninety-nine was the complete opposite. I won it in the javelin. That left the 200-meter dash, which is my favorite track and field event. I love the combination of the power off the turn and the full-out sprint of the straightaway, which is my strong suit. I could still feel the 400 in my aching muscles. But I went out like a tiger — "Always give 'em hell at the start," I could hear Grandpa Jefferies whispering to me — and no one could catch me.

I threw my arms around Gordie.

"Thanks," I said, "for inspiring me to do this."

I said a silent thanks to Grandpa, too, and gave him a wave to the sky.

"Craig is the only handicapped guy we ever met who didn't know he was different," Gordie once said. "Rather than hold out his hand and beg, he only wanted to make it on his own."

Gordie taught me one important lesson. Never give up until you're finished. It's important to give 'em hell from the start, but it's also important to keep pumping through the tape. Capturing 100 gold medals was a goal worth straining for, but it was also a lesson in perseverance. Without perseverance, you can never really reach the important goals in your life.

Showtime! A dare and the fearlessness instilled in me by my parents back in the Soo, led to a life skimming waves and soaring at Cypress Gardens. I found another place to take my full-out attitude, national blind water-skiing championships. When you train among alligators, what do you expect?

Chapter Seven
Go Ahead and Jump

After the shock of not being chosen for the snow-skiing international team in 1983, I didn't have the heart to continue pursuing the slopes. I could probably have won another blind nationals and, having paid my dues I could have been selected to the next international snow skiing competition. I also could've challenged the decision of the selection committee and I might well have won the case. But I was physically and emotionally drained. I would not attend the world championships in Switzerland nor would I ever snow ski competitively again. I was twenty-two, I had won all the gold medals a person could ask for, my body had been through the wringer. I felt I had nothing left to prove to anyone, and nothing left to prove to myself. On the slopes, that is.

Six months later, back in Connecticut licking my wounds, I received a surprise telephone call. It was from Cypress Gardens in Florida, inviting me to be the spokesman for the blind national water skiing championships in late November. I was honored and agreed — under one condition.

Spokesman, heck. Let me compete.

The competition was based on four twenty-second passes, seeing how many wakes you could cross in each given period. You would receive one point for each wake crossing on two skis; two points would be awarded for each crossing on one ski.

Naturally, I made up my mind to go the one-ski route. That's the way I've always attacked everything in my life. Full out. Take the hard road.

I only had one month to train. What sort of chance did I have at that point? I had learned to water ski for the first time at age eleven. That was a long way from national competition. Of course, the odds didn't stop me. Never had.

I knew the drill by now. Find a good teacher, dig in with both feet, shuck off the fear and get the job done. I found my trainer John Swanke near Danbury, Conn., and we went to work on the choppy surface of Lake Zorr.

It might as well have been called Lake Brrrr.

In late October when sane folks are stirring the hickory in their wood stoves, I was pulling on my wet suit in the frigid waters of Lake Zorr to go water skiing.

Call it dedication. Call it stupidity. Whatever you call it, I wanted to give this competition my best shot. I've often found in my career that a little hardship goes a long way toward building athletic character. The weather back in Brantford wasn't always spring-like when I went out for my five a.m. run. I have this thing about life's inconveniences. You've got to ignore them, or you've got to use them to make you stronger. You can't ever let them stop your progress.

Swanke turned out to be an incredible teacher. He was patient. Talented. And a terrific water-skier and bare-footer, himself, who had skied competitively. He had been there. And as a bonus, he taught me how to barefoot.

Let me just say that barefootin' had its moments. A few wipeouts at over thirty miles-per-hour and you're like a beachball on water. That is, until you slow down and figure out where you've been punctured and try to re-inflate your system.

I should mention Swanke is famous beyond the business of towing hapless fellow citizens to their demise behind hundreds of screaming horsepower. He helped design and build the set for the Broadway show, Cats, and several other notable shows. So getting tickets to Broadway was a cinch. I remember one day he took me to tour the set for Cats and to be with him backstage while the production was going on.

That was one of the few breaks we took preparing for water skiing nationals. So as November drew near to Thanksgiving, I was thankful to be in one piece when I boarded the plane for Orlando, Fla. I couldn't wait for this new challenge, though the morning of the competition was overcast and windy. To my surprise, several media crews were there, including "PM Magazine" and "CBS Morning News". Later that day, they would both do film feature stories on me. And those wouldn't be the last.

I was surprised how many other blind skiers were there of all ages. It made my blood run just a little quicker. I wasn't sure how I'd stack up against the others. Nor did anyone else have much of an idea. We were pioneers. Unlike snow skiing which had a history and an old boy network, this was the first Blind National Water Skiing Championships.

What a great stage to play this out. Cypress Gardens. I marshalled my butterflies and took to the water. We skied our two twenty-second passes, then came back to the dock. Once everyone had two passes, the halfway scores were announced.

To my delight — and shock — I was in first place. And by quite a substantial margin. But I knew from my past athletic experience, I should not take any lead for granted. I have learned the hard way to never coast.

By the time we ran our second pass, the wind had come up and the chop on the lake was quite significant. The boat driver, Donny Croft, gave me a couple of quick pointers.

"Stay a little loose out there, since you can't see what's ahead of you," he said. "It won't be such a jolt on your body when you hit those waves."

Of course, I was skiing on one ski to maximize the number of points achievable. I wound up averaging over eighteen crossings per twenty seconds. My timing and rhythm were definitely there. And I think my snow-skiing experience helped mightily. The whitecaps were spanking the bottoms of my skis

and the wind was howling in my ears as the horn sounded
signifying my second run. My quadriceps were burning like all
get out. As I popped over the wake, held tight and popped back
over again, and kept repeating, I was just relieved to still be
standing.

Back to the dock I came, wearily, not too graceful, my legs
and arms spaghetti with rocks tied to the ends of them. I let go
of the rope a little late and crashed into the dock.

It was just a little jab, though — not a knockout punch. A
couple of bruises. Nothing that an ex-wrestler wasn't
accustomed to. It looked worse than it felt.

The rain waited charitably until the competition concluded. It
gently began falling as the medals were handed out. When my
name was called for the gold medal, I smiled slightly and was led
to the podium. I can't honestly say that I was overcome with
emotion. I suppose it was just another day at the office for me in
some ways. As I stood there, I thought, what's the big deal? You
go out, cross the wakes and just try to stay upright. It didn't seem
that demanding. It was the first time for a wonderful idea and
event in a glorious setting. I wasn't knocking it. But it struck me
that better ways could be developed to test blind water skiers.

After I received the gold medal, it was announced that I
would represent the United States at the Blind International
World Water Skiing Championships just outside Oslo, Norway,
in August, 1984.

Now that made me smile.

What an honor. I was beaming inside and out with this
opportunity. But, as everyone was milling around after the event,
I still felt kind of empty about the whole water skiing
experience. I had come a long way since I had first learned to
water ski at Camp Lake Joseph just outside of Parry Sound,
Ontario, at eleven years of age. I really hadn't been on water skis
since, until I started skiing with John Swanke.

So here I hadn't skied that much, but I was the blind U.S.
champion. And then another thought hit me — and honest to
God it hadn't even begun to dawn on me until then. I was the

Go Ahead and Jump

U.S. champion in both water-skiing and snow-skiing, only six months apart and in the same year after arriving in the States.

Then someone in the crowd, bless him, said, "Hey MacFarlane, have you ever ski-jumped?"

"Ski-jumped?" I said. "No. But I'd love to."

That voice in the crowd and my response was all it took. A buzz filtered throughout the dock area.

"Yeah, let's see you do it," another voice cried out.

"Naw, there's no way," another voice yelled. "He'll kill himself."

Now that was really all it took.

"Let me try it," I piped up.

I got my wish. Ricky McCormick, a world water-skiing jump champion lived nearby and they brought him over to the gardens. I couldn't believe it when I first met Ricky. I had met my match. Here was Mr. Energy personified. A heart of gold. And he knew water skiing like the back of his hand — or bottom of his feet. He lived and breathed it. I had just found my Cliff May of water-skiing.

Within minutes, Ricky had me loaded up in a boat with Donny Croft driving. And out to the ramp we went. No skis. I climbed out of the boat and walked around the ramp. Felt how long it was. How wide it was.

This was all happening within a couple of hours of the medals ceremony. Amazingly, no one seemed to have left the grounds. I guess some Evel Knievel Effect had taken over. Like people congregating to see if Evel would leap the Snake River Canyon or leave himself for coyote food in the chasm, folks apparently couldn't tear themselves away from the idea that I might feed myself to the gators.

The ramp was made of fiberglass. It was six feet off the water. I jumped from the end of it. This created a clear mental picture of what would be expected of me when I jumped with skis.

When I would come off the high end of the ramp, it might be only six feet above the water, but the speed I brought into the jump would launch me higher. A sighted ski jumper might go further and higher, but he or she would be cutting into the jump at a more severe angle and at greater speed. A blind jumper would kill himself at that angle. The way I would do it, well, there was only a possibility.

Exploring the ramp harnessed the nervous energy in me about the jump, although granted, it would not erase those butterflies. Of any sport I've ever done, water-ski jumping created more butterflies, droves of butterflies fluttering around my insides. There was no doubt this sport pumped my adrenaline.

One reason is that so many things can go wrong when you hit the ramp. If your ski is on edge, it's like a knife going through butter. You would wipe, big-time. If you're too far back on your skis you fall on the ramp. If you're too far forward, or your arms are extended, you plant your face solidly into the ramp. Also, the boat being on your right side as it tows you onto the ramp, naturally tugs you that way. So you're not going straight up the ramp. There were times you'd come off the top right-hand corner, one ski going one way and one going the other.

Suddenly, you are doing the splits in the air.

Get your skis going in opposite enough directions, now you've turned yourself into a whirlybird. You'll lose it completely in the air. You'll be sideways and upside-down. So you'd better get it together in the air real quick.

All this Ricky was trying to explain to me in what seemed like a few seconds, but actually took forty-five minutes or so.

Ricky helped me into the jump skis. They are longer and heavier than average water skis — they have to be to take the pounding they get. By now I was flush with expectation. Not only were people not leaving. The stands were getting more packed as the buzz went throughout the Gardens.

A totally blind kid was going to try the ramp.

PM Magazine and CBS Morning News had never left. They set up their equipment again, cameras rolling. I truly believe they thought I might kill myself or they wouldn't have stuck around.

As we glided away from the dock, Ricky and I skied side-by-side on two separate ropes, I couldn't help thinking how amazing this all was. A couple of minutes ago, it seemed, I was standing on the podium with no-big-deal spread over my face.

Ricky said as we came to the ramp, he would help steer me into it. He would give me a five-four-three-two-one countdown — one of those again. He shouted out some last-second reminders as we circled out for the jump.

"Keep your knees bent.

"Keep your back straight.

"Don't lean too far forward or too far backwards so when you land you'll be centered over your skis.

"Keep your head up so the boat doesn't pull you over the tips of your skis.

"Keep your arms in a little so you're not overextended when you land."

That was a lot to say in a short amount of time and a lot to remember. I'm not sure I did. Usually I can absorb this kind of information and intuitively put it to use in fairly rapid order.

Now, I was just thinking two instructions to myself.

Jump.

Don't die.

But, truthfully, I never really had the feeling this was going to turn out badly. Neither did Ricky. Had he expressed serious doubts, I might have felt more like backing away. But he said, from the git-go, "Listen Craig. You've got the physique. I can tell watching you ski just a little bit — your balance, your strength and agility. Hey, I know you can do this."

Now, suddenly, the preliminaries were over. No time for more talk. Or thought. No time to ponder or weigh or consider. ...five...four...three...two...

I hardly heard, "One."

My skis chattered as they skidded across the fiberglass. I had time to note that sound, nothing more. The next thing I knew, I was airborne.

And then...splash.

My skis hit the water. Not the most graceful landing. My butt went down and splooshed down on my skis. But I fought my way back up again and skied away. Ricky and I high-fived. We embraced with one arm because we were still holding the tow rope with the other.

I could hear the cheer of the crowd on my right as we skied past the grandstand. I was hooked on that sound. And Ricky was just pumped.

"That was just awesome," he yelled.

There was a ramp at each end of the water-ski show area. We were coming up on it. We were going to take that one, too. ...five...four..three...two...one...

This time I was a little too far forward. I must have looked like an egg-beater as I came off that ramp, arms and legs flailing, fighting to keep my balance. When I hit — not a chance.

Both skis went flying. But as Ricky had taught me, if you wipe out, immediately stick your hand in the air so the boat driver will know you're OK.

I did as instructed. All I could do was laugh. Probably a maniacal laugh at the thrill of it all.

Ricky skied up to me and kept saying, "It's OK. It's OK. Everybody does that. We'll get it. You've already done one."

I was hungry to get back up. I could conquer this thing. I knew what my mistake was. No one had to tell me.

"Give me another shot," I said.

Ricky said, "You got it."

Donny Croft in the boat was awesome. As he circled around to pick us up, he said, "You did it, man. That was amazing. You looked great. Stay confident. You're gonna nail this next one. You're gonna stick it."

I didn't know what sticking it meant at that time, nor did I care. But it sounded like the thing to do. Later I learned "sticking it" means you barely get your ankles wet. A clean, standup landing. It would take me a few more before I could achieve that.

But jumps three and four went better. I landed them both without smacking my bottom in the water, and skied away. Now it was time to come back to the drydock. I was emotionally and physically spent. The old adrenaline drain kicked in. It'd been a lot of water skiing in one day for a kid who had only spent a handful of hours on skis in his life before. That would be enough for me today.

We glided up to the dock, which felt like Astroturf, and as I came to a halt, I was beseiged with questions from reporters and eager fans.

"What'd it feel like?"

"Were you scared?"

"Would you do it again?"

And then there was this comment from a reporter, "Despite the odds, you did it."

My reply: "If no blind person has ever ski-jumped before, then who the heck set the odds?"

Think about it. People are always trying to set the odds for you. They're always saying, "You can't do this" or "You can't do that" or you're too short, or too tall, or not mean enough, or not smart enough, or not good enough. I've been plagued with people setting the odds for me all my life. I've lived to prove them wrong.

Call them odds if you will. To me, they're challenges. And the point of a challenge is to conquer it. When people set the odds for you, the thing to do is laugh. Then get to work.

SHOWTIME: MY BIG SPLASH AT CYPRESS GARDENS

The next day, I couldn't stay away. I had to try this wonderful new toy again. Donny Croft would be driving Ricky and I again between regular shows of the Cypress Gardens Water Ski Spectacular. We landed a lot more landings than we missed — including a few that were very clean.

Before the day was out, the executives from Cypress Gardens approached me about joining their regular ski shows. Four shows a day. Seven days a week, beginning January 1, 1984. I would be paid the handsome sum of $5,000 a month, plus free lodging in the hotel across from the Cypress Gardens gates — meals included.

I let that sink in for a few moments. I was doing it. I was actually getting paid something for my athletic abilities. I didn't tell them, but I'd have been overjoyed if it had been $5 a month. It still would have represented something special to me. But $5,000....that was a decent living wage. It meant I was finally a professional athlete. And it meant financial independence. Financial independence had been my quest from the day I graduated high school. Maybe before.

On January 1, 1984, I joined the water-ski team at 8 a.m. to stretch, run and loosen up, to get ready for the four shows at 10 a.m., noon, 2 and 4 p.m.

I felt like a member of a real professional team — which I was. It takes remarkable athletic ability to ski the routines at Cypress Gardens, even though they make it look so gorgeous. I would go out and jump a couple of ramps each show. On that New Year's Day, I felt more like a kid at Christmas with the best present you could get. Not intimidated. Not hesitant at all. Just rarin' to go.

As the first show drew near, I could hear people filtering into the grandstands. Kids with parents. Grandparents. Teenagers. College kids. The PA system was blaring enthusiastic announcements.

They said, "The world's premier, number one, water ski show." It sent the tingles up my spine.

But that wasn't the focus of the day for me. What held my attention was the camaraderie of the performers. Underneath the fans in the dressing areas, which were first class, all the guys were joking around. And all the girls were just getting to know me.

"Hey, anybody see a blind ski-jumper out there today?" someone would call out.

"Nope. Not me," someone would answer.

It was their way of saying I fit in. I belonged. I was part of a team. As I've said, teamwork is difficult for blind athletes, so we're attracted to solo sports. I had always wanted to be part of something like this, to fit in, to be one of many.

The first day, I didn't miss a single jump in all four shows, although in the first show, I somehow got caught sideways in the air during my second jump and had to fight like crazy to pull myself out of it. When I landed, it was not pretty, but thank God for the leg strength I developed in wrestling. I was able to fight my way back to upright.

The water ski show was timed precisely to the second. My cue was always the same, the Van Halen tune: "Go Ahead and Jump!" When I'd hear that start playing, it was show time. I'd better be on the back dock, skis on, ready to rock.

It's hard to describe that feeling when you leave the dock. Gliding across the water. The noise from the boat motor. The smell of gas in the air. The mist sometimes coming off the water, refreshing your face. The aroma of the flowers all over the Gardens. It's one thing to just go out and jump, but to do it in front of thousands of people every day became infectious. I thrived on it. Here I was, not only part of a team, but skiing with the best skiers in the world.

I'd be the first to admit I probably didn't deserve to be there, from a pure water-skiing experience level. But, I did work hard to improve. And I did get better.

Over the next several weeks, I learned to ski in a variety of conditions. The motto of Cypress Gardens: "Four shows a day, 365 days a year...unless there's lightning."

So, yes, I jumped in the driving rain. I jumped in chop two feet high. I learned how to hold a jump together under severe weather conditions where my timing was literally non-existent.

In the mornings, during our eight a.m. workout sessions, I worked on trios and doubles. Trios is where you and another person beside you had a girl up on top doing various acrobatic moves. Kind of like ballet on water. You'd ski with a harness around your chest so your hands would be free. If you wiped out, the harness would just detach from the rope, so you wouldn't get dragged under.

Doubles were more challenging. It was just me and a girl — with her doing her acrobatic moves. Eventually, I got where I could I perform these in the show. What a rush. This meant mastering a situation where you had the girl's foot in your one hand, and you had to ski. It took an enormous amount of strength. Now, granted these weren't two-hundred-pound women, but it still took great muscle and concentration.

I also skied in the pyramids. At one point I was part of a five tier human pyramid, which has four tiers of girls climbing up on a base of several guys down below.

I used to tease my buddies beside me, "If we ever were going to make a mistake, this would be the ideal opportunity. You'd have four tiers of girls coming down on top of you." That might have been true, but falling knees, elbows and heels in the head don't exactly tickle, which absolutely did happen sometimes in practice. Big time wipe outs. Fortunately we didn't often crash in the show.

I was working hard to get better. I guess, having once believed I didn't belong there, I began to change my perspective at least a little. I'm not saying I was the equal of many of the veteran performers who were unbelievable artists. But, at least I can say I progressed to the point that I was a regular part of the show — on many levels.

I can say, in fact, that I was a normal part of the show, earning my keep. I wasn't just a sideshow freak. I was the first totally blind person to ever ski as part of the Cypress Garden water ski show. And then my over-the-top spirit of adventure topped out too far.

I decided one day to try a helicopter. That's where you wrap the rope around your waist and try to do a three-hundred-sixty degree turn in mid-air — a full rotation spin — coming off the end of the ramp. That was all fine and dandy, but somehow my spin went astray and I wound up landing on Mark, one of the other skiers. My ski cracked his collarbone and half drove him to the bottom of the lake.

I felt terrible. I couldn't understand what went wrong. That ended my helicopter flying but it didn't end my taste for pushing the envelope. Maybe I shouldn't have kept pushing so hard, so fast. But I got bored easy, just doing the regular jumps was becoming routine. I was reaching out for the next frontier.

I decided I'd try a back flip off the ramp. Little did I know that when you're in the air rotating, it's hard to judge when to pull out of that turn without the use of sight. Maybe I should have remembered that from the time I crash-landed off the ten-meter tower at the blind Olympic training camp in Canada.

I had an excellent teacher to help me attempt the back flip. Scotty Clack, a world champion freestyle jumper, would be my partner. This was in the show. I never even practiced it. I put it out there in prime time. I guess I knew how high-risk it was going to be. If it was a one-time thing, at least let the paying customers get the benefit.

I got the countdown to the ramp, went into my rotation. But instead of a three-hundred-sixty, I did a three-hundred-ninety. I was off my axis and got my axis kicked. I smashed into the water cartwhelling off the surface out of control.

My ribs were cracked. My collarbone was broken. But the big blow was that my hamstring was torn away from the bone. It turns out my body just didn't want to bend any of the ways I bent it on this jump. As I lay there in the water, I was saying, "Thank God you have to wear a helmet and a wet suit with flotation in it when you're jumping. Or I might have sunk to the bottom of the lake on impact."

I was dazed. I could sense an eerie hush come over the crowd. The one voice I heard was a little kid's.

"Look, Mommy, he's hurt," the child said.

The kid was right. And I knew it wasn't a small hurt. It felt like my whole body was paralyzed.

A safety boat was quickly on the scene. I was loaded up into it, lying on my back. We sped to the back dock, out of view of the audience. From there, I was put in an ambulance and rushed to the hospital in Winter Haven.

My Cypress Gardens career ended that day. Because I was incapacitated and not much use to Cypress Gardens, I voluntarily decided to step out of my contract. I suppose many people in that instance would have milked it for all it was worth. They would have hung out in the hotel for a couple months, staying on the payroll. Not me. If I couldn't ski and was going to be down for a prolonged amount of time, I would do something else with my life.

If I'd been content to just ride ramps I probably could have been there for years. But it just wasn't in my personality to do things that way. Exactly what I was going to do next, I had no idea. The injury was extremely slow to heal, as anyone who's had torn muscles knows. It hurt so bad, for weeks, that when I went up stairs, I had to go up one step with my good leg and pick the other one up with my two hands. It took me minutes to go up staircases, where normally I'd bound up in a second or two. This was by far the worst injury I'd ever had in a lifetime of wrecking my body. It took me April, May, and June to heal. And even in July, when I was starting to train for the World Blind Water Skiing Championships, my leg was still painful. I could use it, but not fully.

A LONG WAY FROM BRUCE MINES: THAT GABBY KID MAKES GOOD

I didn't need Olympic-level mobility for my next adventure. I needed my gift of speech and a lot of nerve, instead. I was about to test my wings in serious company. My work with the Hartford Whalers and performing at Cypress Gardens had caught the eye of the people running the 1984 re-election campaign of Ronald Reagan and George Bush. They asked me to be part of the Reagan-Bush All Star team, which was a group of athletes who traveled around the country speaking on behalf of the Republican ticket.

At first I thought I was being set up by one of my crazy

buddies with the old fake White House call gag.

"Yeah right," I said when I answered the phone.

Luckily, the White House is used to this kind of response. They convinced me I was actually speaking to the Reagan-Bush people which left me humbled and excited at the same time. I'd never actually taken time to try to define myself in American politics to that point. I'd been in the country less than three years. But, when I thought about it, most of my views were fairly conservative in many ways. I believed strongly in independence and self-reliance — typified by my refusal of my blind pension at age eighteen — and I thought the Republican philosophy was strongly along those lines.

The next thing I knew I was climbing the steps to the Philadelphia art museum — the ones Sylvester Stallone made famous in Rocky — with former heavyweight champs Joe Frazier and Floyd Patterson on either side of me as we kicked off the Reagan-Bush All Star tour. In the coming months I would make 231 appearances in thirty-nine states on behalf of Reagan-Bush. I traveled with the New York Yankee storybook characters such as Mickey Mantle, Whitey Ford and Roger Maris. I roomed with Roger often on the road and discovered what an outstanding man he was, although was often not understood because of his natural shyness. I'm a baseball fanatic, so getting to know the guy who holds the single-season home run record was a thrill.

With each stop on the tour, I began to get more and more understanding and appreciation for the people and spirit that make this country great. My work with the All Star team gave me the kind of visibility that led to my being asked — by President Reagan's office, itself, no less — to help do a leg of the Olympic Torch run through the streets of Washington, D.C., as the torch began its journey across America to arrive in Los Angeles for the Summer Games that July.

Guess who I got to accompany me on the torch run. Gordie Howe.

As we cruised along the Jefferson Memorial Concourse, I'd hear people along our route going, "Who's that running with

Gordie Howe?"

My White House connection brought another bolt out of the blue that year, and it came when I needed it most. I had trained on one good leg and one weak leg for the Blind International Water Skiing Championships near Oslo, Norway. But my performance had been disappointing — to me. I had finished fourth. Before I could completely absorb the reality of not winning, I got a call from all the way across the Atlantic. It was the White House — this time I believed them; I think I was getting the hang of it by now. And this time they asked me something I had trouble conceiving.

They asked if I would speak at the Republican National Convention. I was almost going to have to do it in a wetsuit because I barely had time to dry off and change clothes. I'd have to be in Dallas in two days for the speech.

I never got higher on any of my ski jumps. I was on ecstatic as I flew back to America. Me. This runt from backwoods Canada, was going to be on national television, speaking on behalf of the President and Vice-President of the United States.

Several planes later, I was rushing in a limo to Dallas Reunion Arena. Two blocks from the arena the limo overheated and caught fire. I ran the last two blocks and was pretty rumpled as I hustled in to find my way to the podium.

This was prime-time, center stage. I wasn't the keynoter, of course — not by a long shot. But this was in the evening on network television and I was about four speeches from the main-event. My speech was prepared for me, although I knew I'd be pretty familiar with the material, because it was going to be stuff I'd said on the All-Star tour.

Now I'm standing there fifteen minutes before showtime and how do you think my speech is sitting there waiting for me to deliver it? Think of the worst possible way.

You guessed it. On a Teleprompter.

I started laughing and so did everyone else. Maybe they were hoping I'd regain my sight on prime-time television. That would be news. A real miracle worker story.

Go Ahead and Jump

Fortunately I had a slate and stylus in my bag. I roughed out some notes to the speech on Braille paper. The irony was that I was giving a speech about the administration's concern for the needs of the handicapped. Meanwhile, the blind guy's speech is on a prompter.

The laugh helped relax me. Next thing I knew, I was delivering my old familiar words to a jam-packed Reunion crowd of 18,000-plus and to millions on television and radio. At that moment, my fate as a public speaker was sealed. This was a sub-four minute mile, a bottom of the ninth homerun. And, it had all come to me without asking. I had worked hard to be a good athlete and a good speaker, and good things had come to me as a result.

Reagan-Bush won by a landslide that fall.

I had appeared with soon-to-be President Bush several times during the campaign. He even invited me to jog with him on occasion. I found him to be a warm, sincere, funny and good-hearted man, insightful on so many subjects. And Barbara, of course, is a gentle, intelligent person. No airs. Always herself. So is President Bush. I think that is part of the charm that connected with the American public and eventually swept them into the Oval Office. The two of them had a way of making everyone around them feel special. I was no exception.

"Look, Barbara, it's our athlete extraordinaire," President Bush would say when I came into a room.

I was also honored the next spring, 1985, by Nancy Reagan for my work with youth. The award came at a gathering of thousands at the New York Hilton. There were two guys in the spotlight that day. The Donald and me. Yes. Donald Trump.

'Someday' Arrives

After my political foray, I got back to the serious business of training for international competition in earnest. Finishing fourth at Oslo left a bad taste in my mouth. I'd won the U.S. Blind Nationals again in November of 1984. Now I was back in the hunt for the worlds in August of 1985.

My trainer through the first trip to Oslo and the second U.S. Nationals had been Ken Ransom, a vice president at Eagle Wetsuits. Ken and his wife Tricia had asked me to dinner one night, and, as they told people later, "The guy never left." Through the first trip to Oslo, I lived with them. Ken, a transplanted Englishman, had more patience in training than anyone I'd ever met.

For this second trip to Norway, Ken and I trained at a Boy Scout camp north of Houston called Camp Strake. It wasn't exactly heaven on earth to me because I'd heard about the alligators living there and I had no plans to live the sequel to Crocodile Dundee. I was constantly in fear of running into a future piece of luggage with the jaws and teeth attached.

The first thing Ken and I did when we got to Camp Strake each day was a Gator Run. We circled the lake, looking for alligators. And in more than one instance, we found them toward the ski dock end of the lake, often very close. And Ken would try chasing them with the boat toward the other end.

Skiing in a lake with alligators may sound crazy but it had one advantage. It provided a strong incentive for staying upright on the water rather than in it.

It also meant revamping our signals to each other.

Ken and I had devised codes. Three bangs on the rope meant, "Let go, we're by the dock. Two bangs on the rope meant, "Rough water ahead." One particular day, we were roaring up the lake and an alligator was swimming in our path.

Ken's first thought: "Oh, God. We don't have a code for: Alligator ahead."

All he could hope was that I wouldn't swing out into the path of the gator. I was free-skiing out behind and I might go anywhere. What happened was lucky; the boat went on one side of the alligator and I went on the other side. Within a couple of feet on the other side, I might add. And Ken said later, it was a huge alligator.

"In this instance, thank God you're blind," Ken said when we got back. "You don't want to know what you just missed."

"I don't?"

"Trust me."

"Yeah, I think you just told me. How big was it?"

"Well, let's put it this way. He was big enough to pull you, instead of the boat, if you'd asked him."

"I'll remember that, buddy, if one of 'em ever makes off with you."

A couple days later my skis actually glanced off a small gator as we were coming into the dock.

"Did you see that log back there I clipped?" I asked Ken.

"My friend, that was no log," he said. "That was a tree-trunk with eyes. I think it's a good thing you're going to worlds in a couple days before one of them gets us."

Throughout our escapades, Ken was the perfect teacher, always reassuring, always encouraging, always thinking. He videotaped me and the films helped refine my technique as we skied day and night — yes, sometimes, nights — relentlessly preparing for worlds.

And, as usual for me, hard work paid athletic dividends. My skiing improved dramatically. This time when I went to Oslo I was brimming with confidence. I had a sponsor, Amway International. Their public relations director, Jack Wilke, rode along to Norway to do stories and photographs, so I had my own biographer. Unfortunately, I'm blue and shivering in most of the photographs. I had misjudged the weather, thinking the last time I was in Oslo the chilly weather wasn't really Oslo weather. Of course it was.

Had I brought along a wetsuit? Of course not. Here I was a former spokesperson for Eagle wetsuits, I had trained long and hard with a vice president of Eagle wetsuits, and I didn't think to bring one. It was so cold and choppy in the water, I spent the whole time numb.

The Norwegians thought I had some serious screws loose. They were acclimated to freezing their keisters off in their gorgeous fjords, but not even the hardy Norse were venturing into this competition without wetsuits. In fact, I was the only skier who didn't wear one.

Maybe I was just trying to get out of the water fast. But something clicked — all of Ken's training, the fact I was healthier, the fact I had made up my mind nothing was going to stop me this time.

But I went back into a deep, abiding friend, the Grey Zone. I hit seventeen crosses on my first run and on the second went whizzing back and forth across the wakes like a crazy man. I had no clue how many I hit, honest. It'd gone that quickly, like I was in a trance.

They announced I'd hit a perfect twenty. Craig MacFarlane was the world champion.

A few minutes after receiving my gold medal, I made a call from a phone close to the dock, to a wonderful friend of mine back in Houston. He was a DJ named "Moby" who was emerging as one of the most prominent morning men in America because of his quick wit, charisma and wacky style. I became a good pal and frequent guest on his show. Moby's sportscaster during the morning show was none other than Hannah Storm, who became a friend on her way to NBC sports. So I called Moby, as promised, standing there wearing my medal in Oslo. He immediately put me on air.

Ken Ransom, who was unable to go to Norway because of his job, was listening.

He told me later, "I had Moby and you on as I was driving to work. The level of excitement in your voice made me pull over. I was choked up with emotion. As I sat there, tears were rolling down my face."

Little did I know I would be shedding tears for Ken Ransom just seven years later as I composed myself to offer his elegy. In 1990, Ken was diagnosed with an incurable bone marrow disease. He died October 4, 1992, of a brain hemorrhage related to the disease.

But in 1985, we were both celebrating. Ken and I had already talked about this moment. I wanted it to be my last athletic competition. We both agreed this would be a fitting end, to go out a world champion.

And it all happened exactly as Ken and I talked.

I was certain, right at that instant of winning, that my competitive athletic days were over. I could go out with my head held high. I'd been a champion in wrestling, the blind Olympics, track and field, snow-skiing and water-skiing.

My body had taken a pounding since I was six years old. I was only twenty-three at the time, but it seemed like two lifetimes I had put into pursuing these chunks of hardware and certificates of award.

Mentally, physically, I was weary of it.

I had 136 medals of one kind or another. And 103 of them were gold. That was enough. It was deeply satisfying to go out the way I'd come in seventeen years earlier in my first competition back in Brantford — a winner.

The words of my dear friend, constant confidant and wonderful coach, John Howe, echoed in my mind, on the plane ride home.

"I'm going to be a champion someday, Coach."

"Craig, keep working and I know you will."

When I got back to the States, I spoke at the Lions Club International convention, in front of 21,000 in Dallas Reunion Arena. On Thursday, the keynote speaker was Henry Kissinger. On Friday, the keynote speaker was President Ronald Reagan. On Saturday, the keynote speaker was Craig MacFarlane.

In the fall of 1985, I spoke at the Amway International convention. Sharing the podium with me were Walter Cronkite and Norman Vincent Peale.

Not bad for a kid from a teeny village in Canada, a kid who would never shut up in Mrs. Martens kindergarten class back in Bruce Mines.

Maybe if I had, I never would have arrived.

A duet, Dalton and me. The biggest challenge of my life, and its greatest joy, started with a voice at the drive-up window. But the road was not smooth. I guess it never is.

Chapter Eight
We Are Family

Not every adventure in my life has ended in victory. I've been surprisingly successful on the mat, on cinders, snow and water. But the rigors of athletic competition are nothing compared to the rigors of life. I could train for the slopes of Alta, but I couldn't train for the ups and downs of life. All I could do was try to learn.

Building a successful family life is a mountain that will humble you.

I Could Hear Her Blush

My next big challenge after winning in Oslo began with a sweet voice

"What do you need?"

The voice lingered in my mind.

It was a voice that came out of one of the most unromantic places imaginable. An intercom at a bank drive-through window. I couldn't get the voice out of my mind. It kept teasing my brain, creating a massive yearning in my heart.

I didn't really know at the time why I was so smitten with

the sound of that voice. All I knew was that I had to hear it again.

I'd been riding to the bank with my buddy, Charlie Theurer, with whom I'd been living with in Dallas for some time. We went through the drive-through so I could make a routine withdrawal. It was early morning and just about the last thing on my mind was romance. Nonetheless, this voice on the tiny speaker at the bank struck a chord I didn't know needed playing.

I told Charlie, "I have got to find out who the girl is on the other side of that voice. I just thought of a plan. We'll come back tomorrow, but this time we'll go through backwards and she'll be on my side." Charlie, being just slightly loony like me, thought that was a great idea.

The next day, Charlie whipped into the parking lot, made a U-turn and whipped right up to the drive-through window the wrong way. Five cars were pointed the right way and one car was pointed the wrong way. The girl behind the glass did a pretty good Michael Jordan, leaping about six feet off the floor, according to Charlie. A stunned look crossed her face.

"Uh, may ah hay-elp you?"

"Ah beg yoah pahdon," I said, trying my own Tex-ese on her.

"What do you need?" she repeated her question of yesterday.

I was ready for that one. I rehearsed in case she asked it again. "A phone number to go with the most beautiful voice I ever heard," I said.

She was shy. Painfully so. I could almost hear her blushing. I mean I couldn't see it. But if anyone ever blushed out-loud, so to speak, then it was this girl.

"What is your name, if I may ask?" I said.

"Jami." That's about all she said. Oh, she did also observe, "Ya'll are nuts."

I took it as a compliment — mostly because of the music and amusement and playfulness in her voice when she said it. She didn't give me her home number. But she said I could get in touch with her at the bank, if I wanted.

I called her the next day. And the next day. And the day after that.

Finally, I went into the bank on the fourth day and specifically asked that she wait on me. That finally got me her phone number. But if I have ever been a master of timing in other matters of life, this was what you'd call a disaster of timing. This was in March, 1987, my last day in Dallas before moving. I was taking a job in Schaumburg, Ill., a Chicago suburb, as a spokesman for the National Society to Prevent Blindness.

Jami agreed to go out with me the last day before I left.

I was hooked and I think she was, too. We started working the long-distance lines regularly. In fact, I'm pretty sure I heard Ma Bell dancing in the streets, once Jami and I fell for each other. And the airlines were pretty ecstatic, too.

This was not your typical, everyday, twenty-something courtship. I went at wooing Jami the way I went at wrestling or skiing. Full out. Though my home was supposed to be the Hyatt Hotel in Schaumburg, for the rest of that spring Jami and I lived the life of jet-setters, spending three of the four weekends a month together. Sometimes she flew to Chicago. Other times I flew to Dallas. In July, we flew into Toronto. Through the rest of summer and into autumn, we might be found in New York or Stamford, Conn., where we would stay with my friend Bill Pugliese and his daughter Christina. From there, we basked in the lights of Broadway and the Big Apple. We went to see "Cats", "42nd Street", "Starlight Express" — we saw them all. Every weekend was a romantic adventure. Then when the bad weather started hitting the Northeast on weekends, we headed south, to Florida.

Our favorite spot was the Tradewinds Resort on St. Petersburg Beach. We enjoyed walking on the beach, hearing the waves hit the shore, strolling in water ankle deep, other times fooling around in water much deeper — swimming, laughing. Once in a while I'd run into the occasional innocent bystander who'd get into my line of fire as we played in the water.

I loved the sound of the birds, the gentle breeze, the warm sun. And to top it off, I had a beautiful voice beside me. I often thought, "It doesn't get much better than this."

In January of 1988, I moved to the Cabana Club on Sand Key Beach, Fla., just south of Clearwater Beach. It was an exclusive area. Aside from the beautiful weather, the drawing card was to do some work with the Florida chapter of the Society to Prevent Blindness, whose director has become one of the best friends I've ever had in life. Dick Schultz.

Schultz and I met in the bathroom in Schaumburg at the National Society to Prevent Blindness headquarters in April, 1987. I was reaching around for a paper towel.

"I don't think we've met," he said.

He told me he was from Florida.

"Really? Get ready, man — I'm comin' your way," I said.

In Florida, Schultz became a mentor and a friend. We played hard there. Schultz taught me to shoot baskets and took me to the batting cage where he'd tell me when to swing. I connected big once in a while. That's what muscle memory can do if you're really in tune with your inner self. In exchange, I gave Schultz some insight about blind people. He didn't need much. He was a perceptive, sensitive person.

By February, Jami had moved from Dallas to Florida. Boy, I bet the airlines were really ticked off. She was twenty; I was twenty-five. We had all the energy in the world.

Jami got a job working in a local bank. That was her background....and her family's. She was a teller and handled new accounts. Her mother, Toye, and her step dad, "Mr. D," as we called him, both were involved in banking in Dallas.

Just about that same time, I started a job with Putnam Mutual Funds, traveling throughout the nation, speaking primarily to city-wide broker meetings. If you took out a map and found the 200 largest cities in America, I'd be in every single one at least once — many on several occasions — on behalf of Putnam. It was a little different wrinkle for a mutual funds company to help brokers remember them when it came time to invest the clients' money.

For the next several months, with Florida as our playground, Jami and I had a ball. Disney world. Sea world. Cypress Gardens. Busch Gardens. MGM Studios. Universal Studios. From Naples to Miami, we did it all. And being a kid at heart, I enjoyed each one thoroughly. Disneyworld's Space Mountain was probably my biggest ride. It gets rocking in there so fast in so many directions all at once. It's the thrust, the energy of it that I loved. If you can live on the edge, even at a theme park, well, I'm going to find it.

And through my work with Putnam there were trips to Hawaii. The Caribbean. I remember my first day at Putnam I met a dynamite wholesaler from the Boston area, Nick Corvinous. He said to me jokingly, "Give me a few months, we'll be in the Caribbean together."

He was right. We spent ten days on the island of St. John — Jami and I, Nick and his wife, Irene. I spoke at a few meetings. Then we did a lot of sailing and other water sports. I love the water. I love the outdoors.

One day we were out in two kayaks — one person per boat. They required a certain amount of balance. We got a little further out than maybe we should. Suddenly a quick little storm brewed up, not a severe one, but a little wind and a little rain. Enough to create a few waves. And it was pretty exciting for Nick, through his voice, to try to guide me back into shore. We weren't a great distance out, maybe 400 yards, but enough when it's your first day out, trying to negotiate this silly thing without rolling over, and the waves are beating up on you and the wind howling. Nick was a little hoarse when we got back to the dock.

The Fast Lane Always Ends

After that, Jami decided to take a little time off work, enabling her to travel with me even more. For a girl who'd never flown much before, starting out at 100,000 air miles a year was certainly a change of pace. But we wanted to build a life together and I wanted her to experience my lifestyle. I wanted her near.

Often she said, "I don't know how you find the energy after riding on three airplanes a day to be Mr. Wonderful when you get there."

I'm not sure I have the answer. I guess I've been blessed with a high drive and energy level.

During the fall of 1988, I bought the penthouse at the Cabana Club, situated right on the beach — with a balcony big enough to hold a small tennis match on. I found great solitude from sitting out there, just listening to the water, the wind and the other elements of nature that go with that part of the country. You didn't have to see this beauty to appreciate it. Your mind could wander. You could be creative. The water brings out a certain energy. I guess it taps into the core of who you really are. It makes you reflective.

Jami and I were married on that balcony overlooking the Gulf of Mexico at Sand Key. We had a warm little group of family and friends up there to witness our vows. Then we were off to New Zealand.

Once we tried to ride out a hurricane on that balcony. When the watch was announced, folks were asked to evacuate Sand Key and Belair Beach. Having that spirit of adventure Jami and I decided to hang out there. As the wind came whipping across the Gulf of Mexico, the sky was such a weird color, she told me. I stayed out there as long as humanly possible, but the wind got so intense I decided to retreat indoors. Jami had gone in several minutes earlier.

I wanted to stay and hear and absorb as much of this as I

could but then, yes, even for me common sense kicked in. Eighty-, ninety-, ninety-five-mile-per-hour winds ripped and pelted the shore line. Pieces of siding were literally torn from the side of our building. Jami told me the pieces were flying through the air like saucers or javelins.

The power was knocked out for a few days and parts of the road for the first day-and-a-half were impassable. We had enough supplies that we could hang out for a few days without feeling a pinch.

After the storm passed, we walked out on the balcony and then we went for a walk on the beach. Tons of stuff had washed up down there. Chunks of wood, seaweed, dead fish, sea shells — such an array of stuff all over this unspoiled beach. Parts of the sand were washed away.

It was a humble lesson of the incredible force of nature and just how much havoc it can play and how small we all are. Jami and I were soon to encounter another incredible force of nature.

In August of 1988, we found out Jami was pregnant. We were both ecstatic with the news. Of course we wondered whether it would be a boy or girl — not that it really mattered. I had a great job. We were happy. And this would be a wonderful addition. Towards the end of January of 1989, an ultrasound showed the baby was going to be a boy. As long as the baby was healthy it didn't really matter.

When Jami was eight months pregnant, I was invited on a whim to go to London, England, to speak for the Harris 3M Company. Jami had never been and didn't want to miss it for the world. With the doctors' permission, and all medical records on board with us, we headed to England for one week.

We had a ball, touring Buckingham Palace and Windsor Castle. Jami was a great trooper through it all, lugging the extra passenger around.

Near the end of the pregnancy, I used to put my ear on Jami's stomach and hear the baby kicking. To me this was fascinating. On the evening of March 29, Jami and I were just hanging out, catching the six o'clock, Channel 13 news, as we often did. They were just getting into the sports.

I jokingly put my head down by Jami's stomach and said, "Come on out, little guy. It's time."

I don't know if he was just waiting for an invitation or what. About twenty minutes later, Jami's water broke.

I immediately called my friend, Mike, who lived nearby. He came over and drove us to Bayfront Medical Center, a terrific hospital in St. Petersburg. Jami's contractions weren't close enough together so they had us walk the halls of the hospital for a couple of hours. We were excited. I think she was a little nervous and a little scared, but that was to be expected.

We'd taken Lamaze classes but we hadn't finished the course. We were two classes short of graduation. This little guy was coming just a tad earlier than expected.

I've never been a big fan of hospitals. I appreciate and understand their value. But just the smell and the sound of them makes me edgy. It's not really my cup of tea, unless absolutely necessary. A lot of that goes back to my spending some of my earliest days in hospitals — pain and grief, largely.

But in this place I was hearing a new sound. A new vibe. My adrenaline was pumping. This night the hospital represented life, not death nor despair. This was going to be a great experience, although at the time I don't think you could have convinced Jami of that. Her contractions came much closer and at five-forty-eight a.m., March 30, Dalton Shea MacFarlane was born.

He was seven pounds, six ounces.

As Dalton's head was coming out, Jami's doctor told me to put a glove on.

"Come here and feel the head," she said.

I felt Dalton coming out.

I was awestruck as she laid Dalton on Jami's stomach. I put my head down there tenderly for my first face-to-face encounter with my new son.

He peed on me.

I suppose it was just his way of saying, "Hello, Dad. Nice to see ya." Or maybe because I couldn't see him, he did it to let me feel him. Thanks son.

"Would you like to cut the cord, Pop?" the doctor asked me.

I hadn't even thought about it. She handed me the scissors. I cut the cord and a new life was about to begin. Not only for Dalton, but for us as well.

I remember sitting in the hospital, holding Dalton, shortly after he was born. I'd always known nature does some pretty incredible things that I'd tried to visualize. But for a blind person, this had to top them all. This was something you could hold, touch, feel, squeeze, hug and cuddle. Furthermore, it was a part of me.

As Jami was sleeping. I was sitting beside her bed in a rocking chair, rocking little Dalton, who was sleeping on my chest. This was better than any gold medal, championship or victory that I ever won. And if I had pinpointed the highest moment in my life so far, undoubtedly this was it.

Dalton was badly jaundiced at first and had to spend about four days in the hospital. After the second day, when Jami was released, it was an enormously empty feeling as we walked out of the hospital together, neither one of us saying a word to each other, without our little boy.

I refused to go back to Sand Key Beach. I would stay in a Hilton Hotel near by. I would not stay away from the hospital for more than two hours at a time. I probably spent sixteen to eighteen hours a day there, with or near Dalton.

The doctors assured us it was nothing serious. Thank God they were right. Dalton and Mom were resting in the hospital that first day; my friend Mike and I went to buy him a gift. Oh sure, I was a little zealous. I walked into the hospital with this big boom box.

I didn't totally miss the mark — there were a few rattles and things. But the nurses got a big kick out of that boom box.

Inner Vision

I must say over the years, Dalton has been a little spoiled, to say the least. My intense travel schedule gets me feeling a little guilty that I'm not home with him. Not that you can buy a kid's love, because we have a dynamite relationship, but it always makes me feel good to bring home some special thing that I think he'll enjoy.

In the first two months of Dalton's life, my travel schedule was minimal. I think I was gone four days those two months. I hung out helping with Dalton, bathing him, changing his diapers. Jami used to laugh at me because, whereas a sighted person may use one or two baby wipes to make a clean sweep of the area down there, I would grab about ten of them in my hand — to make sure I got all of it and minimalize the risk of getting much on me. I'm sure baby wipe companies wish there were more blind fathers out there.

Like all parents, I got up lots of nights to rock Dalton when he was fussy. If those early weeks and months have anything to do with bonding, maybe that's why he and I are so close today. I spent an enormous amount of time with him then. It's so important for a father to have that relationship with his kids.

With Dalton's arrival, the complicated life Jami lived with just me was getting more complicated. Living with me can be a challenge. As much as I think of myself as an independent person, a person who lives with me will wind up doing more. For example, she had to do all the driving, although I do volunteer occasionally. When it comes to shopping for clothes, I was at her mercy. I'm just glad she wasn't color blind. Under Jami's care, people began commenting on how smartly I was dressed.

Of course, she had to read the menu to me in restaurants. She was pressed to describe things to me, the inside of the restaurant or the scenery when we drove. She had to be extraordinarily organized at home. If she was finished with the vacuum cleaner, for example, she had to put it back where it belonged. If she didn't, I might be hovering over it two minutes later in mid-flight.

I tried to hold up my end, doing dishes, vacuuming, making beds, laundry. And cooking. I can hold my own in the kitchen, though I'm no master chef.

Soon, we were all ready for a vacation. Toward the end of June, when Dalton was three months old, the three of us took a cruise to the Caribbean. Barbados. St. Thomas. St. Lucia. St. Martens. Dalton was a big hit, especially with the older people.

Dalton started flying at a young age. He was probably about one month old when we flew to Dallas to visit Jami's parents.

In December of 1989, we found out that Jami was pregnant again. On July 2, 1990, Raven Ashley MacFarlane was born.

Eight pounds, eight ounces.

She was a healthy and happy baby. It was such a delight to bring her home. Now with the four of us it seemed like the perfect scenario. This was the way it was supposed to be — first a boy, then a girl.

LEARNING FROM VICTORY IS EASIER...

My whole life had been a struggle to be normal, to fit into the sighted world. I rode my bike just like the other boys, got in trouble with teachers just like the other boys, hunted and fished with my dad, just like other boys. I grew up to be independent, to swim and dance and fall in love, just like everybody else. Being blind, I always wanted to have the life everyone else had. Well, eventually, I got it. Not just the good, but also the bad. The sweet with the bitter.

By the summer of 1989, the relationship between Jami and I was getting a little strained. Perhaps because of my travel schedule with Putnam. Perhaps the demands on my time for free-lance speaking engagements outside my regular work were taking their toll.

A year later, when Dalton was eighteen months, the strain became painfully apparent. One day, it was about eight a.m., I was having Dick Schultz drive me to the airport. My penthouse was on the eighth floor, so I had my bag in my hand and I was walking across our marble floor in the foyer to go down the elevator.

Dalton was behind, chasing me.

"No, daddy," he was saying.

"No daddy. No daddy. Don't go."

As I reached the door, he was hanging onto my pant leg.

"Daddy stay. Daddy stay," he repeated over and over.

He was crying and screaming, very loudly. As Jami came to get him, he clung to me. I dropped my bag and bent over and picked him up, as a boulder rose in my throat. My eyes were watering. He coiled himself around my neck like a snake.

He wouldn't let go.

It's in this instance, you want to say, "The heck with work." You almost forget that it's necessary to survive. I was wishing that I could take him with me. Of course, that wasn't possible.

As I handed him to Jami, picked up my bag and stepped into the hallway outside the door, heading for the elevator, I could still hear Dalton's wailing. The sound cut through the walls and through the door and through my coat and chest and soul.

"Daddy! Daddy!"

As the elevator headed down, I thought to myself, this is a lifestyle I had chosen. But knowing I'd chosen it didn't make leaving easier. So painful. So much guilt.

Sure, my career had its exciting moments, but I didn't realize now with kids it would produce this Niagara of guilt pouring down on me as well. I rationalized that the good things I can provide outweigh some of those horribly negative moments.

As Dalton has grown older, he has begun to understand that my job involves a lot of travel. And he's been a very fortunate boy to reap the benefits of my friendships with celebrities and executives — as sometimes he gets to go to some pretty cool places. Like hanging out in the dugout with the Toronto Blue Jays during batting practice before a game in SkyDome. Or getting into the dressing room of the Hartford Whalers when they visit Maple Leaf Gardens in Toronto.

Though Dalton and I were working on our relationship in those early years, the same thing could not be said for Jami and me. By December of 1990, we both knew we were seriously struggling. I suppose we were looking for a change of pace. We decided to move to Maryville, Tenn. The foothills of the Smoky Mountains.

Dick tried to tell me that it wasn't going to work.

"Craig, the issue isn't where you live, but how you're living," he said. "A change in location is not going to fix the relationship."

He was right.

It was the old Great Escape ploy to solving personal problems, the idea that a geographical cure could be effective. I guess Jami and I thought it could stop the bleeding or maybe put our relationship on a different road.

We spent Christmas in Tennessee. New Years of 1991 came and went. We weren't so much fighting or arguing. Rather, we had just grown apart.

Jami and I had different ways of looking at life. And now some of our interests, dreams and aspirations had changed even more. Now that I had kids, I was even more driven and focused to succeed in my chosen field of public speaking.

Think of it this way: For a blind person, to a certain degree, your options are limited. I'm not a guy who accepts limits easily, but fact are facts when it comes to employment.

You can't even get a job flipping hamburgers if you're blind. You can't get a job driving a truck or delivering the mail, or working construction in the summertime. I had a great career. But I had to work at it. I couldn't take it for granted. To complicate things just a little, I decided at the same time, I would hand in my resignation with Putnam Mutual Funds.

I had been there three years. They treated me well. They treated me fair. But I was looking for a change and I think that maybe says a little about my living-on-the-edge outlook. I wasn't concerned. I still had my free-lance speeches, which would certainly tide me over as I sought out something more permanent and challenging.

Needless to say, I did put myself into a financial crunch, and on January 18, 1991, Jami and I parted ways.

We had talked about it and felt it was best for both of us. Raven would stay with Jami. She was just a little over six months old. Dalton, who was twenty-one months old, would come with me.

The first thing that may come to you is why did we split up the kids. One reason is that Dalton was such a daddy's boy. Jami and her parents and everyone else we knew thought that it would be too traumatic for Dalton to not be with me that much.

Jami was going back to Dallas. I was going to Canada with my parents. My mother had just retired from teaching school for some thirty-eight years. We figured it was the best thing for Dalton because of my travel schedule. Who else would I leave him with? Who else would I trust? No nanny could give him the love and the care that Grandma and Grandpa would. Dalton and I have been there ever since.

Toye and Mr. D., Jami's Mom and Dad, were always wonderful to me. They were great people who believed in me — and even do to this day.

I remember that I left — January 18, 1991. Mr. D, driving Dalton and me and our luggage to the Knoxville Airport. On the way out the door I hugged and kissed Raven. And then Toye. Then Jami.

And I guess in this split moment you do become a little overwhelmed. Because even though we were parting ways, she was the mother of my children. Was and is.

As I held her for the last time, I supposed it would have been easy to change my mind. But I knew as much as it hurt and pained me so deep inside, that this would be better for us in the long run.

It would be hard. I knew Dalton would miss his mother. As we rode to the airport, it should have and could have been a time for reflection. But at twenty-one months, Dalton was a ball of fire and occupied much of my time and energy, as I was looking after his well-being and whereabouts.

We had to change planes in Chicago. I didn't want him running off on me, so that was a challenge. We flew into Sault Ste. Marie, Michigan, or Kinross, eighteen miles south of The Soo, where my parents would pick me up.

If ever there was a dark period in my life, this had to be the back of the cave, the darkest.

Getting divorced.

Stepping out of my job.

Experiencing financial difficulties.

All within the same three-week time period.

It has to get better, I thought. It certainly couldn't get any worse. How bad could it really get?

But when I got home to Canada, maybe it was just touching my feet on home soil that made me feel better. I was flooded with the comforting idea that things were going to be ok.

"I'm glad that's all behind me," I said, when I got home.

I didn't mean it in a callous way. I meant it in the only way I could deal with the situation, by beginning, that second, to look ahead.

During the first part of March, 1991, I flew to Clearwater, Fla., to go before the judge. As I was the one who filed for divorce, I had to appear in court.

It was brief.

A few questions came from the judge. Then he asked, "How're you going to support and look after your son, since you're blind?"

My lawyer immediately piped up, "Your honor, I object. That's discrimination."

His honor stamped the paper. Slid it across the big desk.

"Very well," he said. "You're excused."

"Thank you. Next case."

All of a sudden, what seemed to be a perfect family, would not have the typical storybook ending.

What did I learn from this tough moment in my life? What lesson could I give others from the depths of divorce? I'm stumped, to be honest. It's easier learning from victory than from defeat. I guess in the end, I learned there are some roads you can't conquer. My career wouldn't go away. It was my career, the way I lived, the thing that made me go. We couldn't make our love last. The stars weren't lined up right.

What I did learn is how to be a good father. Dalton and I have forged out a good life for ourselves in Canada. When I'm gone, I'm gone. When I'm home, I'm completely involved. I'm in the Grey Zone of fathering. I guess that's what I learned.

I have not remarried. It's not that I don't want to. But my career and Dalton — and not so much in that order — have certainly taken priority. I feel I have so much to share, so much to give, so much to offer someone in a marriage.

But I know that life is very much a two-way street. And it's nice at the end of a hard day on the road to say, "Hi, sweetie, how was your day? What'd you do?" And share with them what I've done as well.

I think of that sharing, caring and understanding — and most importantly that ability to communicate with one another — has to be the common thread in any relationship.

When the communication breaks down, things start to fall apart, start to crumble. I suppose, looking back, that's partly what happened to Jami and me. She became a little more withdrawn. She was a reasonably quiet person to begin with. But being blind, I'm not going to read your facial expressions. I'm not going to read your eyes. You have to talk to me. Certainly that was not the only breakdown. In every relationship that goes bad people are quick to point the finger. I try not to do that. I shoulder my part of the responsibilities and blame.

The next time, if I get the chance, I hope to do better.

And I will.

*My lifelong passion for music put me in the studios with some
great musician and on the road with a band of my own. OK, so
we played Hastings, Nebraska, not New York City. It was still
rock-n-roll, and I loved it.*

212

Chapter Nine
Music Man

I had no idea it was Huey Lewis stepping into my next dream.

With my athletic career behind me, I could have spent the rest of my life on the road making speeches and motivating people or sitting in the easy chair at home. But my life was not destined for comfort or complacency. It was marked from the beginning for restlessness, the kind of restlessness that pushes for excellence and for the next mountain to conquer. In this case, conquer is not the right word. I didn't really conquer the music industry; instead, I learned to enjoy the climb and focus on the part of my dream I could control.

The music industry is a tough mountain to crack. I dreamed once of platinum and gold records, of endless tours and a rock star entourage. I didn't realize that dream. But, I did get to record my music, and in some pretty special company. And I got to play it, too; maybe it was Boise, Idaho, instead of Madison Square Garden. But being on stage, wired to the amps, with people dancing in the aisles, it's more or less all the same.

I remember where it started. I was at Fantasy Studios in Berkeley, Calif. It was 1 a.m. and the impossible had come to pass. I was living my dream of recording an album.

Recording an album is something I'd wished, hoped and yearned for since I started squeaking and squawking with the clarinet, trombone, trumpet and several other instruments in grade school and high school. Now I was in California, making it happen. I was walking the same halls where Credence Clearwater were fortunate sons, where Journey's lights went down in the city, where The Pointer Sisters got so excited, where Jefferson Starship met Sarah and Eddie Money went to shakin'.

These superstars all recorded their albums at Fantasy Studios. Gold and platinum albums comprised the wallpaper for the foyer and hallways.

So now I'm out here, it's 1985, and I'm taking a break from recording my album, "Love is Blind." By now I am well schooled on the drill. It's cheaper recording at night. And when you're recording at night, most of the work is done from about six p.m. through eight the next morning.

And along about 1 a.m., I go down to the commissary looking to satisfy a serious hunger. I'm standing there and in walks a guy rattling his keys. I assumed it was the janitor, doing his nightly duties.

"Excuse me, sir," I said, flagging him down. "Could you please show me which one of these buttons is the popcorn?"

I still hadn't figured out the vending-machine there. A vending machine may look like an innocent contraption, but it can be a minor nightmare for a blind guy. You punch B-seven to get a Snickers and wind up with Certs.

The janitor was quite willing to help me find the popcorn buttons.

"Once the popcorn tumbled out, I needed a bit more help getting it popped. I hadn't mastered the geography of the commissary yet.

"If you'd be kind enough to stick this thing in the microwave for me and get it rolling," I said, "I'd be really grateful. I'm not familiar with this particular one."

He said sure. The popcorn went in, he hit a few buttons and the microwave fired up.

We stood there and chatted about life in the San Francisco area. We talked about sports. We talked about how, on certain occasions, these nights can seem so long, especially when you string about eighteen or twenty of them together. Sleep gets a little thin. I've never been able to sleep in the day much, even in the best of times, so needless to say I was looking a little haggard. I figured the janitor would understand. I figured he had probably gotten good at sleeping during the day all these years on the graveyard shift.

He laughed and agreed it'd been a long day. Cool janitor, I thought. Got a lot on the ball.

The popcorn was smelling good. I don't think either one of us realized it had stopped popping. Those bags are supposed to go in for about three minutes, give or take. This one may have been in for six, seven, eight minutes...God knows how long.

All of a sudden we hear this huge explosion.

As my new friend rushed over to the microwave, I jokingly said, "That was one huge kernel, wasn't it?"

He opened the microwave and said, "Oh, God, guess there is a time limit on this. Let me help clean this crud up."

He got some paper towels and we went to work, swiping the popcorn out of the microwave. A few minutes later, we dared to nuke another bag of popcorn. I was finally leaving with a reasonably well-cooked bag. I thought I should introduce myself as a common courtesy before I left.

I stuck out my hand and said, "Oh. I'm sorry, I never introduced myself. I'm Craig MacFarlane."

He shook my hand firmly

"It's an honor to meet you. I'm Huey Lewis."

I think my mouth must have dropped to my shoe tops.

"I'll walk back with you," he said.

He hung out in the control room with me for awhile. I was working on a vocal track and he invited me down to his studio the next night to sit in on part of his session. Rapping in the middle of the night with Huey Lewis was the kind of scene I could only have conjured up in my wildest imagination back at the school for the blind in Brantford.

That's exactly where the foray into the music industry began. But that doesn't mean I didn't have crazy dreams. I'd always loved music right from the start at W. Ross MacDonald and — like any kid — I envisioned myself going platinum and making millions.

THE TRUCKERS' DON'T GO FAR, BUT MY DREAM DOES

W. Ross MacDonald wasn't a bad place to dream. There was a heavy emphasis on music there. The music wing was first-class, with approximately twenty individual practice studios, a piano in each. You could learn other instruments as well if you wanted. And when your skills got good enough, you could play in the school band. Of course, we read Braille music. Since most instruments take two hands to play, you would have to memorize your pieces, probably four bars at a time.

By the time I was in the seventh grade and in a practice studio, I'd much rather play a little Elton John — "Yellow Brick Road" — or something like that, as opposed to that other, more traditional stuff they were trying to teach me.

I started taking piano lessons in the fourth grade. For the next few years I would continue to learn the piano, although excelling more in the rock 'n roll vein than in Mozart or Chopin.

In fifth grade I started taking clarinet lessons and in the beginning I think I sounded more like some rare bird species than a clarinet player. But I quickly caught on. It didn't take me long to realize music was in my blood.

In sixth grade, a few of us put together a rock 'n roll band. Eric, Kevin and Kenny were in the band. We played Beatles tunes, Rolling Stones, Elton John. I primarily played piano and did some vocals. We were far from sounding like the Beatles.

As one of my friends put it, "I walked by the studio last night and it sounded like two cats fightin' in there."

We started out calling ourselves The Truckers. God knows why. Maybe it was because when people heard us they tended to say, "Hit the road, Jack."

But our band was always good for a few laughs. Our makeshift studio was a tight fit and when Kenny had the drums set up, it was not uncommon for one of us to blunder into the cymbals and send them flying.

One time I actually knocked a microphone stand over on Kenny when he was playing I bonged him on top of the head. I think we were doing The Eagles' "You Can't Hide Your Lyin' Eyes." I guess in this case the name should have been, "You Can't Hide Your Achin' Head."

Kevin played guitar. Eric played a little guitar and some keyboards. I played keyboards and sometimes I just did vocals. So sometimes I was jumping around the stage with the mike in my hand, feeling the beat, and that's what I was doing when I hit Kenny in the head with the microphone stand.

I guess when you're a blind band you've gotta tone down that Mick Jagger, funky-chicken, strutting-all-over-the-stage stuff. Maybe hold off on those Temptations moves when you can't see. And the life you save may be your own. I've whomped into speakers and pianos and the odd fellow band-member. Maybe we needed a traffic cop more than a bass guitarist.

But we jumped around anyway. Just because it wasn't something you'd expect blind musicians to do didn't prevent us from doing it. In fact, we might have done it because we weren't supposed to.

In grade seven, I was playing clarinet in our school band. As a note of interest, Jeff Healey, from the movie, "Roadhouse," who recorded the hit single, "Angel Eyes," played drums in that same band. Jeff was a couple of grades behind me.

When I attended Central Algoma Secondary School, my music career expanded. I started taking trumpet in grade nine.

Most of the kids at that age are just learning how to play a band instrument so I didn't want to stick with the clarinet, which I already knew. I wanted to tackle something new.

Later that year I played the trumpet in the school orchestra, the fifty-piece concert band. Some of these pieces, I must admit, were a little drab. Some of the band pieces dragged on forever.

In tenth grade, I switched to trombone. I guess I looked on music as a challenge and wanted to master as many instruments as I could. But playing in a band where I was the only blind person was truly a rush. Although, I must say, memorizing all those pieces became a bit of a nightmare.

I loved it when we played special events such as graduation or Christmas programs. Maybe I enjoyed them too much. During the Christmas concert when I was in tenth grade at Central Algoma, in the middle of a song, I opened the spit valve and blew spit all over the heads of the flute section in front of me — all girls. Of course, I did this without missing a beat between songs. I blamed it disgustedly on the fellow beside me.

"How could you do such a thing? That's very rude?" I said indignantly. He took a lot of heat from the row in front of him.

The trombone was a perfect instrument for a trickster. I figured out how to do race-car noises, "Mmmmmweeeowwwwwmm!" or I would do airplane noises, "Nnnnnnyyaaarooom!" as I slid from note to note in the middle of a song. This totally maddened the band director, Mr. Ricci, who thought I could do no wrong and always sharply scolded someone else in the trombone section for the noise — as I bit in on my cheeks to keep from laughing.

When I returned to W. Ross MacDonald School for the Blind in Brantford for my junior and senior years, I continued to switch between trumpet and trombone in the school band. Of course our band was much smaller than the one at Central Algoma. But there were still great opportunities for creating havoc.

We always enjoyed those nights when our dear old friend and foil, Mr. Adams, the blind music teacher, was on duty. We were just too much for him. For blind kids, a studio might be silent some of the time while they were reading and memorizing Braille music. And he didn't have time to investigate all twenty studios. He had a habit of standing down at the end of the hall and not marching around.

So we got to know that pattern. Heck, we'd just come in and he'd check our names off the list.

"Hi, Mr. Adams."

"Is that you, Craig.?"

"Yeah, it sure is, how ya doin', my friend."

"Oh, great. You're in studio seven."

"Thank you very much, Mr. Adams."

Then I'd just cruise right by the studio and never go in. I'd just head right outside and leave. He'd never know. At least I don't think he ever knew.

I continued to play in various little rock bands throughout high school playing school dances in my junior and senior years. And during all that time I kept dreaming harder of recording an album. But as I got older, I realized more and more that unless you get a very lucky break, it's probably not going to happen for you. Even if you've got the enormous amount of money it takes, and you've got the time and you're willing to put in the effort, you've still got to be visited by a lot of luck.

What Am I Doing Here in Studio C? Enjoying Myself Completely, That's What

Once I moved to America, getting a job and surviving were the top priorities. Recording was in a back room of my mind. But in 1985 after the victory at Oslo, I started stretching for that dream. I started looking for a producer to help me record an album. I made a phone-call out to Fantasy Studios in Berkeley, California I told them what I was trying to accomplish and they put me in touch with Elliot Mazer. Elliot had done some stuff with Janis Joplin, Neil Young, Tina Turner, and Linda Ronstadt, just to mention a few.

I was fortunate, to say the least, that we hit it off. And it wasn't long after that phone call, that Elliot was at the Houstonian Club in Houston where I was living, meeting with me, finalizing plans to record an album.

I never envisioned so much work went into recording an entire project like that. I'm not talking days. How about months? When you're talking about writing songs from scratch, putting the studio musicians together and then recording it, mixing it, pressing it, getting the cover designed and photographed, the liners and so forth, it's like maneuvering an army. And I'm sure I'm passing over this lightly. A million details have to be worked out between each of those steps.

In 1985, Elliot and I put together some studio musicians to help me record my first album at Fantasy Studios. The bass player was Ross Valery from Journey. On keyboards was a guy whose nickname was "Banana," and who played with the Youngbloods. In addition, some of the keyboards would be played by Tim Gorman, who played on one of The Who tours. If that's not enough, some background vocals were laid down by none other than Eddie Money.

Eddie didn't do this because of me, obviously — I mean, who was this nobody from the Canadian sticks? He did it out of friendship for Elliot.

I remember the first day, walking into the Fantasy Studios. There were four separate studios housed in this complex under the same roof, so four different sessions could be going on at once.

In one studio, Steve Perry was finishing the vocals on an album for Journey. If memory serves me right, it was the

"Raised on Radio" project. Huey Lewis was in Studio D. I think he was working on "Hip to Be Square." Studio A was occupied by Eddie Money part of the time and Jeffrey Osborne for the other part.

I was assigned Studio C. My first thought was, "What am I doing here, hanging out with all the big boys?" But I learned during break, lounging around in the commissary, that Elliot had informed most of these guys of my athletic prowess. Steve Perry seemed particularly interested in my snow-skiing and water-skiing adventures, and how I maneuvered around, even in the studio halls.

The halls of the Fantasy studio had to be among the trickier athletic feats I've ever tried to perform, actually. The halls were always so crowded, you had to shuck-and-jive like Barry Sanders in heavy traffic. Chairs were strewn around. People were moving equipment in and out and leaving it in the hall. Speakers. Amps. Microphones. Walking around for anyone was quite an adventure, much less for a blind guy.

One time I knocked over a stack of wooden crates and as I did, Eddie Money was walking around a corner. I scored a direct hit on Eddie's shoulder. He shook it off with a laugh.

"Son, don't worry about it," he said. "I knock stuff over around here all the time."

The control room of a studio probably looks like the control panel of a space shuttle. So many buttons, knobs, sliding controls, amplifiers all over the place, speakers large and small, keyboards, microphones, bass guitars, various stacks and racks of special effects. The list goes on. Couches and a few chairs are always scattered around for people to sit on and listen and monitor.

I'd always heard about how a recording is made by layering various tracks but I was surprised to see it in action. In fact, what I discovered is that most of the music on a recording goes down one track at a time. I might have an advantage doing something like that because I've got a mind like a steel trap. When I hear something, or I make a list, or I have to remember a telephone number, I can rarely rely on writing it down, reading it back to myself. Most often, I have to memorize. Keeps the mind sharp. I can usually just remember what's gone down before, every word, every note. That helps when you work piecemeal.

I remember wearing my headphones out there, doing my lead vocal tracks. It was weird to stand in a studio and think of all the great artists who stood in the same spot before me and surely would after. Maybe I hoped some of their talent would rub off on me. But I realized it doesn't work that way. So much of this is up to you.

You can get any mix you want in your headphones. More drums. Less guitar. More bass. Background vocals higher? No background vocals. It's your call. The engineer is there to make you happy and to try to stimulate your best performance.

After a couple months working at Fantasy Studios, the album was finished. I called it, "Love Is Blind." I would not land any big record deal with the project. In fact, it was never officially released. The "timing" wasn't right, I kept hearing. But it was a heck of an education. It was an album even today, of which I'm very proud.

Then in 1987, in Toronto, I recorded another album. I owe a lot of credit to Bill Pugliese, a guy who owned Stamford Insulation in Stamford, Connecticut. He lived around the corner from Andy Robustelli, the former New York Giant Football Hall of Famer, who had been helping me sharpen my speaking skills and market myself in other ways.

Bill lent considerable financial support to my second recording attempt in Toronto. We produced ten songs. Although this album was never officially pressed, these were some of the best songs I've ever written and recorded.

"Just the Thought of Losing You."

"You Set Me on Fire."

"Listen to Me, Baby."

I had financial help trying to get both albums off the ground. With "Love Is Blind" I had financial help from a lot of friends who believed I could conquer the music world the way I did athletic events. On the second album I had Bill Pugilese. And, of course, I used a huge amount of my own cash on all these projects. The primary underwriter was me. "Love Is Blind" exceeded well over $50,000 to produce. The Toronto project probably was more in the $20,000 range.

I took one more shot at the album thing with a third recording session. "Inner Vision" cost another $50,000. This album was produced by a dear friend of mine, Arnold Lanni, who was a star in his own right. He wrote "When I'm With You." Which was a No. 1 Billboard hit, recorded by a group called Sheriff, for which Arnie played keyboards. Then he was the lead singer of a group called Frozen Ghost, which had several big hits in Canada.

Arnie was an awesome producer. More so than anyone else I worked with in the music business. He was honest, which seemed to be a rarity in that industry. Compassionate. Understanding. And he always put my best interests first.

"Hey, if this is coming out of your own pocket, I don't want to spend a lot of money on this project," he would say. "Let's try to get the best results for the least amount possible." He owned the studio so he was talking my language.

The "Inner Vision" album never would have come out the way it did if not for the generosity, understanding, patience and the commitment of Arnold Lanni. The album was recorded at Arnyard Studios — I love that name — in Toronto. Many days we worked sixteen to eighteen hours. It was absolutely grueling, which ran the gamut of high and low emotions.

But to live out this dream was certainly worth every ounce of energy I could muster. To mix the album, we brought over Steven Taylor from England. He'd worked with people like Rod

Stewart, Tina Turner and RUSH. He was one of the industry's premier engineers.

The album is one I'm very proud of today, and was sold in parts of Ontario. And it was the foundation for my Inner Vision Tour during the summer of 1993. The tour was something that I'll never forget, playing in front of hundreds of people a night, sometimes thousands at fairgrounds and venues like that.

A LITTLE DREAMIN' GOES A LONG WAY, WHEN YOU PAY ATTENTION TO THE ROAD

Not making a bigger splash in the music industry was difficult for me to swallow. I was used to going where I set my compass to go. But I learned an important lesson in my musical excursions: I learned to enjoy the experience no matter what the outcome. Great athletes rarely have to learn this lesson. They get the experience and they get to coast around victory lane. But musicians often do great work that stalls before they can get it out on the track.

What I learned is to enjoy making the music. The Inner Vision Tour would provide just the stage for living that lesson.

The tour was, well... wild. One night we might be in Sebring, Florida. The next in Norfolk, Virginia. Then Jennings and Lake Charles, Louisiana. Then, tiny dots on the map like Hastings, Nebraska. Then, Blackfoot, Idaho, for Pete's sake. Sometimes we'd appear in hotter spots, true resort towns like Vail, Colorado.

By then I'd started working for Edward Jones Financial Group, traveling the country extensively, speaking primarily to high schools and groups of youth.

Edward Jones was kind enough to go along with my idea of doing these musical concerts in conjunction with my speaking engagements. That's how I wound up in most of these towns singing. I'd come in, do radio-television-newspaper publicity, do the musical gig and speak.

Much of our tour, we traveled in style in a thirty-six-foot motor home donated by David Hayes, the Bentonville, Arkansas, representative for Jones. Actually, I didn't care how we traveled or where we went. It all seemed good to me. I was in my element wherever we were.

On lots of nights I would sing with a wireless mike so I could run around the stage. That's a small record, I think. It's something I've never heard of a totally blind person doing before. It wasn't that scary for me; don't forget I had once traveled fifty-miles-per-hour downhill on snow-skis. I wasn't going to sit docilely at a piano or perch jauntily on a stool or drool into the mike dreamily standing in one place. No, man. I wanted to put it all out there. We had a few cords on the stage, taped down, kind of in a grid to let me know where I was. But taking things to the edge the way I always seem to do, means things didn't always go the way they were planned.

One night, during a show in Boise, Idaho, my guitar player, Sammie, was in the middle of a solo. It was, as he would say, his "two or three moments of glory" in an evening. The spotlight was on him.

I got a little disoriented, maybe a little dizzy from running around so much. I thought I was somewhere on the stage where I wasn't. I accidentally ran into Sammie and, like Gordie Howe hip-checking some luckless defensemen into the cheap seats, I launched my guitar player into the audience.

Wireless guitar and all.

Not a pretty sound. Or sight.

I heard a few words about that after the concert, as I recall. Sammie accused me "hogging the stage" and ruining his solo. I hardly did it on purpose.

"I just wanted to see if you could fly, Sammie, and still play that thing while doing it," I teased. He did not share my humor on that occasion.

Another time I hurt nobody but myself. I went boppin' up to a speaker and tried to stand on it, only to wind up doing a swan dive off the stage and into the crowd. People caught me in mid-dive, fortunately, let me down and I kept on singing like it was somehow planned that way.

The following day, Michael Theisen, a dear friend of mine from Sault Ste. Marie, who was our road manager for the tour that summer and I were walking down the street in Boise towards our hotel after grabbing a bite to eat. Our tour bus, which we had chartered — one formerly used by the Oak Ridge Boys — was coming back to the hotel to pick us up. It was just driving past.

"There's our bus," Mike said.

And as it passed, he added, "It's also on fire."

Flames were shooting out of the back from the engine. Mike was yelling and sprinting toward the front of the bus to let the driver know. Thankfully, he'd just come to a stoplight.

I could smell smoke filling up my nostrils. People were scrambling from their cars to help. A fire extinguisher was grabbed from the front part of the bus and shot onto the flames. A few moments later, the fire was brought under control. But, wow, did it ever stink.

It burned the wires on the bus. We were laid up an extra day or two until we could get another one. Thankfully, we had a break in our schedule. It could have been much worse, as all of our equipment — guitars, amplifiers, speakers — was on the bus, loaded in the bays.

We got moving again and on we went, rolling up the states. Arkansas. Louisiana. Texas. Idaho. Virginia. Ohio. And then our swing into Florida and Georgia. It was all fascinating to me.

One special night in Boise, Idaho, matter of fact, I got to meet one of the giants of the music industry — and a heck of a nice guy — Steven Tyler of Aerosmith.

Mike took it upon himself to get this done. He went up to the building where Aerosmith was playing, didn't see a security guard, went down a hallway, up another, turned left, hung a right and the next thing you know he's walking into a room with the roadie tuning Joe Perry's guitar. He would use several during the show.

The guy looked at him and said, "How'd you get in here?"

Mike said, "Walked."

Mike went into his spiel about me and what a big fan I was of Steven and the guy says, "No problem. Bring him back after the show."

That's how my friendship with Steven began. I have run into him on numerous occasions since. I know you often hear about Steven Tyler, the wild and crazy guy. But all the times I've been with him, he's been quite down-to-earth, warm and always caring enough to ask specific questions and pay attention when you're talking to him.

In fact, Steven's the type of person who'll always give you a hug when he meets you. I remember the first time, him stepping back saying, "God, you've got a strong back. You're built like a horse."

Mike was fabulous keeping our band all together. Mike Pelleran played base. Mike Saracusa was on drums. The great Flyin' Sammie was the lead guitarist. And Mike Rowland played rhythm guitar. The Inner Vision Tour lasted eleven weeks and about eleven million interviews. So many people all the time. Signs saying we were coming to town, welcoming us.

Not bad for a band that never had a hit.

I think that music is a tremendous outlet. It's a great way to express your innermost feelings. When you're happy, when you're sad. When people listen to the words off the Inner Vision album, there are a few songs they often comment on.

A few of those songs seem to reflect a relationship gone bad.

Lines like, "I'll find love again, but she won't be like you." Or, "Your heart has no conscience." I just kind of smile, because deep inside I know that music is a powerful way to communicate with so many people.

If the feeling is true, if the feeling is pure, chances are many people have shared that same emotion at one time or another in their lives. So songs can be written for other people to understand and take to heart. If songs connect that way, you probably have yourself a winner.

If I had to categorize the style of music, I suppose the Inner Vision album was kind of in the Bryan Adams vein. Bryan is someone I came to know in the spring of 1983 while he was touring the United States, opening for Journey. I was living with Gordie Howe. Gordie got me tickets to the show at the Hartford Civic Center. Through Gordie, I got backstage passes.

I met Bryan's road manager, Graham Langdon and his personal manager, Bruce Allan. They were always kind to me. They brought me back to meet Bryan. For the next four consecutive nights, I was backstage after Bryan's opening act, hanging out in the dressing room with them.

That's back when Bryan's songs "Cuts Like a Knife" and "Straight From the Heart" were hits and a big part of his set. I suppose indirectly on the third night I was partly to blame for Bryan's getting the first stitches he ever got in his life, he later told me.

He offered me a bottle of Perrier water and as he took it out of the ice chest it was in, it slipped out of his hand and smashed onto the floor. The guitar player, Keith, reached down to pick up some of the larger chunks of glass to throw into the trash. As he brought one of the pieces up, Bryan happened to be walking past to hand me another bottle of Perrier water.

Keith didn't see him and the glass sliced Bryan's arm for about five stitches worth. I felt bad about it.

Bryan and I stayed in touch over the years. One year I got a

Christmas card from him saying, "You better appreciate this card. I especially went out and bought it for you myself." The front of the card was this rough-feeling surface. From a tactile standpoint, it was the roughest, humpiest, lumpiest card in the store.

"It was the closest thing to Braille I could find," he said.

His success has been a great inspiration to me. And Bryan has helped remind me just how rugged the musical terrain is out there. Sometimes I think it's a hundred times rougher than skiing down a mountain as fast as some cars on a freeway. The road to musical success is not always a freeway of love. I've lost lots of money. And I know I've only scratched the surface musically. Because behind every song on an album, there's probably forty written and semi-demoed or partially recorded, shelved, scrapped or thrown out for whatever reason.

You don't just show up at a studio, record a song and a few hours later, leave. I'm sure some people, unless they live it, will never truly understand it. My dad always said when I was recording the Inner Vision album, "What are you guys doing down there? You only have ten songs. You should be outta there in a week."

I just laugh. No point in trying to explain it. I don't think Dad would really understand it, anyway. Music's not his cup of tea.

But it's mine and I plan to continue drinking deeply from it. Certainly one of the neatest songs I've ever recorded was a song called "A Little Dreaming Goes a Long Long Way."

It's also the name of a video documentary of my life — narrated by Bob Costas from NBC sports, who has been unbelievably generous of his time with me and become a dear friend. The words to the song were written by Arn Lanni and they go like this:

Sometimes I get scared.
Sometimes I feel all alone,

But every now and then
I cry.
Sometimes I feel strong,
So strong, I'm invincible.
Still every now and then,
I cry.
Oh, I get down,
Lose my ground,
And I feel sorry for myself.
But when I find it hard to smile
I dream awhile.
A little dreamin' goes a long, long way.
A little hope can get me through my darkest day.
Make a wish on a magic star.
A dream can go so far.
Dreamin' goes a long, long way.
Darkness, be my friend,
Oh, comfort me
When I need comforting
Because every now and then
I cry.
Oh, I, I stood tall,
I won't fall
To the thought of what could have been.
Tomorrow's brighter than it seems
When you've got a dream,
Yeah, a little dreamin' goes a long, long way.
And in my time of my own reckoning,
I've cursed this darkness I'm living in.
A little faith helped me
Through it all
Gave me courage,
Gave me hopes
And dreams.

A little dreamin' goes a long, long way.

If you knew nothing else about me, you could know a lot about my feelings on life just by hearing those verses.

The cabin my father built at home in Desbarats where I find soli-
tude, room to raise Dalton and enjoy the company of good neigh-
bors, and connect with the land from which I came.

Chapter Ten
I Can See for Miles

The staccato squawk bludgeons me from sleep.

When you stay in as many hotels as I do, you don't have to think about what that horn means, even when you're shaking off a slumbering haze.

Fire alarm!

My mind takes quick, if groggy inventory. Yes, I'm on the twenty-seventh floor all right. Great view, I suppose. Long way to the ground.

I throw on my pants, grab a shirt, and jam my feet into a pair of loafers. Fortunately, I keep hotel rooms perfectly organized all the time. Nothing out of place, ever. I have to. If I call for a five a.m. taxi to the airport, I don't have time to read the carpet like Braille to find my socks.

I know the routine, too. If you stay in as many hotel rooms a year as I do, you've heard the fire alarm before. You've thought about what to do. The answer is clear: Don't worry about what you're wearing or what you're carrying. Just get out of there, quick.

I've heard fire alarms go off in hotels many times. Almost always a voice came on the intercom before I could make an exit, saying the alarm was accidental.

No voice this time.

This time, what I hear are voices in the hall. This is a large

Los Angeles hotel and it's pretty full, so plenty of other folks are looking to get out.

Then I realize I don't know where the exit is. You'd think a person in my situation would orient himself immediately upon checking into his room. When I first started traveling, I did that. Over a million air miles later, I've gotten blase about it. I've taken for granted I'd never need to know. Like most travelers, I've stopped thinking about it. Until now.

When I get out in the hall, I realize enough people are heading for the stair that I have no problem knowing where to go. And I do have some special experience navigating crowded hallways in a hurry.

I make it down five flights of stairs feeling pretty calm and reassured that I'm going the right direction. I don't feel any heat or smell smoke. No need to panic.

Yet, anyway...

But suddenly, something is wrong. Not with me. With someone else.

I hear a voice, and that voice isn't calm. From the sound of it, I know one thing for certain. That voice is in trouble.

At twenty-three years old, my other senses really have begun to compensate for my loss of sight. My naturally acute hearing has become quite extraordinary.

I'm always hearing sounds that most other people don't. My dad would be amazed when he and I would be fishing from a dock at dark and I could hear the sound that bats make.

I could hear videos two classrooms away in school. In fact, I always thought hearing was a greater advantage than seeing. After all, you can't see around corners. But you can hear around them.

And now that advantage came into play.

I heard, around the corner, as we were hurrying down the stairway, the sound of a woman. Panic was in her voice.

"I need help," she said. "Won't somebody please help me?"

Maybe no one else heard amid the confusion, the clatter of feet on the stairs, people talking anxiously, shouting to each other to move along. The horn was still wah-wah-ing, over and over.

I Can See for Miles

But I heard. I followed that voice into the hallway and heard that it was low to the floor. A few steps later I discovered why. It was coming from a woman in a wheelchair.

Needless to say, the elevators weren't working. You're not supposed to use elevators anyway during a fire, as you well know. She was stranded.

"I can't get out," she said anxiously. "I need some people to help me down from here."

The only "people" I knew for sure were around was me.

I picked her up, wheelchair and all. We started making our way down the stairs. I wasn't exactly sure, but I did quick calculations. I thought I had twenty-two floors to go.

Or rather "we" had twenty-two.

"Don't worry, ma'am," I said. "If I make it down, you're making it down. And I plan on making it down. We're going out of here together."

It didn't take long before I knew clearly I would need all my strength to get both of us down. I'm no weightlifter — I'd just always built myself up through pushups and pullups and situps — but I think the lady, the chair, the whole shooting match, must have weighed about 160 pounds.

Don't ask me why I carried her and the chair down. Heck, maybe I wasn't as calm as I thought I was. It was the heat of the moment. I also thought she would need her chair later. My guess was that her wheels were an extension of her life.

This flashed through my mind, but I didn't stop to take much stock of anything, really.

All I knew was this: She is coming down with me.

I grabbed the two outside wheels and started backwards down the steps. And this lady was saying, "Sir I don't want you to hurt yourself. Be careful."

"Just relax. I have it all under control." I said.

"Don't trip," she said. "Don't fall."

I guess my going backwards movement didn't feel that steady to her. But it was the only way I could figure to do it. It also dawned on me in short order: I can't make much speed carrying a wheelchair, walking backwards, down stairs. Plus, my equilibrium was starting to fail and I was getting dizzy — eight stairs, around the corner, eight stairs, around the corner.

My arms were starting to kill me.

I am not going to put this lady down to rest, I thought. First, I don't think we have time. Second, I don't want to unsettle her anymore than she is already.

I couldn't hear anyone else coming down behind me.

Nobody to ask, "Take the other end of this thing, please?"

It was she and I.

"Just keep going," I told myself. "You can do this."

It occurred to me that I was thankful for some old workouts I used to do, running up and down the YMCA Tower in Ottawa when I was going to school at Carleton. I wasn't competing for anything. I just did it for conditioning. Each day I'd run twenty-two stories. Up, then down again. Over and over and over.

God truly does work in mysterious and funny ways, doesn't he? In the hallway, with this woman and her wheelchair in my arms, I'm thinking: How bizarre that I used to run up and down stairways. I doubt there is anything I could have done in the world that would have better prepared me for getting this woman and myself down these stairs.

I do a quick calculation. Maybe ten flights to go. Maybe eleven. I'm trying to reassure my comrade: "Don't worry. A lot of times, the alarm just goes off for no reason. We might not even have a fire here."

No sooner do I say this, gasping for breath, than the smoke starts hitting my nose.

I think, "Oh my God, this is the real deal."

She smells the smoke, too, and says, "Oh, God, we're going to be trapped."

"Just give me another couple of minutes and we'll be out of here," I say to her. "I promise you, we're gonna get out of here."

That is my voice. My mind is saying, "Get the heck outta here — fast."

I started quickening everything up. I was running on

adrenaline, sliding into the grey zone I knew so well on the slopes and the mat. I was exhausted. Her legs were dangling into me, sometimes out to the side of me, as we rounded corners. A couple of times I could feel her slipping forward. I braced my shoulder to keep her in the chair.

Another quick calculation. Can't be more than a few flights to go. Two maybe. Not three, I pray. I was whipped, beyond exhaustion. A small wildfire had started in my arms and legs. My fingers weren't there; they were beyond feeling. I felt like I had melted. I was a five-foot-seven inch sack of Jell-o trying to hold her up. I felt like, any second now, this chair would just fall out of my hands and she would topple down the stairs.

I was staggering backward, fishing with numb feet for the next step. The smoke had thickened considerably the last few floors and I had lost some control. The chair clanged off the railing, the wheels banged off the wall. My elbows were scraped up from swinging around the corners.

God, do these steps ever run out? I thought. Then I felt the cold air blow against the sweat pouring down my back through my drenched shirt.

We swung out into the sidewalk. Safe.

A few minutes later we ran into a friend of hers, who had been staying on a different floor. She wasn't in a wheelchair. They hugged and greeted each other and I kind of stood there. People were talking about how I'd brought this lady out of the hotel, down twenty-something flights of stairs.

I just said, "It was what I was supposed to do."

I certainly wasn't going to walk past a lady in a wheelchair in a fire and get myself out alone. That was beyond me.

You know, fate works in funny ways. I had been preparing all my life to be a hero at that moment. Everything in my life had moved me toward it. Perhaps no other human being would have been properly equipped to do what I did. All these 'inconveniences' in my life were actually training for the most important race I ever ran.

Think about it. The simple, virtually random accident that

took my sight at age two, may well have saved another person's life two decades later. The way my parents raised me to be as normal as possible, hunting, setting traps, riding my bike, throwing bales of hay, created a man who was anything but fragile when the chips were down. Those nights Eric and I used to sneak out of the boys' residence at W. Ross MacDonald and climb up the corner bricks of the girls' residence then creep along the ledge, must have been preparation for the treacherous flights of stairs I somehow made it down through the smoke. And the strength I was driven to create in my upper body and legs for wrestling — few other people in that hotel could have maneuvered a woman and her wheel chair the way I did.

Think about this. A sighted person may well have become completely disoriented when the smoke filled the stairway and visibility went to zero. Not me. I was perfectly equipped to maneuver in the dark.

I don't say this to boast. I say it to drive home one point. If I can do it, so can you. If I can live the exciting life I've lived, so can you. And if everything in my life led me to this point, then ask yourself, where is your life leading you? What special duty are your "inconveniences" leading to? For what special duty are you right now in training?

The question for you is simple. How has your life prepared you to be a hero? If I can be a hero, so can you.

On the lighter side, as I stood there on the sidewalk being congratulated, I couldn't help a smile coming to my face. It had just dawned on me. I'd come to Los Angeles to give a speech for AT&T.

"Is this what they mean by reaching out and touching somebody?"

God knows, people had been doing that for me all my life, lifting me up through highs and lows. I was just grateful for a chance to return the favor this particular night.

Coming back: The questions kids ask keep me flying

Today, my life is better than ever, largely because God has always helped me grasp the next rung on the ladder even when it seemed like I was losing my grip. And He's always provided somebody to give me a boost up, just when it seemed I was sagging the most.

Case in point: The job I have today.

It came along in 1991. At this time, I had resigned from Putnam, split up with Jami, jingled around in my jeans and found very little jangling in there. I was down about as low as I've ever been. I felt the needle slipping over to the "E" mark on my emotional tanks.

But I was determined not to slip into a hopeless bog. I'd been through too much and strived too hard to achieve excellence in my life. I started scratching around and dug up a few free-lance speaking engagements.

Getting even the first one put some pep back in my step. An old quote came to mind: "Yesterday is history; tomorrow is a mystery; today is a gift and that's why we call it a present."

As I took off for that first free-lance assignment in Tampa, Florida, I told myself that what happened next to Dalton and me was entirely on my shoulders. I could fold up or I could fire out in a new direction.

The speech I gave that night was one of the most important of my life. Not, perhaps, for those listening, but for me. Their applause and affirmation were medicine to my bruised ego and balm to my soul.

Afterward, I came back to Desbarats where Dalton and I were living with my parents. My next phone call was to a buddy of mine named Jim Schmidt. I'd met Jim when I was working for Putnam and spoke at a major Chamber of Commerce gathering in Sault, Michigan. Jim was a broker there for Edward Jones Co., and they have a strong involvement in all kinds of civic functions.

Jim said he had an idea for me to be a goodwill ambassador

for Edward Jones. What initially intrigued me about the company was their approach to the brokerage business. They pioneered the concept of "one-broker branch offices." They believed that investors deserve to deal with someone who lives and works near them, someone who works with them closely and frequently, someone who truly understands their personal concerns.

Each office was run by one investment representative and an assistant, so clients would always know who they were talking to when they called. It was Wall Street rocking on your front porch with you. Wall Street sitting down for a sip of coffee in your kitchen. It was big business personalized and tailored to small-town life, or you might say the Wall Street to Main Street approach.

Small town life ran through my blood like maple sap out of the trees in our backyard. And being blessed to travel throughout my native Canada, my adopted homeland, America, and a dozen countries from Europe to the Pacific Rim, I had come to know a wide variety of major players in powerful positions all over the corporate map.

I was made for Edward Jones, I felt. And, they were made for me.

That had not always been the case for me in the corporate world. More often, corporate managers had said they'd seen something in me, but they just didn't have anything for me "at this time." I didn't seem to fit a preconceived mold or a wedge on some pie-chart or some box on an organizational flow chart.

"We'll take a good hard look at it and get back to you."

"We'll pass it on to our management committee."

"Personally, I like it but I'm not sure I can sell it to others."

"We've never done anything like this before."

"It's not in the budget."

"We're not sure if it's a fit."

Frankly, what I was hearing was the classic runaround a lot of people get. Some people talk a great game about giving someone with a supposed limitation a chance. But it's gasbag stuff bigger than the Hindenburg when you get down to the nitty-gritty. Another door slams in your face.

It gets pretty old after awhile hearing the same lame excuses when you know you're able to do a great job for someone.

That was almost seven years ago. After a six-month trial period that didn't last the whole six months, I was officially made a member of the team. My job, then and now, is to travel the country speaking primarily to groups of kids in high schools and junior highs, delivering my message of PRIDE and encouraging them to reach for the stars and follow their dreams and realize their potential to the fullest. What I tell kids is this: If I can do it, so can you.

Over the last twelve years, I have spoken to roughly 1,700 high schools, and an estimated one-and-a-half million students. I love their questions.

"Do you ever go to kiss a girl and miss?" one girl asked.

Answer: Not often. I may bumble and stumble and miss the mark on a lot of things, but if there is one thing the Good Lord gave me, it's a pretty unerring aim when it comes to lips. It's way too much fun to spoil by missing.

"Do you dream in color?" another asked once.

Answer: I do not. What I see would be like me asking you what does pure water taste like. It's an absolute nothing — not black, not white, nor light or dark. I don't remember what color looks like.

"Do you remember seeing anything before the accident?" another asked.

Answer: Virtually nothing. Crazy, but the one image that has ever come to mind is a porcupine running along a ridge in the woods. At least I think it's a porcupine from descriptions of them. A blurry, fuzzy creature with sharp ends on it. Of all the things on God's great green earth, why would only the image of a porcupine linger?

I'm stumped. Maybe God will answer that one someday.

"How do you know whether a girl is good-looking when you meet her?" another student asked. As you can tell, a fairly strong thread through the questioning is boy-girl stuff.

Answer: It was frustrating for a long time not being able to see girls and make eye contact. But I taught myself — and others helped me — to be comfortable in social settings. I don't cock my head or face off somewhere when girls — or others — are talking to me. Mom and Dad taught me from before I can remember, "Face straight toward someone who's talking. It makes them know you're really there with them, having a conversation."

But a really nice side benefit to all this is that it's taught me to listen carefully and sense and seek out the inner beauty in people. I'm not saying physical appearance isn't important. I like being with an attractive girl just like anyone else. But the inner person is the thing I connect with the most. It has the most meaning. I'm not sure I would feel that to the extent I do if I could see. It's the inner beauty that talks to me and that I have to connect with; perhaps blindness has an advantage when you first meet someone. You don't judge them by appearance but what they have to say and the level of integrity with which they say it.

One advantage of being blind is when you first meet someone, you don't judge by the color of their skin, the clothes they wear, the color of their hair or any other physical attributes. You judge them from the inside out. You judge them by what they say and the level of integrity you feel in the way they say it. You listen for the sincerity in their voice. I believe if more people could put the blinders on periodically they wouldn't be so judgmental; they would take time to get to know people and care for people in the manner that blindness has made me care about people, from the inside out.

One question that always seems to fascinate kids — adults, too, for that matter — is, "How do you get around from place to place." I'll have as many as 200 speaking engagements in a year all over the world. And, actually, getting around is pretty interesting stuff to me, too.

Answer: I don't use a dog or cane in the streets. I rely on my "facial perception," as I've explained before, to get around most of the hallways, sidewalks, streets and so on. I can usually sense where doors are, or steps, or dips and rises in the sidewalks.

But I still do rely on the generosity and kindness of a lot of people. A prearranged driver picks me up and deposits me at the airport. Usually an airline attendant helps me get to my gate. If I'm going from a car into a building with which I'm not familiar, I'll lightly touch someone's elbow as they guide me to the auditorium or gym or wherever I'm speaking or staying. In fact, I use this method a lot in lobbies of hotels. I can usually get from my room to the elevator and downstairs in a hotel. But I may need someone to help me from there to a hotel restaurant or gift shop, until I learn the ropes.

I become very friendly with bellmen and depend on them a lot. They'll take me to a workout room or the swimming pool. I have to be sure to remind them to come and get me at the pool. I've stayed out there until I was chicken-fried Craig more than once.

In fact none of my methods are perfect.

Take facial perception. I'm pretty proud of walking around so you couldn't always tell right off I'm blind. But one time I got stranded in the middle of a street. The cars were whipping around. I didn't know where I was for a few worried moments. I was lucky I didn't come away with the grillwork from a Buick where my teeth normally are.

"What kind of stuff do you do besides skiing and wrestling and running and things like that?" kids will ask.

Answer: Just about anything that comes to mind. I've gone parasailing, jet-skiing, snowmobiling, white-water rafting, body-surfing in the ocean. I've worked out in the gym with Evander Holyfield, which they find interesting.

I tell the kids that one of the greatest ways to build

confidence is to find something you enjoy — music, soccer, a hobby — and put much of your energy into it. When you find something enjoyable, it doesn't seem like work to practice it. When you acquire good practice habits, you can apply that to the rest of your day.

I think an idea like this can turn a kid's life around. If you enjoy playing soccer two or three nights a week, you know you can look forward to practice. It gives you a sense of purpose, a sense of belonging.

I really want kids to understand how important attitude is. When you wake up in the morning, when you put that game face on — that smile — it's part of the game plan that makes you a winner. When you show up at school, don't drag your feet down the hall, head down, shirt half-untucked. That's not the stuff of champions. Regardless of how you feel, put your game face on then walk out of the house with some bounce in your step ready to face life's challenges or hurdles.

I encourage kids to work hard, to have fun and, most importantly, to be responsible for their actions. You can't always be a leader, but you can make darn sure you follow the right crowd.

Nothing bothers me more than mediocrity in people, someone who is lollygagging, not interested in what he or she is doing, going through the motions. Put a wholehearted effort into it. When you get out of bed and look in the mirror, what looks back at you is who you are. The mirror does not lie. The only person who can really make a positive change in your life is you.

You can overcome anything if you truly want to. Maybe you don't have a stable home environment. Maybe you don't think you come from the right place to achieve success. I can relate to those feelings about not coming from the right place. From age six to eighteen, I was only home two years plus holidays. Even though I had awesome parents, they were almost 500 miles away. And when I was home, I was in a town of only 400 people.

Another person might accept these as disadvantages but I didn't. I saw the world as my playing field.

You can always make something of your life if you do two things: First, get help from teachers, coaches, and others who care about you. Second, get involved in positive activities.

It's up to you to make your life what you want it to be.

For whatever reason, young people are able to relate to my story. I can communicate in their language. Maybe eighty-five percent of the time I get a standing ovation. Whatever it is that connects, whatever seems to be getting through, believe me, I am extremely grateful. I don't think it's any great credit to me, anyway. I just think this is God using me in a way that seems best to Him and it works out for that reason.

JUST ANOTHER HAPPY ENDING

The kids I work with on the road are important to me. But the kid I have at home is the one who focuses my life. He's a tether for me. I swing out around the globe to do my job, but I always wind up back at home. I have a job to do there, as well.

Dalton is the North Star in my universe, the one person I am always moving toward and returning to, in my mind and in my heart. He's also the person I'm constantly returning to from jet liners and hotel rooms.

I think being there is extremely important to a kid. It's one thing to carry my little nine-year-old son in my heart. Well, he's not that little anymore at fifty-seven inches tall and 115 pounds. It's another to act my love out in person. No matter how many books they write or pretty speeches anyone gives on child-rearing, one eternal truth remains. It's the oldest cliche in the book: Kids spell love, T-I-M-E.

Speaking at a high school once, I remember running into a wonderful young man who was seventeen. He said his father had never seen him participate in sports. It's demoralizing to young people to put their heart and soul into something and not have parents care enough to honor and support it. I made up my mind, no matter how wacky my travel schedule was, I would put Dalton's activities at the top of my list.

Many times I've flown across country to be home for twelve hours so I could see something he's involved in, before zinging out again. A recent trip comes to mind.

Friday was Halloween, October 31. I wanted to be home for that. On Friday morning, I spoke in St. Louis, Missouri. In the early afternoon, I spoke in Chicago. Late that afternoon I landed in Soo, Ontario, so I could be home to go with Dalton trick or treating that evening and then to hockey games on Saturday.

I had commitments Saturday night and Sunday morning in New York. Yes, it would have been much easier to go directly from Chicago to New York. But, Dalton had hockey games sixty miles from Desbarats in a town called Blind River. Blind River is two hours from Sault Ste. Marie, Ontario Airport, where I had to fly from late that Saturday afternoon.

Dalton was scheduled to play two games, one at 10 a.m. and one at 1:30 p.m. Novice level games don't last more than an hour, so by the end of his second game, it would be 2:30 p.m. I had a flight leaving at 4:45 p.m. from Sault Ste. Marie to New York. Now, these were huge engagements with hundreds of people in attendance. I could not miss either of them.

But I also could not miss Dalton's games. That was one unshakable commitment over all others. So I hurriedly got Dalton into the dressing room after the second game, helped get his skates off, got him dressed in his street clothes and then went on a mad dash to the airport.

With my girlfriend Patti playing the role of Mario Andretti, we squealed into the Soo airport with less than five minutes to spare.

More important to me, I didn't miss any of Dalton's slap-shots. Lots of parents were saying, "Why don't you leave early? We'll take Dalton back to Desbarats and you can be sure you make your flight." But I just couldn't do that to Dalton. That's the same stubborn guy talking who decided no Salt Lake City, Utah, hospital could hold him the night before the blind nationals in skiing.

Dalton scored four goals and had two assists and hit four goalposts to lead his team to victory that Saturday afternoon. It was definitely one of his best games, although on numerous occasions Dalton has scored three, four, even five goals in a game. Last year he led his team in scoring with thirty-eight goals and twelve assists for fifty points. Matter of fact, he's led his team in scoring the last two years.

It gives me great pleasure being at his hockey games because, of course, it was a dream of mine to be a professional hockey player.

But if it sounds like Dalton's success is the reason I'm so hot to make these games, it's not. The point isn't whether he scores or leads or stars, and I mean that. It's that he participates — and does so to the fullest extent of his abilities. It wouldn't really matter if he wanted to play the piccolo all day. I'd want to be there to listen. It so happens he loves hockey and, naturally, I think that's cool.

But it's not just for Dalton that I like being involved. Currently I'm managing the Tier One team out of Desbarats, which is a select group of talented kids who play tournaments and exhibition games. It's a great privilege and joy to work with all these kids, not only my own.

Dalton was three when he first learned to ice skate. He started playing organized hockey at five. Teams in his league travel as far as a hundred miles on road trips. In Desbarats, that just goes with the territory. Sometimes, at his games, the excitement in the stands is greater than at NHL games. Heated rivalries among these communities gets the parents' blood boiling. After Dalton scores a goal, it's always nice to hear his coach, Eric Ableson, yell from the bench, "nice deek and great shot" and Eric's wife Terry yell over to me after his fourth goal,

"What did you feed that kid at lunch? Next weekend let's feed it to the whole team."

I just try to feed him love.

During the summer, Dalton plays Rookie League baseball. I've shared the stage with lots of great major league players, including the late Mickey Mantle. And I've visited SkyDome, home of my ballclub, the Toronto Blue Jays. I remember the day Patti helped take me on a tour of the Skydome field before a game, with the blessing of the Blue Jays. Just to feel the height of the mound, the warning track, the padding on the walls, the dirt they slide in, to discover how gritty and sandy it is, helped bring the game alive for me. To walk from home plate to the fences was amazing. It gave me a new feel for just how strong and athletic hitters must be to blast one out.

The home run fence on the field where Dalton plays is 160 feet from home plate. Patti and I like to sit just behind the fence. That way I'm close to the action when Dalton is playing the outfield, usually center field. I can hear the ball smack into his glove if he catches a line drive or a pop fly. I can also hear the ball hit the fence on a ground ball deep into the outfield.

I suppose one of my proudest moments as a father was in a playoff game in 1997 when Dalton hit four consecutive home runs including ten RBI. By the time he came to bat in the bottom of the last inning, his teammates were chanting "home run, home run." Just like in the movies, he delivered. His fourth home run, other fathers told me, soared at least thirty feet high when it cleared the fence.

When we're not at ball games or hockey matches, we sometimes spend the evenings in the log cabin my father built on the back portion of my 300-acre farm. It's authentic; Dad cut the logs, peeled them, notched and caulked them. He did all that with his own two hands. He carried every stick of it, except for one big heavy beam which our good neighbor, Ray Matheson, helped put in place.

When the sun begins to go down, you'll often find Dalton

and me and Mom and Dad, Ray and Sheila Matheson, along with other close friends. It's a very relaxing place for us to gather.

When you're sitting on the front deck, you're looking at the beaver dams on the creek. You can watch the beaver and muskrats and hear them in there swimming. Oftentimes, deer bound across the field. The farm is also a hunter's paradise. Most recently, Ian, who lives in Indiana now, came up and got two bear.

The place just teems with life, both the wildlife and the comfortable life which good, hard-working, decent people have hacked out of this wilderness. It's a mingling of the wildness and the taming of it that blend together in a wonderfully reassuring way.

A gravel road about three-quarters of a mile long runs from my farmhouse back past my dad's cabin. Often I go for walks there. Feeling the familiar pits in the road, I'm warmed and fed and energized by the solid Ontario earth firmly underneath my feet. I live in two opposite worlds. One hectic. One full of solitude.

When I come home, the world seems to stand still, at least when I'm at the cabin. I walk out along that road and I get the breeze singing soft woodwind melodies to me out of the pines. A coyote croons his haunting refrain. A woodpecker drums out his percussion solo on a distant tree. The cicadas whisper that nightfall is near.

I catch the smell of a woodstove and the aroma of Dad's eternal pan of bacon frying. The smell of fresh-cut hay comes out of the property where Ray and Sheila are running cattle and the herd's familiar pungency, like an old friend, lingers in the air.

These all speak to me as I walk along the road.

A smile comes to my face as I remember all the wonderful times I've shared with Ian's kids, my niece Crystal, and my nephew, John.

As I walk, I often think of what my mother said.

"Craig, there must be some purpose to what happened to you as a child. We'll just wait to find out what God intended it to be."

And as I walk and hear my mother's voice, I hear other voices working below the hum and sigh of the dusk settling into the hush of firs.

I hear a kid who came up to me in Mississippi, a young African-American kid, who said he had spina bifida. He said he'd been told all his life he couldn't do certain things. He was lucky to be able to walk, he was told.

He grabbed my hand hard and said in a clear, strong voice:

"Man, I've been letting everyone feel sorry for me and tell me what I could and should be. I don't think I've had it as hard as you. I can see. From now on, I'm going to be the one who decides what I can and can't do.'

I could hear the rising excitement in his voice, the stiffening conviction and I could feel the tightening of his hand in mine. I couldn't help it this time. Tears flowed from my eyes.

Walking down that gravel road, I hear the kid who came up to me in Texas and said his parents had recently been killed in an automobile accident. He'd been struggling with being left alone, with the feeling that no one cared, that there was nothing left for him. He told me what I'd said had moved him.

"I'm going to show respect for my mom and dad by going on with life," he said.

And walking down that road, I hear the kid in Florida who'd lost an arm and was trying to play baseball. His would-be teammates and even his coaches had scorned his efforts. We talked about standing on his own two feet, ignoring the ridicule, making up his mind to do whatever he wanted to do. Not his detractors.

"I promise I will," he said.

In those moments, it seems clearer than at any time since my childhood what God had in mind.

Still, I'd be lying if I said I didn't wish I'd been able to keep my sight. Every minute of every day I would count as an unspeakable joy to be able to see, to see Dalton's face and those of my mom and dad and all my friends who've stuck with me throughout my life. To go back to those mountains and gaze at them. To stare and drink in the majesty of the ocean. To soak up the rugged lushness of New Zealand or even the grit of New York City. To look longingly into the eyes of the woman I love.

In a heartbeat I'd take my eyesight back. You bet I would.

But would my life have been better?

I think of the kid from Mississippi, the kid from Texas, the kid from Florida. And I think of the one on the gravel road next to me, gripping my hand, looking up at me and saying, "Pretty great evening, huh Dad? It's cool being out here, just you and me."

And as I walk on the good earth of the northwoods with my son, I can see down that road with the inner vision God in his mercy and wisdom has granted me.

And I see that the road goes on forever. It never looks back in worry or anger or regret.

It just goes on, His finger beckoning me, always around the next beautiful bend.

AFTERWORD
A FINAL WORD FROM A FRIEND...

Knowing Craig MacFarlane has enabled me to be a better person. We all tend to complain about our lot in life, trivial upsets cause us to become angry or full of self-pity, and we feel the whole world is against us.

Knowing Craig enabled me to remove the negatives from my life by concentrating on the positives. I soon realized I had far more good things in my life than bad. My family became the most important thing to me. Problems became secondary and almost insignificant.

The "new me" was seriously put to the test in May 1990, when I was diagnosed with primary amyloidosis, a rare, incurable disease in which the bone marrow produces a corrosive protein (amyloid) that attacks any part of the body where there is a concentrated blood flow.

I've been fortunate in that the amyloid's first target was my kidneys, so I was able to start dialysis at home in January 1992, and this has proven very successful in replacing my normal kidney function.

The average life expectancy of an amyloid patient is one to three years. My family and I were devastated when we heard the diagnosis, but Craig's attitude toward life has played a major part in helping all of us deal with the situation. We have concentrated on the good, rather than complaining about what is bad.

Craig's two visits to me in the hospital were the best possible tonic, especially the one when he wheeled me around the entire hospital complex in a wheel chair!

Craig's suggestion that we start each day with the thought, "What can I do today to make life just a little bit better than the day before?" has been invaluable, especially on those days when my health took a turn for the worse or everything seemed to be going wrong.

Craig forces himself to have faith and believe in himself and his God-given abilities, even when nothing appears to be going right. His example has helped me do the same, even when the obstacles have been overwhelming. Counting one's blessings may sound trite, but I've found it to be the path to happiness and success.

"Success" means different things to different people, but to me success is sharing a loving, supportive relationship with my wife and family, being fortunate enough to have enjoyed every job I've ever worked at, including delivering newspapers, pattern-cutting, flying with the RAF Red Arrows Aerobatic Team, serving in several business capacities, managing a wildlife park, teaching water-skiing and attempting to help tell the story of Craig's life.

I hope this book will inspire readers to believe that anything is possible if you believe in yourself. All you have to do is get started, take one step at a time, and keep putting one foot in front of the other.

Sir Isaac Newton said, "If I have seen further, it is by standing on the shoulders of giants."

Craig MacFarlane is a five-foot-seven-inch giant; he helps us see beyond our own individual fears, doubts and insecurities.

KEN RANSOM
SEPTEMBER 1992

Ken Ransom, husband, father, businessman, pilot, athlete, coach, friend and lover of all God's creatures, died Sunday, October 4, 1992, of a brain hemorrhage related to his disease. He donated his body to medical science in the hope that what could be learned from his case might help others. We thank his wife, Tricia, for allowing us to include a part of his work in this book.

253

ABOUT THE AUTHOR

Craig MacFarlane is on the road 200 days a year, motivating students and adults in Canada and the United States. In addition to his work with Edward Jones, Co., speaking to brokers, community groups and schools, MacFarlane is in demand as a freelance speaker. He has made presentations to small companies and large corporations from Wal-Mart to Ford Motor Co., I.B.M., Whirlpool, and a host of others.

His speaking career has allowed him to talk to a diverse groups of audiences. Lou Holtz, former coach of the Notre Dame Fighting Irish football team, invited him to address the squad. Later, Dennis Erickson invited him to speak to the Miami Hurricane football team. Coach Barry Alvarez invited MacFarlane to speak to the Wisconsin Badgers; coincidentally, they won the Rose Bowl that year. He's been asked to motivate the Iowa Hawkeyes, the Clemson Tigers, and the Washington State Cougars.

In 1996, MacFarlane was keynote speaker at the National Speakers Association Annual Conference. In 1997, he addressed the National Sportscasters and Sportswriters Association.

MacFarlane has spoken to the Republican National Convention three times, Lions Club International and Rotary International, and the annual Wal-Mart convention. He has logged over two million air miles in the past thirteen years.

ABOUT THE AUTHOR

MacFarlane has won 103 gold medals in a variety of sports: wrestling, track and field, snow-skiing, and water-skiing. By the age of 19 , three documentaries had aired on National Television thoughout Canada, depicting Craig and his numerous accomplishments. He lives at home in Desbarats, Ontario, Canada with his nine-year-old son Dalton.

For information about booking MacFarlane for personal appearances, you can reach him on the World Wide Web at: www.lyon-publishing.com.

His E-Mail address is: cmacfarl@lyon-publishing.com. or write to P.O. Box 456, Sault Ste. Marie, Michigan 49783.